Routledge Revivals

Social England in the Fifteenth Century

Annie Abram was born in London in 1869 and died in Sussex in 1930. She contributed significantly to the twentieth-century historiography of late medieval England, researching the social, cultural and religious mores of the English laity and clergy. First published in 1909, this title explores the impact of economic changes on society during the fifteenth century. This was a period of important developments both socially and economically, which witnessed the rise of the middle class through industrialisation, agrarian change, and the growing economic and commercial character of towns. The chapters discuss these areas, as well as the industrial position of women and children, the economic position of the Church and the development of a national character. This is a fascinating classic work, which will be of great value to students researching the socio-economic history of late medieval England.

Social England in the Fifteenth Century

A Study of the Effects of Economic Conditions

A. Abram

Routledge Revivals
Routledge
Taylor & Francis Group

First published in 1909
by George Routledge and Sons, Limited

This edition first published in 2013 by Routledge
4 Park Square, Milton Park, Abingdon, Oxon OX14 4RN

Simultaneously published in the USA and Canada
by Routledge

605 Third Avenue, New York, NY 10017

Routledge is an imprint of the Taylor & Francis Group, an informa business

Publisher's Note

The publisher has gone to great lengths to ensure the quality of this reprint but points out that some imperfections in the original copies may be apparent.

Disclaimer

The publisher has made every effort to trace copyright holders and welcomes correspondence from those they have been unable to contact.

A Library of Congress record exists under LC control number: 10008277

ISBN 13: 978-0-415-71882-0 (hbk)
ISBN 13: 978-1-315-86780-9 (ebk)

THE RESEARCH LIBRARY

SOCIAL ENGLAND

IN THE

FIFTEENTH CENTURY

A STUDY OF THE EFFECTS OF ECONOMIC CONDITIONS

Thesis approved for the Degree of Doctor of Science (Economics) in the University of London

BY

A. ABRAM

B.A. CAMBRIDGE HIST. TRIPOS

LONDON

GEORGE ROUTLEDGE AND SONS, LIMITED

NEW YORK: E. P. DUTTON & Co.

1909

PREFACE

In the following pages I have endeavoured to show the effects of the development of Industry and Commerce upon Social Life in England in the fifteenth century. So great an interest is now felt in Social questions, that there is no need to justify my choice of a subject. The fifteenth century is a particularly attractive period, not only because it witnessed very important Economic changes in this country, but also because it formed a prelude to the Age of the Renaissance and the Reformation.

I desire to express my thanks to Mr. Hubert Hall, of the Public Record Office, for much help given to me in the course of my work. I am especially indebted to him for advice as to the use of original sources; at his suggestion, I examined the *Early Chancery Proceedings* and found them full of information of all kinds. I have by no means exhausted them, and I hope they may be of use to other students of Social and Economic History.

I also wish to thank the London County Council for very kindly giving me copies of some of the entries in the *Court Rolls* of Tooting Bec Manor.

Miss E. M. Delf has made some valuable criticisms upon my work, and Miss E. Earle has read my proofs; to both of them I owe many thanks.

A. Abram.

CONTENTS

PART II

THE EFFECTS PRODUCED BY ECONOMIC CHANGES UPON ENGLISH SOCIAL LIFE IN THE FIFTEENTH CENTURY

INTRODUCTORY NOTE

THE fifteenth century was not marked by an epoch-making catastrophe, like the one which preceded it, or glorified by an outburst of literary activity, like that which followed; but it was none the less a most critical period in the history of the nation. Momentous events took place in the spheres of industry and commerce, which shaped its destiny in future days. England had hitherto depended largely upon her neighbours in these matters, but at this time she began to be conscious of her own powers, and entered upon the career, which she has never since quitted. Industrial development caused great changes in social life; it introduced new ideas, trained new faculties, and brought into prominence men who had been of little account in the past, and thereby it overthrew old modes of thought and old institutions. A century is, however, an arbitrary division of time, and the origin of some of the changes which swept over England in the fifteenth century may be found in the fourteenth. Other changes were not fully accomplished until long after the fifteenth century had reached its close, and they, in their turn, exercised a great influence upon conditions of life in the sixteenth century.

Economic environment is only one of the many forces which mould social life; religion, political institutions, and war are factors which must be taken into account, and they might have lessened the effects of the economic changes had not circumstances diminished their own strength. Religion was discredited by quarrels in the Church, and respect for the priesthood was decreased by its worldliness. Political institutions, however admirable, are of little practical use, unless they are well administered, but during the greater part of the century the Government was weak and inefficient. The authority of the Crown was lessened by a defective title and by wars of succession, and the nobles, who should have been its chief support, were absorbed in their private affairs, and cared little for the public good. War, it must be admitted, affected the characters of those engaged in it, and the deterioration of the baronage may be partially attributed to the demoralizing influence of the French War. But after the death of the Duke of Bedford the French War languished, the people took little part in it, and they had even less share in the Wars of the Roses. Moreover, in so far as war reduced the numbers and lowered the prestige of the nobles, it acted in conjunction with Economic forces, which deprived them of superiority by raising other classes to their level.

Thus economic forces were not only able to hold their own, but also materially to affect the development of other tendencies; and so religion and politics were tinged by a commercial spirit, and commercial intercourse formed the subject of much diplomacy. Consequently England made great strides as an industrial country; but her devotion to trade prevented her from paying much attention to other affairs, and she was hardly aware of the great awakening of thought which was going on in the South of Europe. A comparison of the progress of this country with that of other nations would be an interesting study, and though space does not permit it here, perhaps this slight attempt to describe life in England may furnish some data for this purpose. From several points of view, therefore, the Economic History of the fifteenth century has a special value for ourselves, for our own age must inevitably witness a like process of transition—new ideas are constantly presented to us, and new interests are beginning to demand our attention. Possibly, then, we can gain from the past some wisdom to guide our future policy.

ABBREVIATIONS USED IN THE REFERENCES OF THIS WORK

A.C. : Ancient Correspondence.

A.P. : Ancient Petitions.

Cal. : Calendar.

Early Chanc. Proceed. : *Early Chancery Proceedings.*

Early Eng. Wills : *Fifty Earliest English Wills*, edited by Dr. F. J. FURNIVALL.

Hobhouse : *Churchwardens Accounts of Croscombe, Pilton, Yatton, etc.*, edited by Bp. HOBHOUSE.

Howard Household Book, I : *Accounts and Memoranda of Sir John Howard.*

Howard Household Book, II : *Household Books of John, Duke of Norfolk, and Thomas, Earl of Surrey.*

Italian Relation : *Relation of the Island of England.*

Rot. Parl. : *Rotuli Parliamentorum.*

SOCIAL ENGLAND
IN THE FIFTEENTH CENTURY

PART I

ECONOMIC CHANGES

CHAPTER I

INDUSTRIAL CHANGES

AMONGST the Economic Changes of the fifteenth century none was more striking in its rapidity or more far-reaching in its consequences than the development of manufactures. In the time of Edward III the wealth of England still consisted mainly in raw products, and her industry was but little advanced,[1] but in the fifteenth century manufactures were springing up in every town[2]; and the most important of these was the manufacture of cloth. In 1352 the Commons told the King that wool was 'la Sovereine Marchandise and Jewel . . . d'Engleterre'[3]; a hundred years later they declared that 'the makeyng of Cloth' was 'the grettest occupacion & lyving' of the poor people of the land[4]; and in another petition they protested against the taxation of English cloth, be-

[1] Cunningham, *Alien Immigrants to England*, pp. 100–1.
[2] Ashley, Introduction to *Econ. Hist.*, Part ii, p. 6.
[3] *Rot. Parl.*, II, p. 246. [4] *Ibid.*, V, p. 274. No. 5.

cause it would in course of time cause little cloth to be made, and be 'a meane of distroiyng' the navy.[1] Contemporary writers, extolling the glories of England, boast equally of its cloth and wool.

> 'Ffor the marchauntes comme oure wollys for to bye,
> Or elles the cloth that is made theroff sykyrly,
> Oute of dyverse londes fer byyond the see.'[2]

So speaks the author of a little poem 'On England's Commercial Policy'; while Fortescue ranks 'wolleyn clothe' as the fourth of his 'Comodytes of Englond,' and declares that there is enough 'redy made at all tymys to serve the merchaunts of ony two kyngdomys Crystenye or hethyunye.'[3] A practical illustration of the value set upon cloth may be seen in an incident revealed by the Correspondence of Bekynton: Henry VI wished to obtain the goodwill of the Pope, and to induce him to grant privileges to Eton, so he sent him a gift of the best English cloth[4]; the Pontiff was evidently very gratified by the present, for his chamberlain expressed warm thanks in his name, and described how he had heard him praising Bekynton.[5] The choice of the gift was the more remarkable because the Pope was at that time residing in Florence, where the finest cloth in Europe was manufactured.[6] Nor were the humbler varieties of cloth less valued in their own proper sphere, for John Paston asked his wife to send him some worsted for doublets, and added that William Paston had a 'tepet of fyne worsted, whech is almost like silk.'[7]

Not only do deeds and words alike testify to the importance of the manufacture of cloth, but the

[1] *Rot. Parl.*, V, 269. [2] Wright, *Political Songs*, II, 283. [3] Fortescue, *Works*, I, 551. [4] Bekynton, *Letters*, I, 227. [5] *Ib.*, 241. A similar gift was sent to the Bishop of Utrecht, Rymer's *Fœdera*, VIII, 244. [6] Dixon, E., *Florentine Wool Trades*, in *Trans. Roy. Hist. Soc.* N.S., XII (1898), p. 171. [7] *Paston Letters*, IV, 188.

legislation of the period enables us to trace its growth and development and the efforts of the Government to foster and regulate it. An Act passed late in the fourteenth century mentions Somerset, Dorset, Bristol, Gloucester, and Essex as seats of the industry.[1] From other sources we learn that it had been established also in Norfolk, Suffolk, Kent, Westmoreland, Lancashire, Yorkshire, Sussex, Devonshire, Worcester, Hampshire, Berkshire,[2] and Coventry.[3] In the fifteenth century it spread to London,[4] Cambridge,[5] and Cornwall[6]; and there were so many worsted weavers in Norfolk that four wardens were needed to supervise the craft throughout the county, as well as four within the city of Norwich.[7] Cloth was also made at Guildford[8] and Salisbury.[9] Another sign of the growth of the industry may be seen in the extraordinary number of different kinds of material which were made. The petition concerning the regulation of the industry in Norfolk specified more than a dozen varieties of worsteds.[10] A later enactment mentions also 'Clothe called Vervise, or Plounkett, Turkyns or Celestines,' 'Carsey,' 'Vessees,' 'Packyng whites,' 'Florences with Crenyll listes,' 'brode cloth,'[11] 'Saillyng Ware,' 'Bastardes,' 'Kendales,' and Friseware.[9] Even this list was not exhaustive; there were in addition, 'Cloths,'[12] russet, blanket, 'Drap de Cremosyn,'[13] 'Fustian, Bustian . . . Scarlet Cloth,'[14]

Development of the manufacture of cloth.

[1] 13 *Ric. II*, No. 1, c. 11. [2] Fuller, *Church Hist. of Britain*, II, 287. [3] *Rot. Parl.*, III, 437. [4] 7 *H. IV*, c. 9, and 18 *H. VI*, c. 16. [5] 7 *Ed. IV*, c. 1. [6] *Rot. Parl.*, IV, 52. [7] 23 *H. VI*, c. 3. [8] 15 *Ric. II*, c. 10; and see page 12. [9] 1 *Ric. III*, c. 8. [10] 'Worstedes appellez Boltes,' either 'streits or brodes.' 'Mantelles . . . si bien les motles, paules, chekeres, raies, flores, pleynes, monkes-clothes'; chanon-Clothes '. . . and Worsted-beddes.' (*Rot. Parl.* III, 637.) [11] Broad cloths and broad dozens. (*Rot. Parl.* IV, 451.) [12] 20 *H. VI*, c. 10. [13] *Rot. Parl.*, III, 506. [14] *Ibid.*, V, 505.

says and serges,[1] stamyns,[2] and mustrevalers.[3] Equally significant are the statutes passed to protect English manufacturers against foreign competition, or to ensure a sufficient supply of raw material,—such as the orders that sheep should not be transported beyond the sea without licence,[4] and that foreign cloth should be forfeited on importation,[5] and the restrictions placed upon the purchase of wool by aliens, because the clothmakers of the realm could find wellnigh none to be sold by the growers.[6] Acts for the regulation of the industry, specifying the measure of the cloth,[7] the methods of sealing it,[8] the duties of the aulnager,[9] and other details, are numerous, and in some cases they were supplemented by the ordinances of the crafts[10] and the laws of the towns.[11]

Evidence of the growth of the manufacture of cloth may be seen in the decrease of the customs on wool, of which the Commons complained more than once.[12] In 1348 the subsidy on wool was valued at £60,000, and in the twenty-eighth year of Edward III the customs and subsidy on wool brought in more than £111,000[13]; this sum, however, was unusually large, and the gross proceeds of the customs two years later amounted to £66,830.[14] But the estimated yearly net value of the Custom Revenue between Michaelmas, 1428, and March 3rd, 1461, was only about £31,500 net, or £32,000 gross.[15] This extraordinary decrease of revenue from the customs on the export of wool was prob-

[1] Fuller, *op. cit.* [2] W. Beck, *Drapers' Dict.*, 325. [3] *Ibid.*, 71. [4] 3 *H. VI*, c. 2. [5] *Rot. Parl.*, V, 563. [6] 4 *Ed. IV*, c. 4. [7] 11 *H. IV*, c. 6. [7 and 8] 4 *Ed. IV*, c. 1; 7 *Ed. IV*, c. 2; and 8 *Ed. IV*, c. 1. [9] 18 *H. VI*, c. 16. [10] *Little Red Book of Bristol*, II, 127–8. *Coventry Leet Book*, Part i, 92 and *seq.* [11] Ordinances of Worcester, in *Eng. Gilds*, 378 and 382. [12] 27 *H. VI*, c. 2. [13] Stubbs, *Constit. Hist.*, II, 578. [14] *Ibid.*, 579 note. [15] Ramsay, *Lanc. and York*, II, 267.

ably due to the fact that much of the raw material was kept in England, to be made up into cloth here. Moreover, during the latter half of the fifteenth century, it is clear that the duty on cloth was becoming an important item of revenue, and the returns of the Customs in the reign of Edward IV indicate 'a steady decrease in the return from wool, and a corresponding increase in that from cloth,' which leads us to believe 'that the English cloth industry was swiftly gaining ground.[1] Schanz points out that the Hansards exported 4464 pieces of cloth in 1422, 6159 in 1461, and 21,389 in 1500.[2] The Merchant Adventurers also exported cloth, and their increasing prosperity is another indication that the industry was developing.

The silk manufacture.

The cloth manufacture was not the only industry which took root in England in the fifteenth century. By 1455 the 'occupation of silkewerk within the citee of London' had advanced so much that the 'silkewymmen' petitioned against the importation of 'wrought silk throwen, rybens, and laces falsly and deceyvably wrought, and corses of silk.'[3] Nine years later the artisans protested in a similar manner against the competition of aliens, and begged for the prohibition of the import of various kinds of wares 'beyng full wrought and redy made to the sale,' 'wollen bonettes . . . tyres of silke or of gold, sadles,' 'aundyrnes . . . hamers . . . gloves . . . gurdels . . . peltry ware . . . shoen . . . knyves . . . daggers . . . cisours . . . pynnes . . . candelsticks . . . ladles . . . hattes,'[4] and many other small articles.

According to the *Débat des Hérauts* coal-mining

[1] Alton and Holland, *The King's Customs*, 47. [2] Schanz, *Englische Handelspolitik*, II, p. 28. [3] *Rot. Parl.*, V, 325; *Ibid.*, 506; and 33 *H. VI*, c. 5. [4] *Rot. Parl.*, V, 506. See Appendix A.

was carried on to a considerable extent in England.

Mining. The English Herald claims that his people have 'charbon de pierre ardans, de quoy on fait le feu et se chauffe on ou dit pais, et en porte on vendre a grant habondance en plusieurs lieux,'[1] and the French Herald does not deny the fact.[2] The Newcastle coal trade was certainly large enough to require regulation by statute.[3] There were also other miners at work digging up the 'richesse dessoubz terre,'[4] 'mynieres d'estain, de plonc, de metal, d'alabastre, de marbre noir et blanc . . . de coutz de raseur.'[4] The *Early Chancery Proceedings* mention a free-stone quarry in Devon, of which the profits were said to be £30 a year[5]; and Mrs. Green draws attention to the iron works in the Forest of Dean.[6] Some of these industries had been in existence for a long time, and were very flourishing; but salt could not be produced in sufficient quantities in England to supply all that was needed for agricultural and domestic purposes,[7] and by the French Rolls we see that sixty persons were brought from Holland and Zealand, by John de Shiedame, to manufacture salt in England,[8] and they were established at Winchelsea.[9]

Beer-brewing. Another industry which owed its inception to aliens was the manufacture of beer, which was introduced by Dutch settlers in the eastern counties. This beer was different from the old-fashioned English ale, and those who made it were called 'bere-bruers' or 'brasiatores de scitrol.'[10] The French Herald

[1] *Débat des Hérauts*, p. 36. No. 97. [2] *Ibid.*, 46. No. 128. [3] *Rot. Parl.*, IV, 148 and 9 *H. V*, c. 10. [4] *Débat des Hérauts*, p. 36. [5] *Early Chanc. Proceed.*, 226/38. [6] Mrs. Green, *Town Life in the Fifteenth Century*, I, 54–5. [7] Thorold Rogers, *Hist. of Agriculture and Prices*, IV, 390. [8] *French Rolls*, 1439–40, m. 27. Feb. 8. [9] *Ibid.*, 1440–1, m. 4. Aug. 9. [10] Redstone, in *Trans. Royal Hist. Soc.*, N.S., XVI, pp. 174 and 186.

declares 'vous gastez plus blez pour faire vostre boisson, c'est assavoir vos servoises, que pour vostre mangier;'[1] but Dutch beer was made of malt and hops.[2] When Elizabeth Stonor was coming to London, Thomas Henham wrote and asked her whether she would have 'bere or hale' provided for the household.[3] The names of Dutch beer-brewers frequently occur in the Chancery Proceedings,[4] and the trade must have grown considerably by the end of the century, as Henry VII granted letters of denization to Hillary Warner, 'bere-bruer,' a native of Germany, with licence to export thirty tons of beer yearly, and to import hops[5]; and beer was also exported to Flanders.[6]

Brick-making.

The Dutch were also instrumental in starting the manufacture of bricks,[7] or in reviving an old industry, which had, at least partially, died out. They made these bricks very cheaply, and William Elys 'supplied two hundred thousand for the repair of Dover Castle (20 Edward IV), at the rate of two and a half hundred for a penny.'[8]

Manufacture of guns.

Guns were also manufactured in England, and many Flemings and Germans found employment here as gun-masters.[9] In the reign of Henry VII 'the master founder and maker of all cannons and guns in the Tower of London and elsewhere' received as wages eighteen pence a day for himself, and twelve pence a day for two men under him.[10]

A comparison of the statutes regulating wages in the fifteenth century shows that ship-building

[1] *Débat des Hérauts*, p. 43. No. 120. [2] Redstone, loc. cit., p. 176. [3] *A.C.*, Vol. XLVI. No. 240. [4] *Early Chanc. Proceed.*, 46/278, 59/44, 64/299. [5] Campbell, *Materials for the Reign of Henry VII*, II, 512. [6] *Early Chanc. Proceed.*, 65/22. [7] Redstone, loc. cit., 176. [8] *Ibid*, 177. [9] Wylie, *Hist. of the Reign of Henry IV*, II, 269. [10] Campbell, I, 219–20.

must have made progress. The Act of 1495[1] deals with shipwrights, master ship-carpenters, other ship-carpenters, hewers, clinchers, and caulkers, none of whom are even mentioned in the Act of 1444.[2] The English also seem to have acquired greater skill in ship-building; at the beginning of the century men-of-war had only two masts and two sails, by the end of it, they were three- or four-masters, with top-masts, topsails, bowsprits, and spritsails.[3] The first dry dock known in England was constructed at Portsmouth, in 1495–6, and no foreigners were employed on the work.[4]

Ship-building.

Some other industries existed at this time—there were linen-weavers in London,[5] and bell foundries in London, Salisbury, Norwich, Gloucester and Bridport. Carpets and tapestry were made at Ramsay.[6]

A review of the progress of Industry as a whole during this period shows that although aliens still influenced its development to some extent, their interference was more and more resented by the native workmen. Quarrels between denizens and foreigners were frequent,[7] and in some cases gild ordinances forbade the employment of alien apprentices or workmen.[8]

[1] 11 *H. VII*, c. 22. [2] *Rot. Parl.*, V, 112. [3] Oppenheim, *Admin. of the Roy. Navy*, I, 29. [4] *Ibid.*, I, 39. [5] The alien Clothmakers complained to the Chancellor that the Wardens of the Linenweavers would not suffer them to live within the city as heretofore, yet they demanded the same contribution from them (*Early Chanc. Proceed.*, 45/30). [6] *Town Life*, I, 56–7. [7] The Dutch Cordwainers in the suburbs of London brought a petition before the Chancellor against the English Cordwainers (90/23), and Hamond Tayloure, a 'foran' working in the franchise of London, was imprisoned at the suit of the tailors of London (78/113). Disagreements of English and alien weavers (*Rot. Parl.*, III, 600 and IV, 162). Alien goldsmiths ordered to submit to the wardens of the London craft (*Ibid.*, VI, 185). See also [5]. [8] *The Glovers of Hull in 1499*, quoted in Lambert, *Two Thousand Years of Gild Life*, p. 216; *Little Red Book of Bristol*, II; *Weavers' Ord.*, p. 128; *Hoopers'*, 163; *Cordwainers'*, 178–9.

The development of manufactures naturally led to great changes in the organization of Industry. The growing complexity of the work and the employment of a larger number of workmen caused the differentiation of processes and the division of labour.

The Organization of Industry.

"... gardyng, spynnyng, and wevyng,
Ffullyng, rowyng, dyyng, and scheryng"[1]

were all separate employments; there were even subdivisions of some processes, for the 'Libel' speaks of 'toukers' as well as dyers.[2] We know also that the occupations of the Brown-baker[3] and pye-baker[4] were distinct, and that the same person was not allowed to sell both brown and white bread[5]; and the employments of coverlet weavers,[6] honey-men,[7] pouchmakers,[8] girdlers,[9] and foystours,[10] (the makers of the wood-work of saddles), must have been highly specialized. The cutlers declared that every knife was prepared by three crafts—the blade by the bladsmyths, the handle and other fitting work by the cutlers, and the sheath by the sheathers.[11] The result of this splitting up of the crafts was the formation of a number of new gilds. Every occupation that engaged a score of men came, in the fifteenth century, to have an organization of its own[12]; even unskilled labourers, like the waterleders and porters of York formed misteries.[13] There were, indeed, ninety-six organized trades in York.[14] Discord, of course, arose frequently between the different gilds regarding their respective

[1] The 'Libel', in Wright's *Polit. Songs*, II, 284. [2] *Ibid.*, 285. [3] *Early Chanc. Proceed.*, 45/300. [4] *Ibid.*, 67/214. [5] Denton, *op. cit.*, p. 244. [6] *Early Chanc. Proceed.*, 48/50. [7] *Ibid.*, 64/1055. [8] *Ibid.*, 51/236. [9] *Ibid.*, 32/283. [10] Sharpe, *Wills*, II, 389. [11] Lambert, *Gild Life*, 263. [12] Ashley, *Economic Hist.*, Part ii, 74. [13] *Ibid.*, 75. [14] Wylie, *Henry IV.*, Vol. III, p. 187. See Appendix C 2 for further illustrations of the subdivision of industry.

spheres of action and other matters. The Cobblers and the Cordwainers of London quarrelled[1] so seriously that neither their own officials nor the civic authorities could settle their grievances, and the Cobblers applied to the Chancellor.[2] Sometimes trades, which had long been associated, desired to be parted; the 'taillours, shermen, & fullers' of Coventry, who had 'as one feliship yerely chosen a maister to rule them,' found they could no longer agree, and asked that the 'taillers and shermen' might be separated from the fullers.[3] On the other hand, unions of gilds are also found in the fifteenth century,[4] but they were utilized for religious, as well as for industrial purposes.[5] There is an interesting example of a union of crafts in the Coventry records—a complaint against the ordinances of the Wiredrawers states: 'hit is like myche of the kynges pepull, and in speciall poor chapmen and Clothemakers, in tyme comeng shullon be gretely hyndered; and as hit may be supposed the principall cause is like to be amonges hem that han all the Craft in her own hondes, That is to sey, smythiers, brakemen, gurdelmen and Cardwirdrawers'; and the petition goes on to show what evils may arise through the misdeeds of the man 'who hathe all thes Craftes.' He may force the 'Brakemon' and the 'girdulmon' and the 'cardwiredrawer' to use his iron, even if it be 'dissayvabely wrought,' because they must do as their

[1] Riley, pp. 570–1 and 571–4. [2] *Early Chanc. Proceed.*, 59/129. [3] *Ibid.*, 16/490*a* and 490*b*. [4] The Gild of the Holy Cross, Stratford-upon-Avon, apparently joined two other fraternities, the Gilds of Our Lady and of St. John the Baptist (*Eng. Gilds*, Part ii, 219–20). Union of Crafts at Walsall (Gross, *Gild Merchant*, I, 121–2). [5] Mrs. Green describes a confederation of Gilds at Canterbury grouped together to maintain the pageants of the town, in 1490 (*Town Life*, I, 151). Gross explains that in 'many towns there was a Corpus Christi Gild which embraced most of the Crafts,' all of which took part in the pageants on Corpus Christi Day (*The Gild Merchant*, I, 118, n.).

master bids them.[1] This incident is significant because it seems to point to the presence of the capitalist employer, whose advent is one of the most important of the economic changes of the fifteenth century. In the earlier period small masters, employing two or three men, made and often sold finished goods; [2] but this simple arrangement was only possible as long as the market was small. The expansion of trade and the demand for larger supplies of goods made production on a greater scale inevitable, for which more money was required than a small master possessed; therefore a new class of men arose, commanding an adequate amount of capital,[3] who were able, as we have seen at Coventry, to bring a comparatively large number of workers into dependence upon themselves.[4] In the cloth industry these men were called clothiers, or cloth-makers; they gave the 'wolles' to the 'carders, spynners, and all other Laborers' to be wrought,[5] paid them for their labour, and thus arranged for every stage of the manufacture.[6] When the cloth was made, the clothiers in their turn sold it to the drapers, another class of traders who owed their special functions to the development of Industry. The drapers were both makers of and dealers in cloth when they obtained their first charter of incorporation, in 1364,[7] but the growth of the manufacture rendered it desirable to have a class of dealers in cloth distinct from the makers,[8] and the drapers therefore became exclusively dealers. The London drapers tried to obtain the monopoly of the sale of cloth, and were so aggressive that Parliament was obliged to pass

[1] *Coventry Leet Book*, 181–2. [2] Ashley, *Woollen Industry*, 72. [3] *Ibid.*, 75. [4] *Ibid.* [5] *Rot. Parl.*, V, 502, No. 17, and 4 *Ed. IV*, c. 1. [6] Ashley, *Woollen Industry*, p. 81. [7] *Ibid.*, 63 [8] *Ibid.*, 58.

an Act to protect the rights of the country drapers.[1] Developments of a similar nature occurred in other trades, and so there was a regular gradation of classes in the industrial world—the artisan, the manufacturer, the middleman, and the merchant; and this was a state of affairs which differed greatly from the simple arrangements of earlier days. We find one or two anticipations of modern methods of industry in the use of machinery,—fulling-mills are mentioned at Hawkesbury, Bisley and Chalford in Gloucestershire, and Guildford.[2] The King was asked to forbid the use of 'gygymlles and Toune Milles' in 1463–4,[3] and of fulling-mills in 1482.[4] Both petitions were answered in the affirmative, nevertheless, Henry VII granted several leases of fulling-mills in the Duchy of Lancaster.[5] It was said that a mill could full more in a day than eighty men, so no doubt the employment of them was very profitable. The grants of mill-streams at Stroud and Bisley show that men were beginning to realize the industrial value of water power.[6] A curious instance of an approximation to modern modes of industrial warfare may be seen in the combination of the dyers of Coventry in order to enhance the price of dying cloth.[7] A petition against them was laid before the King in 1415.[8] A complaint made to the Chancellor by Thomas de Feriby and other dyers of Coventry against Egynton and W. Warde, also dyers, may perhaps refer to the same incident; in any case it affords an illustration of the way in which dissentient fellow-

[1] 7 *H. IV*, c. 9. [2] *Victoria County Hist. of Glos.*, II, 157. The sum of £27 is stated to have been spent on repairing fulling-mills near Guildford (*Early Chanc. Proceed.*, 89/69). [3] *Rot. Parl.*, V, 502–3. [4] *Ibid.*, VI, 223. No. 29. [5] Campbell, *op. cit.*, II, 329–30, 332, 367, 399, 441. [6] *V.C.H. Glos.*, II, 151. [7] Dormer Harris, *Life in an Old English Town*, 265. [8] *Rot. Parl.*, IV, 75, 21.

workers were intimidated. Egynton and Warde, it was stated, 'firent faire ore tarde une congregacion a Coventre de toutz ceux de ceste mestier, et la firent les ditz suppliantz countre leur gree iurrer entre autres de faire & excercer certeins choses en desceit de la poeple.'[1] Mrs. Green traces 'rude beginnings of a factory system,' and gives as an instance the malt made by the brewers of Kent, whereas it had been hitherto bought from the people[2], and Miss Dormer Harris alludes to a movement among the Journeymen Weavers in Coventry which was like a modern strike.[3]

Distribution of the products of Industry.

It might perhaps be expected that the growth of trade would cause improvements both in the means of communication between different parts of the country and in the methods of transporting goods. Upon these points modern writers do not agree. Thorold Rogers insists that in this century 'the means of communication were fairly good,' and the principal roads, even in winter, were in decent repair[4]; and he gives as his reasons for this opinion the lowness of the cost of carriage,[5] the existence of a common carrier,[4] and the length of the journeys, both on horseback and in carts, which were undertaken in a single day.[6] Dr. Cunningham, on the other hand, is convinced of the decay of the roads.[7] Fortunately we have descriptions of the streets and highways from persons living at the time. We read in the Statute Book that the road from Abingdon towards Dorchester, 'over the Water of Thames by the Places of Burford and Culhamford . . . was lately by the Increase

Roads.

[1] *Early Chanc. Proceed.*, 7/23. [2] *Town Life*, II, 89.
[3] *Life in an Old Eng. Town*, 278. [4] *Work and Wages*, 135.
[5] *Agriculture and Prices*, IV, 692. [6] *Ibid.*, 693.
[7] Cunningham, *Growth of English Industry and Commerce*, I, 450.

of Water so much surrounded, that no one could pass there, nor make any suche Carriage there without Danger of losing their Lives, Goods, Chattels, and Merchandises.'[1] Steps, however, were taken to repair the road and the bridges over the river. In Bristol, one of the most prosperous towns in England, the paving in the streets was 'decayed, broken, and holowid and pitted, by water fallyng out of Gutters, by Ridyng and Cariage, to great hurt and disease of the Kyngs Liege People.'[2] The wills of the period contain many bequests for the repair of 'foundrous ways'[3] and of 'noyous jeoperdes'[4] ones, in all parts of the country, 'betwen Hillindon and Akton,'[5] 'betwene London and ware,'[6] 'beside Portmannes Crosse fast by Briggenorth,'[7] so it is clear that the evil was not confined to any one district. The safe return of a traveller was a matter for great thankfulness, and did not pass without comment. 'Rychard Cely was at norlayge . . . and ys com hom in savete,' writes old Richard Cely to his son George.[8] From a rather unexpected source we have further evidence of the existence of 'perilous highways.'[9] The Coroner's Rolls for the county of Leicester attribute an extraordinary number of deaths to falling out of carts. One man was bending over to whip his horses, and fell out and was killed[10]; in another case the cart turned over, and part of it crushed the driver's head[11]; one instance is recorded in which both man and cart fell from a bridge into the water[12]; and more than once a wheel came off

[1] *Statutes of the Realm*, 9 *H. V*, c. 11. [2] *Rot. Parl.*, VI, 391.
[3] Sharpe's *Wills*, II, 487 (1437). [4] *Ibid.*, 599 (1497).
[5] Furnivall, *E. E. Wills*, 11 (1402). [6] *Ibid.*, 15.
[7] *Ibid.*, 31 (1418). [8] *Cely Papers*, Letter 28, p. 28 (1480).
[9] Sharpe's *Wills*, II, 422, 430, 432, 433.
[10] *Coroners' Rolls*, 63, m. 2, No. 1. [11] *Ibid.*, 60, m. 4.
[12] *Ibid.*, 63, m. 2.

and caused a fatal accident.[1] It seems almost impossible that so many accidents of this kind should have happened if the roads had been in a safe state for travelling. The jury added in one account that the cart was rickety,[2] but as a rule they offer no explanation, and treat the affair quite as a matter of course. Nor do the methods of transport employed lead us to suppose that the roads were very good: 'the common carrier' apparently conveyed the 'fardells' on horseback.[3] We hear of plate which is to be 'pakked in the cariors pakke of Exeter,'[4] of cloth sent by 'cariers' to Oxford,[5] and of fish carried in 'paniers vpon horsis to London.'[6] The 'mere tracks,'[7] which Thorold Rogers repudiates, would have been quite sufficient for horses, and it is probable that the roads in some districts were little more than bridle-paths and unfit for vehicular traffic. In one of the Paston Letters (dated Jan. 30, 1443), it is stated that the Chief Justice dared not come to the Assize on horseback, because he had a sciatica, but for the 'remanent of the assizes' he would 'purvey to be there by water';

[1] *Ibid.*, 61, m., 4, cf. ms. 6 and 7. Other cases in the same county are 61, m. 10; 63, ms. 2 and 5; 60, m. 6. Instances in other counties in Rolls 168 (Stafford), and 145, m. 2 (Shropshire). Very few Coroners' Rolls for the fifteenth century are in existence, and as I have omitted those published by the Selden Soc., rolls for only four counties were left, Middlesex, Stafford, Leicester, and Shropshire; the records for the first two are rather scanty, and Shropshire was in an exceptional position, on the borders of Wales and exposed to attacks from that country, so I thought it better to use Leicester to illustrate this subject. [2] Coroners' Rolls, 63, m. 2, No. 3.

[3] The horse in Lydgate's 'Horse, Goose, and Sheep' boasts

> 'Leede, ston, and timbre cariage eek for bellis,
> We brynge to chyrches (of trouthe, this is no tale);
> We lade cloth sakkis and many a large male
> And gladly someres ar sent euyr to-forn
> With gardeviaundis how myht we be for-born.'
>
> *Political, Relig. and Love Songs*, p. 21.

'Someres' means pack-horses, 'gardeviaundis' a chest for food or valuables.

[4] *A.C.*, Vol. XLVI., Letter 160. [5] *Early Chanc. Proceed.*, 9/124.

[6] *Pecock, Repressor*, 30. [7] *Agriculture and Prices*, IV, 693.

'the absence at that period of any carriage-road between London and the Assize town of one of the home counties is worthy of remark.'[1] Similarly, in a communication to the Privy Council it was announced that the King was ill, and could not travel, especially not on horseback, but he hoped to come from Windsor to Staines that night, and thence to London by water.[2] In 1463 Sir John Howard's steward was obliged to hire 'a gyde to gyde' his master's draper to Long Stratton[3] (Norfolk), so there must either have been no road at all, or one that was very bad and hard to find.[3] Carts were no doubt used sometimes, especially for the transport of heavy articles, and we find several entries in Household Books of payment for the cartage of provisions,[4] or fuel,[5] or other goods. A few grand people had carriages; the 'chariet' of the Duchess of Buckingham is mentioned in her Household Book once or twice.[6] And when Henry VI wanted to welcome Margaret of Anjou he borrowed 'many horses, as wele palfrieies, as for chares, chariетts, someres, and other.'[7] The majority of people, even women, made journeys on horseback. Margaret Paston never thought of travelling in any other way, and Elizabeth Stonor asked her husband to send her horses when she wished to go to him[8]; so no doubt this method was the one best suited to the roads. On the whole we may reasonably conclude that they were in a very bad state during the greater part of the fifteenth century, but the civic authorities made some attempts to improve them. The repairing of the

[1] *Life of Sir John Fortescue*, I, 8–9. [2] *Proceed. Privy Council*, I, 290. [3] *Howard Household Book*, I, 154. [4] *Add. MSS.* 34, 213, f. 25 dorse, f. 31 d., f. 77. *Howard Household Book*, I, 387 and 498. [5] *Add. MSS.*, 34, 213; 33. [6] *Ibid.*, ff. 64, 65 d., 79 d. [7] Ellis, *Original Letters*, Third Series, 81–2. For cost of transit see Appendix C, 1*a*. [8] *A.C.* 46, Letter 115.

road between Abingdon and Dorchester has already been mentioned; it was carried out, not by the Abbot, through whose franchise it ran, but by the people of Abingdon.[1] An order was issued in Coventry, in 1423, that every man must repair his pavement in front of his tenement, before the next Leet.[2] About twenty years later it was decreed that the mayor should provide paviors to pave the streets, and that their wages were to be raised by distraint.[3] In 1430–1 the Mayor of Northampton obtained from Parliament the right to force persons owning free tenements, 'buttant sur ascun hault chesmyn ou rue du dit ville,' to contribute to the making and repair of the same.[4] During the last thirty years of our period, the towns of Gloucester,[5] Canterbury,[6] Taunton,[7] Cirencester,[8] Southampton,[9] Winchester,[10] and Bristol,[11] all sought and gained similar powers. This desire to improve their streets surely betokens an awakening sense of the necessity for better means of communication on the part of the trading classes, and may fairly be attributed partially, if not entirely, to the growth of Industry; but their efforts were directed only to the improvement of the streets within the city-walls, and the roads outside remained neglected.

Probably the reason why 'foule and feble' roads were so long tolerated in England was that the great use of water carriage enabled people to do without them to some extent. Coal was brought to London from Newcastle by sea,[12] and wheat was

[1] *Statutes of the Realm*, 9 *H. V*, c. 11. [2] *Coventry Leet Book*, 58 Worcester ordered every man to keep his path clean, and his pavement in repair (*Eng. Gilds*, 384).
[3] *Coventry Leet Book*, 199. [4] *Rot. Parl.*, IV, 373, 23.
[5] *Ibid.*, VI, 49, 54. [6] *Ibid.*, VI, 177, 21. [7] *Ibid.*, 179, 22.
[8] *Ibid.*, VI, 180, 23. [9] *Ibid.*, 180, 24. [10] *Ibid.*, VI, 333, 64.
[11] *Ibid.*, VI, 390, 9. [12] *Early Chanc. Proceed.*, 15/160.

sent from Walberswick in Suffolk in the same way[1]; and ships, going via Newcastle to Edinburgh, took provisions to the English Army in Scotland.[2] Rivers were the great highways within the country, the means by which 'all Manner of Merchandise, and other Goods and Chattels' were conveyed to the districts through which they flowed. The alarm of the people of Tewkesbury when their turbulent neighbours in the Forest of Dean attacked the boats on the Severn[3] shows how greatly they valued the right of free passage on the river. Entries in *Compotus Rolls* also illustrate the employment of rivers for this purpose: the Duchess of Buckingham paid four bargemen sixteen pence for conveying goods from 'Queynhith' to Westminster.[4] The *Howard Household Books* are full of payments for 'botehyre' to barges which brought salt, cheese, wine,[5] and other necessaries; and the churchwardens of Tintinhull record the transit of 'ij wey of cole' by water from 'Ronam' (Rownham-on-Avon) to Kingston.[6] The Government, which apparently cared nothing about the condition of the roads, took the utmost pains to keep the waterways open. Not only were the statutes of Edward III,[7] forbidding the formation of weirs and other obstructions to boats, confirmed[8] and enlarged,[9] but commissioners were appointed to ensure the execution of the Acts,[10] and they were well paid for their labour[11]; and in one case they were empowered to take a toll of fourpence from

[1] *Early Chanc. Proceed.*, 187/30. Other references to transit of grain by water, *Rot. Parl.*, V, 31, *Cal. Patent Roll*, 1433, m. 24.
[2] *Accounts, Excheq. Q. R. Army*, 42/32 (1 *H. IV*). [3] 8 *H. VI*, c. 27. [4] *Add. MSS.* 34, 213, 74 d. [5] *Howard Household Bk.*, I, 518, 523. See Appendix C 1*a* for cost of transit by water.
[6] *Hobhouse*, 117. [7] 25 *Ed. III*, st. 3, c. 4, and 45 *Ed. III*, c. 2.
[8] 1 *H. IV*, c. 12, and 1 *H. V*, c. 2. [9] 9 *H. VI*, c. 9, and 12 *Ed. IV*, c. 7, and 2 *H. VI*, c. 19. [10] 1 *H. IV*, c. 12. [11] 4 *H. IV*, c. 11.

every boat passing down the river if money were needed for their work.[1] So heinous was disobedience to these statutes considered that a penalty of a hundred shillings was inflicted for each default.[2]

The growth of Industry caused a demand for better facilities for the sale of goods. A few of the old fairs fell into decay. 'The importance of St. Ives mart' declined in the fourteenth century[3]; Boston Fair had entirely ceased by 1416[4]; and St. Giles, Winchester, was greatly reduced by 1471,[5] because the centre of trade had shifted; the manufacture of cloth, to which it had owed its prosperity, had almost died out there.[6] London profited by the decline of her rivals, and Stow narrates the grant, in 20 *H. VI*, to the Master, Brothers and Sisters of St. Catherine's, of a new fair to be held upon Tower Hill,[7] and there were already three great fairs in the suburbs of London—at Westminster, Smithfield, and Southwark.[8] Stourbridge Fair continued to flourish, and from the accounts of the Priories of Maxtoke and Bicester, in the time of Henry VI, it is seen the monks visited it yearly, although the place was at least a hundred miles distant from them.[9] The fair in the North Hundred of Oxford derived importance from the sale of books.[10] Fairs must have been a fruitful source of income in the time of Henry VI, for that monarch endowed Eton with four,[11] and the town of Lincoln petitioned for the right to hold two a year, that it might be enabled to raise money to pay its fee-farm.[12] In the latter part of the fifteenth century great dissatisfaction was caused by the

[1] 9 *H. VI*, c. 9. [2] 2 *H. VI*, c. 19. [3] C. Gross, *The Law Merchant*, Vol. I, xxxiv. [4] Riley, *op. cit.*, 637. [5] Cunningham, *Growth of Eng. Industry and Commerce*, I, 452. [6] Lambert, *Gild Life*, 79–80. [7] Strype's *Stow*, I, 72. [8] Ashley, *Econ. Hist.*, Part ii, 214. [9] Walford, *Fairs*, 63. [10] T. Rogers, *Agric. and Prices*, IV, 155. [11] *Rot: Parl.*, V, 78 and 131. [12] *Ibid.*, IV, 418.

aggressions of the courts of Pie powder, and their encroachment upon other local jurisdictions,[1] and certain rules were laid down by statute to remedy these abuses,[2] but they probably did a great deal to injure fairs in general.[3] The statute of 1487, though it speaks of the importance of the fairs of Salisbury, Bristol, Oxenforth, Cambrigge, Netyngham, Ely, and Coventry, unconsciously suggests that their vigour was waning; if it had not been so, they would not have been in danger of 'utter destruction' merely because the Common Council of London had forbidden its citizens to carry goods for sale to any fairs or markets outside the city.[4] Nevertheless, fair moots continued to flourish,[5] and Henry VII not only confirmed existing rights to hold fairs and markets, but allowed several new ones to be established,[6] even in places where other fairs were held.[7] Taking all these circumstances into consideration, we may conclude that the value and usefulness of fairs had not entirely passed away. It is clear, however, that they no longer afforded enough opportunities for the increasing amount of trade that was carried on at this time. The Drapers of London bought Blackwell Hall and turned it into a market for country drapers, and business was carried on there for two whole days every week.[8] 'London Lickpenny,' a little poem attributed to Lydgate, gives us a lively picture of the tradesmen of London and their eagerness to sell their wares:—velvet, silk, lawn, and Paris thread were on sale in the Cheap,[9] cloth 'throughout all Canwyke street,'[10]

[1] 17 *Ed. IV*, c. 2. [2] Gross, *Law Merchant*, Vol. I, xviii. [3] Cunningham, *op. cit.*, I, 452. [4] 3 *H. VII*, c. 9. [5] Gross, *op. cit.*, Vol. I, xvii. [6] Campbell, *op. cit.*, I, 390, 480–1. [7] *Ibid.*, Vol. I, 455; Vol. II, 335–6. [8] Ashley, *Econ. Hist.*, Part ii, 215. [9] *Minor Poems of Dan John Lydgate*, edited by J. O. Halliwell (Percy Soc., 1840), p. 105, verse 10. [10] *Ibid.*, p. 106, verse 11.

and hot pies and ribs of beef abounded in East Cheap[1]; and the noisy bustling sellers seemed to be doing a brisk trade. No doubt similar scenes took place, though upon a smaller scale, in many a country town, and they are typical of the effects produced by industrial changes in the fifteenth century.

[1] *Ibid.*, p. 106, verse 12.

CHAPTER II

AGRARIAN CHANGES

CHANGES of such magnitude as those which took place in the industrial world in the fifteenth century could not fail to exercise much influence upon the other factors of the economic system, and the development of manufactures in England was not without serious consequences for husbandry, because it provided new and profitable careers for the people. Complaints of the scarcity of agricultural labourers, which had begun in the fourteenth century, and was unquestionably due in the first place to the ravages of the Black Death, continued and increased. Thomas Billop, servant of Sir William Plumpton, at Kinalton, writes and tells his master that he cannot get his corn carried, because every man is so busy with his own, and that his malt has not been winnowed because he could get no help.[1] By the statute of Cambridge, passed in the reign of Richard II,[2] any person who had laboured in the service of husbandry up to the age of twelve was ordered from henceforth to abide at the same labour, and this Act was confirmed early in the fifteenth century, with, however, an exception in favour of those whose parents possessed lands of the yearly value of forty shillings, or goods worth forty pounds.[3] But even these severe measures were not sufficient to check the evil, and

Scarcity of agricultural labourers.

[1] *Plumpton Correspondence*, p. 21 (1469). [2] 12 *Ric. II*, c. 5.
[3] *Rot. Parl.*, III, 501, 59.

in 1406 a more stringent Act was passed, which shows that the superior attraction of industrial employments was considered the chief cause of the trouble. No man from henceforth was to apprentice his child, even under the age of twelve, to any mistery in any city or borough, unless he possessed lands to the value of twenty pounds a year, but children were to follow the occupations of their parents, or such labour as their conditions demanded.[1] This Act was no doubt evaded in some cases, for in the year 1444, Justices of the Peace were empowered 'to take all Servauntz, witholden with eny persone by colour of Husbandrye and not dewly occupyed aboute it, . . . oute of ye servyse of theire Maisters, and to compelle theym to serve in the occupation of Husbondrye.'[2] In spite of legislation, it was impossible to entirely stop the flight of agricultural labourers to manufacturing towns, and by the end of the century it was necessary to raise their wages[3] in order to retain their services.

Condition of agriculture.

Statistics of the export of grain throw some light upon the condition of agriculture. Export was permitted if a licence were obtained from the King, but the Council was authorized to restrain it when it seemed necessary.[4] The use made by the Council of the discretion left to it does not appear to have had much correspondence with the wishes of the land-owners,[5] and was therefore probably not very beneficial to husbandry. The *French Rolls* and the *Patent Rolls* show that very few licences were issued during the reign of Henry V, and not a very much larger number between 1422 and 1442. The years

[1] *Rot. Parl.*, III, 601–2 and 7 *H. IV*, c. 17. [2] *Ibid.*, V, 113.
[3] 11 *H. VII*, c. 22. [4] 17 *Ric. II*, c. 17, and 4 *H. VI*, c. 5.
[5] Faber, *Die Enstehung des Agrarschutzes in England*, p. 83.

in which the most grants were made are 1426–7, 1427–8, and 1431–2.[1] The *French Rolls* record that twenty-nine licences were issued in the year 1426–7 to forty-two persons, forty-one licences in 1427–8 to sixty-nine persons, and thirty-two in 1431–2 to thirty-seven persons. Merchants of London,[2] Kingston-upon-Hull,[3] Maldon,[4] Southwold [5] and Kent [6] were amongst those who most often obtained permission from the Council to export grain. The small number of grants of licences gives the impression that agriculture was not in a very flourishing condition. In 1437–8 the people of Cornwall were allowed to trade with Ushant, because corn was scarce in England[7]; and there was also great scarcity in 1439.[8] The *French Rolls* give us information occasionally as to the districts from which grain was obtained. Corn came from Berkshire,[9] Kent,[10] and Gloucestershire,[11] grain was bought in Dorset, Somerset, and Devon[12]; but these were not the only corn-growing districts; all the counties immediately north of London, from Suffolk to Gloucestershire, and the southern districts of Leicester, Stafford,[13] and Cambridge,[14] produced good wheat. It was, however, found that restriction of the export of corn, even in a modified form, was not wise. The farmers, it was said, could not sell their corn but at a bare price, so Parliament, anxious to foster husbandry, decreed that wheat might be exported when the price of it did not exceed six shillings and eight pence a quarter, and barley when it did not cost more than three shillings a

[1] *Cal. French Rolls*, sub annos. [2] *Ibid.*, 1426–7, MS., 16–14, 8, 7, 2. [3] *Ibid.*, 1427–8, MS., 17–14. [4] *Ibid.*, 1426–7, MS., 13, 6. [5] *Ibid.*, 1427–8, m. 16; 1431–2, m. 8. [6] *Ibid.*, 1426–7, m. 8; 1427–8, m. 8; 1431–2, m. 8. [7] *Ibid.*, 1437–8, m. 11. [8] Syllabus to Rymer's *Fœdera*, II, 665. [9] *Cal. French Rolls*, 1440–1, m. 8. [10] *Rot. Parl.*, IV., 307. [11] *Cal. French Rolls*, 1422–4, m. 16. [12] *Ibid.*, m. 13. [13] Denton, *England in the Fifteenth Century*, 144. [14] Denton, *op. cit.*, 145.

quarter.[1] Even this concession was apparently not enough to make agriculture thrive; in 1463 a complaint was raised that 'Occupiers of Husbandry . . . be daily grievously endamaged by bringing of Corn out of other Lands and Parts into this realm . . . when the corn of the growing of this Realm is at a low Price.' So it was enacted that wheat, rye, and barley should not be imported when the prices did not exceed six and eight pence, four shillings, and three shillings a quarter respectively.[2] Another sign of the desire to encourage agriculture was the reduction of the toll on a horse-load of corn far below that charged for other commodities.[3] In spite of these protective measures the agriculture entered upon a period of decline. The *Paston Letters* afford a very good illustration of the decreasing value of agricultural land in the case of the parsonage of Oxnead: 'William Paston, Justice, qwan he cam fyrst to dwell in the maner of Oxned, paid to the parson that was than for the corne growyng on the parsonage londys and for the tythynges, ondely but in corne whan it was inned in to the barn, xxiiij li. And the same yere the parson had all the awterage and oder profytes be syde the seyd xxiiij li. It is yerly worth, as the world goth now, x li.'[4]

The Cloth Industry not only enticed labourers away from husbandry, but led to the gradual substitution of sheep-farming for tillage.[5] Increasing

[1] *Rot. Parl.*, IV, 500 and 15 *H. VI*, c. 2, which was continued for ten years, 20 *H. VI*, c. 6, and made perpetual, 23 *H. VI*, c. 5. [2] 3 *Ed. IV*, c. 2. [3] Campbell, *op. cit.*, II, 332: in the castle and honor of Hertford, in 1488 a corn-laden beast was charged a farthing; others a penny or a halfpenny. [4] *Paston Letters*, No. 934, Vol. V, 326. [5] The return to the Inquisition for Belawe (Norfolk), in 1517, states 'et causa est quod sui infra idem hundredum occupant misteram siue facturam de le worsted & parpuipendunt iconomiam ad detrimentum dicti hundredi.' Mr. Leadam in *Trans. Royal Hist. Soc.*, N.S. VII (1893), 202–3.

supplies of wool were needed to satisfy the demands of English manufacturers, as well as those of foreigners, and sheep-farming grew so profitable that land-owners were tempted to enclose their cornfields and to convert them into sheep-runs. It is not easy to tell exactly when the movement began, but Miss Davenport has drawn attention to one or two instances in the closing years of the fourteenth century, in the manor of Forncett. She also points out that a tenant of the same manor paid for a licence to have a fold for a hundred sheep, in 1401, and that in 1404 the first protest against enclosing appears in the *Court Roll*. By that date several tenants had enclosed their lands, and sixteen of them paid fines for so doing.[1] The *Court Rolls* of Launton state that 'the jurats present that all the tenants, freeholders and villeins assembled and brake an hedge of land which marked off a recent enclosure, and carried it away in contempt of the lord.'[2] In 1420 Sir Robert Plumpton granted a licence to the prioress of Esshold to enclose two assarts.[3] It is also interesting to notice that the enclosing of woods and forests was sanctioned by the enactment (22 *Ed. IV*, c. 7) that owners might enclose land in the forest for seven years, if the wood had been cut down.[4] Sometimes the lord of the manor enclosed part of the demesne himself,[5] or let it to a tenant, who had the privilege of enclosing it. William Scargille, who obtained a lease of demesne land from Henry VII, was allowed 'to cut and throw down hedges growing

The enclosing movement.

[1] Miss Davenport, *Econ. Development of a Norfolk Manor*, pp. 80–1.
[2] Denton, *op. cit.*, 157 note. [3] *Plumpton Corr.*, xlvii, note.
[4] Ochenkowski, *Englands wirthschaftliche Entwickelung*, p. 33 and note. [5] John Fisher, serjeant-at-law, enclosed the lordship of Clopton. *Early Chanc. Proceed.*, 223/25 (date, 1493–1500).

in the said land, for fuel and enclosures.'[1] Occasionally land was let on the express condition that it should be enclosed. The lease of a meadow called Tropemede, in the county of Hertford, stipulated that the tenant should enclose it at his own cost, and at the end of his term leave it sufficiently enclosed.[2] In the reign of Henry VII the enclosing movement had reached such dimensions that it attracted the attention of Parliament, and attempts were made to stop it. Two statutes were passed with this object: one dealt especially with the Isle of Wight,[3] the other was of general application.[4] Both deplored the desolation and depopulation caused by sheep farming, the 'wilfull waste of houses & Townes . . . and leyeng to pasture londis whiche custumeably have been used in tilthe,' whereby two or three men were occupied instead of two hundred, and husbandry had greatly decayed.[4] The Acts were, however, quite ineffectual, and in 1517 Commissioners were appointed to inquire what houses had been thrown down and what land enclosed since Michaelmas, 1488. Many of the returns made to the Commissioners have been preserved at the Public Record Office, and Mr. Leadam has examined them and published his results. He tells us that between the years 1485 and 1500, 15,709½ acres of land were enclosed within the counties of Northampton, Buckingham, Oxford, Warwick, and Berkshire, of which 2347½ acres were devoted to agriculture, and 13,362 to pasture.[5] Professor Gay thinks that Mr. Leadam has overestimated the amount of land which was enclosed with the object of improved cultivation, and nothing more,[6] but both agree that depopulation

[1] Campbell, *op. cit.*, I, 597. [2] *Ibid.*, II, 313. [3] 2 *H. VII*, c. 16.
[4] 4 *H. VII*, c. 19. [5] *The Domesday of Inclosures*, I, 41. [6] E. F. Gay, 'Inquisitions of Depopulation,' in *Trans. Royal Hist. Soc.*, N.S., Vol. XIV (1900), 241 and *seq.*

was caused. Mr. Leadam has also calculated that 1205 acres of land were enclosed for pasture in Stafford, the East Riding of Yorkshire, Cambridge, Gloucestershire, Norfolk, Hereford, and Shropshire, between 1486 and 1499.[1] The total amount of land enclosed may not seem very great, but these calculations only cover a short period of time, and only deal with a small number of counties. In addition to the official records we have other evidence of the prevalence of sheep-farming in the comments of the writers of the fifteenth century, who were very much struck by it. The author of the 'Libelle of English Polycye,' writing in 1436 or 1437, asks regretfully—

> 'Where bene oure shippes? where bene our swerdes become?
> Owre enmyes bid for the shippe sette a shepe.'[2]

Sir John Fortescue, in the *Comodytes of Englond* (written before 1451), maintains that 'the third Comodyte of this land ys that the grounde therof ys soo goode and comodyous to the shepe, that beren soo goode woll and ys soo plentyous thereof that all the merchands of two londs may not by that one merchandyz.'[3] England had always enjoyed a great reputation as a wool-producing country, but apparently her wool improved both in quality and quantity at this time. The English Herald in the *Débat des Hérauts* (written probably between 1458 and 1461) boasts that England has 'par especial de bestes a laine, comme de brebiz qui portent la plus fine et la plus singuliere layne que on puisse savoir nulle part.'[4] The testimony of the writer of the *Italian Relation*, at a later date,

[1] 'Inquisitions of 1517,' I. S. Leadam in *Trans. Royal Hist. Soc.*, N.S., VI (1892), pp. 310–11. [2] Wright, *Political Songs*, II, 159. [3] *Works of Sir. J. Fortescue*, I, 551. [4] *Débat des Hérauts*, 35, No. 96.

corroborates the statement of the English Herald. 'Above all,' he says, speaking of the English, 'they have an enormous number of sheep, which yield them quantities of wool of the best quality.'[1] Many allusions in documents of various kinds confirm the impression produced by the literature of the time. We learn that Sir John Howard 'ad at Bray and in the Kontery a bowete morre than xjc schepe'[2]; and there is on record the case of a Dorset gentleman who owned fourteen thousand.[3] Persons of less wealth had fewer sheep, but even they had a fair number. A man named Richard Dalby complained to the Chancellor that four hundred of his sheep had been seized by a 'man of grete myght,' against whom no law could be executed[4]; two other petitioners stated that two hundred of their sheep had been carried off[5]; and four hundred and forty, belonging to the Abbey of Walton, were taken on the plea of non-payment of a pension.[6] Another Chancery petition illustrates the stocking of the tenant's land by the landlord, and shows the market-value of sheep,—Dame Katherine Chideok held certain lands and tenements of the prior of Christchurch, Twynham, for the 'terme of hyr lyfe,' and two hundred 'wedyr shepe for the instoryng of the seid londez and tenementez,' on the condition that they should be returned immediately after her death, or a payment of twenty pence for each.[7] That sheep were very profitable to keep is evident. Sales of wool and fells figure largely among the receipts of Metyngham College,[8] and even a great man like the Duke of Norfolk did

[1] *Italian Relation*, 10. [2] *Howard Household Book*, I, 555. [3] Atton and Holland, *The King's Customs*, 48. [4] *Early Chanc. Proceedings*, 27/359. [5] *Ibid.*, 27/421. Date of Bundle 27, 38 *H. VI* to 5 *Ed. IV.* Date of *Italian Relation* about 1500. [6] *Early Chanc. Proceed.*, 31/440. [7] *Ibid.*, 27/61; for date see above. [8] See Appendix, C 1*b*.

not think it beneath his dignity to make money out of his shearlings and hides.[1] The *Court Rolls* of the fifteenth century indicate the increasing number of sheep-pastures. The tenants of Hawkesbury Court, in 1466, issued orders stinting the number of sheep that might be kept on the common called 'Les Mores.'[2]

Thus the fifteenth century witnessed the beginning of 'the greatest of those agricultural revolutions which have in successive ages swept over this Country'—the transition from arable to pasture farming.[3]

[1] See Appendix, C 1*b*. [2] *Victoria County Hist. Glos.*, II, 156.
[3] I. S. Leadam, *Trans. Royal. Hist Soc.*, N.S., VI, p. 169.

CHAPTER III

COMMERCIAL CHANGES

THE rise of English foreign trade, and the consequent interest in national shipping, distinguishes the fifteenth from any previous century.[1] The *Patent Rolls* of the fourteenth century give safe-conducts for merchants and their servants in various parts of the realm,[2] but the records of the fifteenth show that they went to all the civilized maritime countries of Europe, and even occasionally beyond the limits of this continent. The earliest triumphs were won by the merchants, who traded with Holland, Zealand, Brabant, and Flanders. So many of them had settled in these parts beyond the sea by 1406, that Henry IV granted them by charter the right to have an assembly, to choose governors, to administer all kinds of justice, to make laws, and to punish offenders[3]; privileges which were confirmed by Henry V and Henry VI,[4] and increased by Henry VII.[5] The *French Rolls* contain many grants of licences to various persons to trade with these parts and the surrounding countries[6]; but we associate this branch of commerce especially

Enlargement of the area of trade.

[1] Giuseppi, in *Trans. Royal Hist. Soc.*, N.S., Vol. IX, 76.
[2] Law, *Ibid.*, 57. [3] *State Papers, Dom.*, ch. ii, Vol. XXVII, 1–5.
[4] *Ibid.*, 5. [5] *Ibid.*, 6 and *seq.* [6] *Cal. French Rolls*, 1422–4, m. 12; 1426–7, ms. 17, 8; 1428–9, m. 6; 1429–30, ms. 9, 8; 1430–1, ms. 19, 10, 5; 1431–2, ms. 15, 11, 7; 1432–3, m. 17; 1433–4, m. 10; 1435–6, m. 3; 1436–7, m. 7; 1437–8, m. 4; 1438–9, m. 3; 1439–40, ms. 28, 26, 16, 13; 1440–1, ms. 39, 37, 32, 27, 26, 22, 21, 18, 15, 8, 7, 6, 4, and other instances in other years.

with the traders who were known in the latter part of the century as Merchant Adventurers. Their career is interesting because it illustrates some of the most important economic changes of our period. Unlike the Staple, which was the financial organ of the Government, they were free and independent,[1] and whereas the older organization had the monopoly of the export of wool, they dealt chiefly in cloth.[2] Under these circumstances it was inevitable that a struggle should be waged between the two bodies of merchants, and traces of it can be seen in the petitions of the Staplers to the King, praying for the maintenance of their privileges,[3] and also in the prohibition of the payment of fines to them.[4] As the Cloth Industry developed the Staplers declined in wealth and power, while the Merchant Adventurers grew stronger.[5] They apparently remodelled their somewhat loose form of organization,[6] and by 1497 they had become so exacting that other merchants declared that they were kept away from the marts in Burgundy by the large fines demanded by the Adventurers, and Parliament consequently ordered them to lower their entrance fee to ten marks.[7] They were typical of their age, not only in their successful opposition to the Staplers, but also in their antagonism towards alien merchants: the company was entirely composed of Englishmen, and no member was even allowed to marry a foreigner.[8] Their settlement at Antwerp in 1407, gave them a point of vantage in the Netherlands, of which they made such good use that by the end of the century they dominated the

[1] Schanz., *op. cit.*, I, 332. [2] Schanz, I, 338.
[3] *Rot. Parl.*, IV, 250, V, 149, 273.
[4] *Ibid.*, V, 276. [5] Schanz, I, 339.
[6] *Ibid.*, 339-40. Lingelbach in *Trans. Royal Hist. Soc.*, N.S., XVI, pp. 33-4.
[7] 12 *H. VII*, c. 6. [8] Gross, *The Gild Merchant*, I, 148.

cloth trade in that country. The author of the 'Libelle' declares that he has heard it said—

> 'And yff the Englysshe be not on the martis,
> They bene febelle, and as noughte bene here partes;
> Ffor they bye more, and fro purse put owte,
> More marchaundy than alle othere rowte.'[1]

Even more significant is the complaint of the Flemish drapers, which was embodied in a proclamation in 1464, that the English every day sold great quantities of cloth, more than they had ever sold before, and at prices lower than the Flemings could afford to take, with the result that their sales were falling off, and their industry greatly diminished.[2] English cloth and wool were in consequence excluded from Flanders for a time, but the English retaliated by forbidding the importation of any merchandise, except provisions, from the lands belonging to the Duke of Burgundy,[3] and the Flemings soon gave way. Negotiations were carried on by Henry VII,[4] and culminated in the *Magnus Intercursus*, which guaranteed freedom of commerce to both nations.[5]

A great increase of English commerce with the countries round the shores of the Baltic also took place in the fifteenth century. The Hanse merchants were very powerful during the early part of the period, but the English had already obtained a footing in Norway, Sweden, Denmark,[6] and Prussia,[7] and a war between the Norwegians and the Hansards enabled them also to open communications with the Teutonic knights in Prussia.[8] In 1449 Henry VI desired the favour of the Master General of the Order for the factor of William

[1] Wright, II, 180. [2] Varenbergh, *op. cit.*, 521–2. [3] 4 *Ed. IV*, c. 5. [4] Gairdner, *Letters of R. III and H. VII*, II, 69–70. [5] Rymer's *Fœdera*, XII, 578–91. [6] Cunningham, *op. cit.*, I, 415. [7] Syllabus to Rymer's *Fœdera*, II, 550. [8] Cunningham, *op. cit.*, I, 417.

Canynges, of Bristol;[1] and various other Bristol merchants also employed agents in Prussia.[2] Trade with this country was of great value because timber, which was needed in England, could be obtained there. The *French Rolls* record that a licence was granted to a merchant of York to sail to Prussia, with four ships, in quest of wood for spears and bows, because there was such a scarcity of it in England.[3]

Trade with Iceland was very lucrative because stockfish, which could be caught near the island, were in great demand,[4] but the kings of Norway forbade the English to go there without special licence from them.[5] The marriage of Philippa, daughter of Henry IV, to Eric of Norway brought the two monarchs into friendly relations, and the English kings required their subjects to have a licence from them[6] as well, but in spite of this double set of restrictions merchants went there frequently. The *Icelandic Annals* show that the English visited the country between the years 1412 and 1430. In one year five ships came, in another six, and in 1419 as many as twenty-five were wrecked round the coast.[7] In 1430 the *Annals* end, but the *French Rolls* supplement them, and prove that the trade was continued.[8] It is not likely, however, that these records give an adequate idea of the business which was carried on during these years, because there was so much smuggling. The 'Libelle' tells us that the men of Scarborough and of

[1] Syllabus to Rymer's *Fœdera*, II, 679. [2] *Early Chanc. Proceed.*, 9/223. [3] *Cal. French Rolls*, 1435-6, m. 3. [4] Schanz, *op. cit.*, I, 253. [5] *Ibid.*, I, 252. [6] *Ibid.*, I, 254. [7] Laird Clowes, *Royal Navy*, I, 396-7. [8] *Cal. French Rolls*, 1438-9, m. 11; 1439-40, ms. 28, 26; 1441-2, ms. 17, 7; 1442-3, 11; 1443-4, ms. 16, 13, and 9; 1452-3, m. 9; 1454-5, by merchants of Kingston-on-Hull, m. 14; 1455-6, by merchants of Newcastle, m. 34; 1457-8, m. 21; 1459-60, m. 21.

Bristol went to 'Yseland,'[1] and the *French Rolls* mention amongst others John Taverner of Holderness,[2] and William Canynges of Bristol,[3] as well as various unnamed merchants of London, Kingston-on-Hull, and Newcastle. For some time the English Government encouraged smuggling, but the protests of the Norwegians became louder and louder, and threatened to lead to open war; so proclamations were issued in 1429 and other years strictly forbidding it.[4] In 1434 it was announced that in consequence of injuries done by the English to the subjects of the King of Denmark, Norway, and Sweden, especially in Iceland and Finmark, a staple had been established at Norbern. The King of England resolved that no one should contravene this ordinance on pain of forfeiture of goods and imprisonment,[5] and Edward IV treated offenders very severely.[6] Henry VII inaugurated a new era, and obtained important concessions for his subjects,—they were allowed to trade direct with Iceland on payment of toll, to possess land in Bergen and other Scandinavian towns, and to govern themselves in their settlements.[7]

Even more striking changes took place in the commerce of Southern Europe, which was almost entirely in the hands of Italians in the early fifteenth century. This branch of commerce was very important, because the products of the East came through Italy. All kinds of Italian merchants came to England—Venetians,[8] Florentines,[9] Genoese,[10]

[1] Wright, *Polit. Songs*, II, 191. [2] 1439–40, m. 3. [3] 1450–1, m. 14. [4 and 6] Schanz, I, 255. [5] *Proceedings of the Privy Council*, IV, 208–10. [7] Rymer, *Fœdera*, XII, 381–7. [8] *Cal. French Rolls*, 1419, m. 11; 1415, m. 21; 1420, m. 8; 1421, 11; 1422, 1; 1425–6, 4; 1432–3, m. 11; 1435–6, m. 21; 1439–40, ms. 30, 18; 1441–2, m. 18. [9] 1415, m. 9; 1419, m. 8; 1420, m. 5; 1422–4, m. 13; 1428–9, m. 1; 1442–3, m. 15; 1446–7, m. 6; 1455–6, m. 9; 1470–1, m. 4. [10] 1414, 13; 1435–6, m. 9; 1446–7, m. 8; 1444–5, m. 10; 1451–2, 16; 1455–6, ms. 21, 16; 1455–6, m. 4; 1456–7, m. 22; 1470–1, m. 9.

men of Milan,[1] and of Lucca.[2] The 'Libelle,' reflecting public opinion no doubt, complains bitterly that they bring 'thynges of complacence' and 'trifles that litelle have availede,'[3] and 'bere hens oure best chaffare, Clothe, wolle, and tynne.'[4] The lists of goods of various kinds in the possession of alien merchants, supplied by their English hosts, in accordance with the Statute, shows that they brought fine cloths of silk and gold, as baudekyn, cloths of Damascus, satin, velvet, tarterin, gold of Venice, wines, pepper, cinnamon, spices, sugar-candy, woad, alum, and paper. The merchants of Lucca brought armour from Milan.[5] English merchants, however, soon began to trade with the Mediterranean, and as early as the reign of Henry IV they petitioned that they might be allowed freely to ship staple merchandise and other goods 'en les parties de West, passantz les estroites de Marrok, outre les Mounteynes.'[6] The blow which Venice suffered by the loss of trade with Egypt (1442)[7] assisted the development of the English. In 1449 John Taverner of Hull received a licence to export goods to Italy, through the 'straits of Marrok,'[8] and Henry VII also granted many licences to merchants to carry wool beyond the 'straits of Marrok.'[9] Robert Sturmys of Bristol must have carried on a considerable trade in the Levant,[10] for the Genoese were obliged to pay him nine thousand marks for capturing his ships[11] (37 *Henry VI*). The Venetians greatly resented

[1] 1418, m. 4; 1420, m. 3; 1428–9, m. 5; 1435–6, m. 11; 1438–9, m. 1; 1440–1, m. 38; 1441–2, 5; 1446–7, m. 19; 1448–9, m. 8. [2] 1414, m. 20; 1418, m. 5; 1450–1, m. 9. [3] Wright, II, 172. [4] *Ibid.*, 174. [5] *Trans. Royal Hist. Soc.* N.S., IX, p. 88. [6] *Rot. Parl.*, III, 662, No. xi. [7] Green, *op cit.*, I, 114. [8] Syllabus, Rymer's *Fœdera*, II, 680. [9] Campbell, *Materials for the Reign of Henry VII*, Vol. II, 339, 365, 432, 446, 449, 459, 468. [10] Fabyan quoted in Ricart's *Kalendar*, 42. [11] Ricart, pp. 41–2.

the growth of English commerce. When they found that the English were interfering extensively with their commerce in the Levant, they imposed heavy duties upon English shipments from Candia. The English retaliated by laying 'a duty of eighteen shillings a butt, on malmsey brought to England in alien shipping,' and at the same time fixed the selling price of malmsey at a rate which the Venetian ambassador, in a statement to the Senate, declared ruinous to Venetian trade.[1] The Florentines, on the contrary, welcomed English merchants, and a very advantageous treaty was signed in 1490, by which the English agreed that the bulk of their wool should be shipped to Pisa, the port of Florence.[2] They already had a settlement and a consul of their own[3] at Pisa, and Florence gave them permission to form a company and elect their own officers.

The commercial relations of England and Portugal up to the year 1485 have been described by Miss Shillington in a recent work. She tells us that by the beginning of the fifteenth century there was an English factory in Lisbon, and that so many Englishmen lived in the city that they needed a chapel of their own.[4] They chose their own proctor, and a charter protected them from extortionate duty on the wine they exported.[5] Indeed, so many privileges were granted to them that by the middle of the century the Portuguese complained that the English were treated better than themselves.[6] The Portuguese imported various commodities into England, especially wine, wax, salt, and sugar[7]; but

[1] Atton and Holland, *op. cit.*, 54.
[2] Rymer, *Fœdera*, XII, 389–93. [3] Syllabus of Rymer's *Fœdera*, II, 720. [4] Shillington, *Commercial Relations of England and Portugal*, 65. [5] *Ibid.* [6] *Ibid.*, 69. [7] *Ibid.*, 108, the kinds of wine mentioned are bastard, wine of Algarve, and osey: sugar was brought in increasing quantities after 1466; it came from Madeira.

the English had the larger share of the trade between the two countries. In six months from November, 1465, the total value of Portuguese merchandise brought to Bristol was £4800, and of this the value of the goods imported by the English amounted to more than £4700.[1] Of 1062 pieces of ungrained cloth which left Bristol for Lisbon, 1042½ belonged to English merchants, and only 19½ to Portuguese.[2]

There must also have been a considerable amount of commercial intercourse between England and Spain.[3] The trade seems to have been mainly in the hands of merchants of Bristol,[4] London,[5] and Southampton.[6] Traders also came to England from various parts of Spain—from Catalonia,[7] Aragon,[8] Barcelona,[9] Bilbao,[10] Seville,[11] St. Sebastian,[12] Saragossa,[13] Biscay,[14] Loredo,[15] Navarre,[16] Deve,[17] and Guipuzcoa.[18] The Spaniards and the Portuguese brought iron, kid and beaver skins, red wine of Biscay, and liquorice.[19] In 1410 the sheriff of Kent was ordered to publish the articles of a commercial treaty with Castile concerning captured goods.[20] In 1416 negotiations were commenced with the King of Aragon to arrange the

[1] *Ibid.*, 52. [2] *Ibid.*, 105. [3] Licences were granted to English merchants to trade with Spain, *Cal. French Rolls*, 1422-4, m. 8; 1452-3, ms. 15, 12; 1453-4, m. 12; 1455-6, m. 34; 1459-60, ms. 27, 22, 21, 19.
[4] *Cal. French Rolls*, 1413, m. 13; 1422-4, m. 10; 1426-7, m. 5; 1427-8, m. 9; 1431-2, m. 3; 1434-5, m. 6. [5] 1414, m. 26; 1422-4, 8; 1432-4, m. 5. [6] 1424-5, m. 10; 1428-9, m. 3; 1431-2, m. 7; 1437-8, m. 4. [7] *Ibid.*, 1413, m. 4; 1419, m. 10; 1422-4, m. 19; 1424-5, m. 9; 1426-7, m. 11. [8] 1415, m. 9; 1427-8, m. 7. [9] 1419, m. 9; 1424-5, m. 10; 1431-2, m. 5; 1433-4, m. 15; 1436-7, m. 5. [10] *Ibid.*, 1424-5, m. 3; 1425-6, m. 9; 1429-30, m. 6; 1440-1, m. 12; 1442-3, m. 15. [11] 1424-5, m. 6; 1425-6, m. 5; 1440-1, m. 7. [12] 1429-30, m. 6; 1431-2, m. 13. [13] 1429-30, m. 7. [14] 1437-8, m. 3. [15] 1440-1, m. 15. [16] 1456-7, m. 17. [17] *Ibid.*, 1430-1, m. 14. [18] Hardy, Syllabus of Rymer's *Fœdera*, II, 706. [19] *Trans. Royal Hist. Soc.* N.S. IX., p. 89. [20] Hardy, Syllabus of Rymer's *Fœdera*, II, 565.

terms of commercial intercourse between the two countries.[1] In 1482 a mercantile treaty, to last ten years, was signed with the little province of Guipuzcoa.[2]

In spite of the Hundred Years' War trade between England and France was wonderfully active.[3] Wine was at all times a costly beverage; in 1420 a bottle of Bordeaux was sold in London for eight pence, and a bottle of white wine for sixpence.[4] In times of truce English merchants went freely to Bordeaux and Bayonne,[5] but when these towns fell into the hands of the French they changed their route, and took their wool to Rouen.[6]

Commerce with Brittany continued throughout the whole century, and in 1486 Henry VII concluded a treaty of mercantile intercourse with its duke.[7]

Trade was also carried on between England and Ireland. The chief articles imported were butter, salmon,[8] and hides,[9] but the 'Libelle' also includes among the commodities of Ireland 'hake, herynge, Irish wollen, lynyn cloth,' and skins of 'otere, squerel, shepe, lambe, and fox.'[10] The Act of 1465, which forbade the import of foreign cloth into England, made an exception in favour of Ireland.[11] Bristol and Southampton seem to have played the most important parts in this branch of commerce, and sometimes merchants exported goods from

[1] *Ibid.*, II, 595. [2] *Ibid.*, II, 713. [3] Michel, *Histoire du Commerce et de la Navigation à Bordeaux*, I, 345. [4] *Ibid.*, I, 339. [5] *Ibid.*, I, 340–3 and *Cal. French Rolls*, 1425–6, m. 6; 1430–1, m. 9, m. 4, and m. 3; 1434–5, m. 2; 1435–6, m. 2; 1436–7, m. 8; 1437–8, m. 5; 1440–1, 15. [6] Michel, I, 360. [7] Hardy, Syllabus to Rymer's *Fœdera*, II, 720.

[8] Fifty pipes of salmon were brought from Ireland to Bristol, *Cal. Patent Rolls*, 1441, Part II, M. 24d. [9] Licence for W. Payn and W. Soper, of Southampton, to take wine and salt to Ireland, and to bring back fresh salmon, hides, and other merchandise. *Ibid.*, 1426, Part II, m. 22. [10] Wright, *Polit. Songs*, II, 186. [11] 4 *Ed. IV*, c. 1.

Ireland to the continent. William Canynges of Bristol states in a petition that he 'fretta en Irelande 60 lastes de quirs en petites vesseulx' to go to Calais[1]; and another Bristol merchant went to Ireland for the herring fishery, and then took course to Lisbon.[2] That the intercourse between Ireland and Bristol was intimate is seen by the bitter complaints by Bristol artisans concerning the employment of Irish workmen.[3]

Great attention was paid to fishing in the fifteenth century; not only did Englishmen go to Iceland for this purpose, as we have seen, and to Ireland, but also to the coast of Aberdeen.[4] The fisheries of Norfolk and Suffolk were considered so important by Henry VII that a commission was issued to Sir William Vampage to impress mariners and soldiers for ships, to proceed to sea for their defence.[5] In 1487, Sir John Paston was amongst those who were appointed to oversee the masters of the wafters, which protected these fisheries, and he was empowered to levy contributions from the fishermen for the expenses of the wafters.[6] A special clause in the *Magnus Intercursus* stipulated that fishermen who for any cause took shelter in the ports of Flanders should be allowed to depart freely.[7]

Not only was the area of English trade much enlarged, but the transactions of English traders increased in magnitude. Although the staple as a whole had begun to decline, individual merchants were sometimes very successful in trade. On one occasion 2448 Cottiswold fells, belonging to Sir William Stonor, merchant of the Staple, were shipped to

Increased magnitude of commerce.

[1] *A.P.* 299/14910. [2] *Early Chanc. Proceed.*, 45/41.
[3] *Little Red Book of Bristol*, II, 128 and 163.
[4] Macpherson, *Annals of Commerce*, I, 611.
[5] Campbell, *Materials for the Reign of Henry VII*, II, 103.
[6] *Ibid.*, II, 193. [7] Rymer, *Fœdera*, XII, 583.

Calais.[1] In May, 1476, Stonor's agent acknowledged the receipt of fifty-one sarplers[2] of wool, and the cargo must have been worth a large sum of money, as in August, 1475, the Celys sold eighteen sarplers for £611 7s. 6d.[3] Richard Cely also did good business;—in 1478 he wrote that he had shipped or would ship 'xl sarplerys of cottyswolde woll and x packys of fell or more.'[4] Some of the *Early Chancery Proceedings* incidentally give information both as to the value of merchandise, and of the places to which it was sent. We learn that a merchant of Ipswich delivered to his factor '4 pakkes of Wollon cloth vnto the valour of £200, to carie them to Spruce' (Prussia) 'and fro thens to retoune with merchaundise of the seide Countrey.'[5] One petition describes an agreement between Thomas Ward, of York, and merchants of Bordeaux, by which he was to receive fifty-six tuns and one hogshead of wine at £4 a tun, amounting to £225.[6] Some other merchants of Bristol laded a ship with Gascon wine, iron, saffron, lampreys, and armour, to the value of £439.[7] A complaint was made in Parliament that the Danes had taken goods to the value of £25,000 from English merchants, in one year (1432).[8] To estimate the magnitude of these transactions aright, the difference between the value of money in the fifteenth century and the present day must be taken into consideration.

Shipping.

It would be interesting to know how far English commerce was carried on in English ships; the frequent allusions to them in contemporary books and documents lead us to believe that they were employed more frequently than in the previous century. It is true that

[1] *A. C.*, Vol. XLVI, Letter 100. [2] *Ibid.*, 171. [3] *Cely Papers*, pp. 1–3. [4] *Ibid.*, p. 8. [5] *Early Chanc. Proceed.*, 16/427. [6] *Ibid.*, 16/164. [7] *Ibid.*, 27/262. [8] *Rot. Parl.*, IV, 402–3.

Richard II's *Navigation Act*[1] nominally inaugurated the Mercantile policy as regards shipping, but it is exceedingly unlikely that its rigorous prohibition of the use of foreign ships by English merchants was carried out at the time. Another Act of the same reign repeats the command that English merchants must use English ships; but it adds the significant clause, 'provided that English ships take reasonable freight.'[2] Petitions in the next year,[3] and in 1399,[4] that the Act might be observed, suggest that the legislation on the subject was ineffectual. The reason seems to have been that it was a little premature, and that there were not enough English ships to meet the increasing demands of English traders. Some information as to the condition of shipping may be gained from a study of the navy accounts, because any vessel could be commandeered for the King's service, and warrants were issued, from time to time, for the arrest of ships.[5] Indeed, with the exception of a very small number of ships which belonged to the King, all vessels used in war in those days had been built for merchantmen, and were used as merchantmen in times of peace; hence the connection between the navy and the commercial prosperity of the country was very intimate.[6] Henry V built several 'grete shippes,'[7] and their character shows that they were provided for sea-going purposes, and not merely for transport or the escort of ships, which had been the object of previous kings.[8] Some of them were hired by merchants when they were not needed for warfare,[9] but the majority fell into decay during the reign of Henry VI, and for a short time

[1] 5 *Ric. II*, st. 1, c. 3. [2] *Rot. Parl.*, III, 278. [3] *Ibid.*, 296. [4] *Ibid.*, 444. [5] Rymer's *Fœdera*, IX, 218, XI, 21, XII, 160. [6] Laird Clowes, I, 348. [7] Wright, *Polit. Songs*, II, 199; [8] Oppenheim, *Admin. of the Royal Navy*, I, 11-12. [9] *Excheq. Accounts, Army*, 44/24.

ships for the navy were furnished by contractors.[1] But even if the Government neglected the up-keep of the navy, there are very clear indications that the people were keenly alive to its value and to that of the merchant service.

'The trewe processe of Englysh polycye,' says the 'Libelle,'

'Is thys, that who seith southe, northe, est and west
Cheryshe marchandyse, kepe thamyralté,
That we bee maysteres of the narowe see.'[2]

In the *Débat des Hérauts*, the French Herald admits 'la grant puissance'[3] of 'le gros navire d'Angleterre,'[4] so we may at least conclude that England possessed more vessels than France, at the time when this little dialogue was written. One or two other circumstances also lead us to think that the number of English ships increased in the course of the century. Pilgrimages were exceedingly popular, especially to St. James of Galicia, and in the majority of cases the pilgrims were transported by Englishmen in English ships. Our information on the subject is obtained from the licences granted to the masters of the ships, and in many cases the name of the port to which the vessel belonged is stated. Some of the ships were allowed to carry as many as one hundred and twenty pilgrims;[5] and in one instance licences were granted to sixteen persons owning vessels belonging to fifteen different ports.[6] Mention is made of the *Trinity* of Shoreham,[7] the *George* of Poole,[8] the *Katherine* of Penzance,[9] the *George* of London,[10] the *Trinity* of Hull,[10] the *Mary* of Plymouth,[11] the *Trinity* of Bideford,[12]

[1] Oppenheim, *op. cit.*, I, 24. [2] Wright, *Polit. Songs*, II, 157–8. [3] *Débat*, p. 25, No. 65. [4] *Ibid.*, p. 29, No. 75. [5] *Cal. French Rolls*, 1427–8, m. 14. [6] *Ibid.*, m. 13. [7] *Ibid.*, 1422–4, m. 15, May 18. [8] *Ibid.*, 1422–4, m. 14. [9] *Ibid.*, 1424–5, m. 5. [10] *Ibid.*, 1427–8, April 20. [11] *Ibid.*, Feb. 3. [12] 1433–4, m. 14.

the *Trinity* of Bristol,[1] and many others. The Earl of Oxford applied to Henry VI for a licence to carry pilgrims to Compostella, in a ship called the *Jesus* of Orwelle, of which he was owner.[2] A very old sea song, probably of the time of Henry VI, gives a quaint account of the troubles of those 'that saylen to seynt Jamys.'[3] We also find allusions to a good many English ships in the complaints regarding piracy and similar misdemeanours sent to the Court of Chancery. Accusations are made against ships of 'Rye, Wynchelsee, and Hastynges'[4] —the *Little John* of Sandwich was another offender.[5] The *Edward* of Fowey, of which Sir Hugh Courtenay was part owner,[6] is said to have seized a carrack of Genoa.[7] The *Katherine* of Humflete was taken by 'certein men of werre of two englissh Shippes'[8]; Philip Mede, of Bristol, petitioned against the *Palmer* and the *Julian* of Fowey[9]; and many similar cases might be quoted. It appears that not only did English ships increase in number, but that they were of a larger size and greater value. John Taverner, of Holderness, possessed a ship, *La Grace de Dieu*, which was so large that when it traded with Iceland it could not be taken into port, but was laden and unladen in the open sea.[10] This ship was exempted from the payment of harbour dues at Calais for the same reason.[11] Another merchant, John Shipward, prayed for permission to ship goods in a vessel of three hundred tons.[12]

[1] *Ibid.*, m. 13. [2] Ellis' *Orig. Letters*, 2nd series, p. 110. [3] *Naval Songs and Ballads*, edited by Firth, p. 4. [4] *Early Chanc. Proceed.*, 6/130. [5] *Ibid.*, 9/414. [6] *Ibid.*, 13/16. [7] *Ibid.*, 11/204. [8] *Ibid.*, 17/161. Many references to English ships could be given from petitions dealing with other subjects. [9] *Ibid.*, 22/14. [10] *Cal. French Rolls*, 1439–40, m. 3. [11] *Ibid.*, 1444–5, m. 9. A ship of the same name and from the same port, but attributed to other owners, was discharged from the King's service, in 1443, because 'he draweth so depe' (*Proc. Privy Council*, v, 282). [12] *Ibid.*, vi, 254–5.

The *Giles* of Hull was a ship of two hundred and forty tons.[1] The *Margaret Cely* cost £28,[2] and her tonnage was about two hundred tons.[3] The merchantmen, used for the transport of soldiers to Aquitaine, in 1451, included fifty ships of a hundred tons and upwards.[4]. Henry VII granted bounties to persons who built large ships, and amongst the earliest recipients were three men of Bristol who owned a ship of four hundred tons.[5] Another sign of increase of English shipping may be seen in the formation of a Fraternity of Mariners[6] at Bristol, which was one of the towns which profited most by the growth of commerce. To the increasing demand for English ships may perhaps be ascribed the development of the industry of shipbuilding, which has already been discussed.[7] An example of the results of this development may be seen in the *Kervelle*, which was built for Sir John Howard.[8] Edward IV encouraged trade, and devoted steady attention to the recovery and maintenance of the dominion of the sea.[9] Richard II's *Navigation Act* was repeated during his reign.[10] England was beginning to struggle for a share of the carrying trade; one of the complaints raised against the Hansards was that they brought goods which were not their own products.[11] Henry VII forbade the importation of wine and woad from Gascony in any but British ships,[12] and from the discontent which his legislation aroused amongst foreign merchants we may infer that it was a success.[13]

One of the results of the growth of the mercantile

[1] *Early Chanc. Proceed.*, 27/8. [2] *Cely Papers*, 176. [3] *Ibid.*, Introd., 37–8. [4] Oppenheim, *op. cit.*, I, 20. [5] *Ibid.*, I 37–8. [6] *Little Red Book of Bristol*, II, 186. [7] p. 7. [8] *Howard Household Book*, I, 197. [9] Laird Clowes, I, 349. [10] *Rot. Parl.* V, 504. [11] Schanz, I, 185, and II, 425. [12] 1 *H. VII*, c. 8. [13] Giuseppi, *Trans. Royal Hist. Soc.*, N.S., IX, 77.

classes in England was the severe treatment accorded to alien merchants. The native merchants had always been jealous of foreigners, but hitherto their ill-feeling had been held in check by the Crown. Edward III, in particular, favoured alien merchants.[1] The kings of the fifteenth century were, like Henry VI, too weak to enforce their will, or they thought, like Henry VII, that it was more to their interest to support their own subjects. Consequently existing Acts against aliens were supplemented by more rigorous restrictions of their trade. They were not allowed to sell merchandise to each other, and they were forced to lodge with 'certain people called hosts,' who must be privy to all their sales and contracts, and who must send an account of all business done by them to the Exchequer.[2] This statute was in force for six years, but there is no evidence that it was renewed after that time.[3] A special tax was, for the first time, imposed upon aliens resident in the country in 1439—householders paid sixteen pence a year, and those who were not householders sixpence.[4] In 1449 a subsidy of six shillings and eight pence was levied upon alien merchants, and twenty pence upon their clerks or factors; and all who stayed more than forty days were liable for the tax.[5] In 1453 the rate on alien householders was increased to forty shillings, and that on clerks to twenty shillings.[6] This taxation must have been mainly due to a desire to injure aliens, and to prevent them staying in the country, as there were not enough of them to make it a satisfactory source of income. The subsidy rolls show that there were

Treatment of alien merchants.

[1] He permitted 'Gascoignes et touz autres aliens . . . venir en dit roialme (England) ove lour vins, & franchement vendre' (*Rot. Parl.* II, 287). [2] 18 *H. VI*, c. 4. [3] Giuseppi in *Trans. Royal Hist. Soc.*, N.S., IX, p. 90. [4] *Ibid.*, 91. [5] *Ibid.*, p. 92. [6] *Ibid.*

on an average forty to sixty alien merchants in London, and about twice that number of clerks, and five to ten merchants in Sandwich and Southampton, and a corresponding number of clerks.[1] The majority of these merchants were Italians, as it was against them that most enmity was felt, and a special Act was directed against them in the reign of Richard III.[2] Not only were alien merchants thus subjected to heavy taxation, and hindered by stringent regulations, but they were also often annoyed by petty insults,[3] and were sometimes the victims of outrage. A merchant of Genoa complained to the Chancellor that his woad had been seized by the sheriffs of London without any cause[4]; and many appeals were made to him against false action of trespass,[5] and wrongful imprisonment.[6] Frequently petitioners declared that juries had been unfair to them. Francis Dore, merchant of Genoa, stated that the jurors said they would credit no Lombard.[7] The Hansards, we know, in 1499 refused to submit the matter in dispute between them and the English to English judges, because 'there might be great parcialitie in the said judges and favour in the examinacion of witnesses, and also the parties might instruct and corrupt the saide witnesses.'[8] Sometimes assaults were made upon aliens,[9] and occasionally riots broke out against them.[10] It may perhaps be urged as some slight excuse for this bad behaviour that it was retaliation for similar treatment meted out

[1] I am indebted to Mr. Hubert Hall for this piece of information. [2] 1 *Ric. III*, c. 9. [3] 'der Londoner Mayor keine Gelegenheit vorübergehen die Hansen zu schädigen' (Schanz, I, 186). [4] *Early Chanc. Proceed.*, 109/55. [5] *Ibid.*, 110/36 and 19/22. [6] *Ibid.*, 24/252. [7] *Ibid.*, 32/439. Similar cases in 64/995 and 66/374. [8] Schanz, II, 422, quoting MS. of Lord Calthorpe, X, 206. [9] *Early Chanc. Proceed.*, 67/194. [10] *Ibid.*, 27/273, and Giuseppi in *Trans. Royal Hist. Soc.*, N.S., IX, p. 80, attack on the steelyard in London.

to Englishmen in many foreign countries. 'What reason is it,' asks the 'Libelle,' 'that wee schulde go to oste?'

> 'In there cuntrees, and in this Englisshe coste
> They schulde not so, but have more liberté
> Than wee oure selfe?[1]

The same authority tells us that Englishmen were forced in Brabant to discharge their 'marchaundy' in fourteen days, and to charge again in fourteen days.

> 'And yf they byde lenger alle is berefte,
> Anone they schulde forfet here godes alle."[2]

In 1440 Henry VI was obliged to request the Master General of the Teutonic Order to prevent the continued ill-treatment of the English at Danzig, and at the time the King desired from Lubeck and other Hanse towns redress for English merchants who had been imprisoned and plundered.[3] M. Michel has given an account of the inconveniences which the English suffered in Bordeaux, after it was taken by the French: they were only allowed to walk about in the town from seven in the morning till five at night, and even then they were ordered to carry a red cross attached to their clothes, so that everybody might know them; and they were forbidden to go into the country at all without the permission of the mayor, who sent an archer with them, at their expense.[4]

Even in Portugal, although they enjoyed the favour of the Crown,[5] and were not objects of hostility to the people,[6] English merchants were

[1] Wright, *Polit. Songs*, II, 178. [2] Wright, *Polit. Songs*, II, 179. [3] Hardy, Syllabus of Rymer's *Fœdera*, II, 667. [4] Michel, *op. cit.*, I, 380. [5] Shillington, *Commercial Relations of England and Portugal*, p. 69. [6] *Ibid.*, 70.

often very badly treated. The Customs officials forced them to pay extra duties,[1] and they subjected them to many annoyances in connection with the 'dizima,' or tithe on cloth, a duty which was levied in kind. They carried off the clothes and bedding of the unfortunate merchants, on the pretext that cloth might be concealed in them,[2] and when this was stopped, they handled the cloths so carelessly that many of them were spoilt, and the owners were treated very rudely if they tried to look after their goods themselves.[3] In addition to these grievances the English found great difficulty in obtaining payment for their cloths,[4] and vexatious lawsuits were frequently brought against them.[5] Worst of all, they were not allowed to carry arms, and so were in continual danger of robbery and violence.[6]

All these restrictions and aggressions—except those in France, which were probably mainly due to political causes—are signs of the importance which was attached to trade in the fifteenth century, and of the determination of each nation to drive away commercial rivals. The existence of a poem like the 'Libelle of Englysshe Polycye' is a proof that the nation was keenly interested in commerce, and fully aware of the benefits to be derived from it. It is written in the vernacular, it is illustrated by allusions which the people could understand, and it takes into consideration their views and their needs. It not only paints a graphic and accurate picture of the commercial life of the time, but gives very sound advice as to the best way to encourage and maintain trade. The necessity for the 'kepinge of the see,' upon which it insists so strongly, is still one of the most fundamental principles of our

[1] Shillington, *op. cit.*, 112. [2] *Ibid.*, 114. [3] *Ibid.*, 115.
[4] *Ibid.*, 122. [5] *Ibid.*, 120. [6] *Ibid.*, 125.

national policy. A later poem 'On England's Commercial Policy,'[1] though not nearly as clever as the 'Libelle,' is another example of the same appreciation of the importance of industry and trade. Equally significant is the careful attention paid by diplomats to commercial affairs. Some mercantile treaties have already been mentioned, but they are only a very few out of a very large number. M. Varenbergh has traced the diplomatic relations between England and Flanders in the Middle Ages, and the impression gained from his book is that the two nations never left off negotiating during the whole course of the fifteenth century. A practical proof of the importance of commerce may be seen in the prosperity of those seaports which had the largest share of trade. Bristol was very flourishing: it traded with Ireland, Denmark, the Baltic, Iceland, with France, Spain and Portugal, and with the Levant[2]; and it was rich enough to give Edward IV three thousand marks on one occasion.[3] Sandwich appears to have been very prosperous,[4] although the other members of the Cinque Ports had fallen into poverty. Plymouth and Chester are mentioned as rising ports,[5] and London did so much trade that it was necessary to increase its staff of controllers of the Customs.[6] Southampton was the chief port on the south coast, and the great emporium for imported wines and miscellaneous goods[7]; its returns to the Customs were considerable, often second only to London,[8] and its importance is shown by the fact that its jurisdiction extended from Portsmouth

[1] Wright, *Polit. Songs*, II, 282–7. [2] Hunt, *Bristol*, 94.
[3] *Ibid.*, 99. [4] Atton and Holland, 46.
[5] *Ibid.* [6] *Ibid.* [7] Hall, *Custom Revenue*, II, 31.
[8] For example, in 1483–4, Mich. 1–2 R. III, and 1484–5, Mich. 2–22, Aug. 3 R. III, Ramsay, *Lanc. and York*, II, p. 559.

to Weymouth, and included the Isle of Wight.[1] These circumstances and the complaints of those towns which did not share largely in the benefits of trade alike show that commerce and industry were important sources of wealth in the fifteenth century.

[1] Hall, II, 32.

CHAPTER IV

FINANCIAL CHANGES

THE changes which had taken place in other phases of economic life caused changes in finance also.

Employment of capital. To meet the new needs of an age of expansion it was necessary to render the financial system more flexible, and to employ methods which had not been used by previous generations. In the early Middle Ages industry and agriculture had been carried on without the intervention of capital, as we now understand the term.[1] In the fifteenth century it is clear that the use of money was general.[2] The horror caused by the attempts of the cloth-makers to force their workmen to take part of their wages in pins, girdles, and other wares proves how entirely the old order of things had passed away; a sympathetic writer bewailed the woes of 'the pore Pepylle.' 'Lytyll thei take for theyre labur,' he said, 'yet halff ys merchaundyse'[3]; but this 'hewsaunce'[4] did not last long, as it was forbidden both by national legislation[5] and by Gild ordinances.[6] Instead of hoarding money or using it entirely for military and other unproductive purposes,[7] men

[1] Cunningham, 'Economic Changes' in *Cam. Mod. Hist.*, I, 497.
[2] Cunningham, *Growth of English Industry and Commerce*, I, 459.
[3] Wright, *Polit. Songs* ('On England's Commercial Policy'), II, 285.
[4] Custom or usance. [5] *Rot. Parl.*, V, 502, and 4 *Ed. IV*, c. 1; but it was quite allowable to give workmen food instead of part of their wages, 11 *H. VII*, c. 22. [6] 'Ordinances of Worcester' in *Eng. Gilds*, 383. [7] *Cam. Mod. Hist.*, I, 498-9.

began to invest it in commercial and industrial enterprises. The effects of the employment of capital in the cloth industry have already been discussed, and enclosures, whether for the improvement of tillage or for sheep-farming, were usually the work of Capitalists, as they entailed considerable initial expense. Capital was no less necessary in commerce when it was prosecuted on a large scale, by men like Sturmys of Bristol (who took a hundred and sixty pilgrims to Palestine in his own ship),[1] or William Canynges, who is said by William of Wyrcestre to have possessed no less than ten ships at the time of Edward IV's visit to Bristol.[2] The payment of customs and subsidies alone must have obliged merchants to keep a large supply of ready money. On one occasion they cost George Cely £110 5s. 8d.,[3] and this was not an exceptional occurrence. Further evidence of the existence of the capitalist trader may be seen in the complaints of monopoly by both aliens and Englishmen. 'Ther ys but lytyll Cotteswolld woll at Callez and y understond Lombardys has bowght ytt up yn Ynglond,' wrote George Cely to his father.[4] The most novel form of monopoly was that practised by a small body of English capitalists: they secured the control of the means of transport to and from the Continent, and then trebled the charges for traders and their pack-horses, and made the room do duty for twice the usual number of passengers and animals.[5]

[1] Fox Bourne, *Eng. Merchants*, I, 68. [2] Quoted by Pryce, *Memorials of the Canynges' Family*, 127; even allowing for exaggeration, Canynges must have done a large trade. [3] *A.C.*, Vol. 53, No. 125. Other instances, *Ibid.*, 58, and *Cely Papers*, pp. 36 and 44. [4] *Cely Papers*, p. 48; and this was in spite of the prohibition of buying wool before the sheep were shorn, by the Act of 4 *Ed. IV*, c. 4, which was repeated, with special reference to aliens, 4 *H. VII*, c. 11. [5] H. Hall, *Custom Revenue*, I, 99.

The demands of merchants and manufacturers for capital rendered the maintenance of an adequate supply of money in the country exceedingly important, and great care was bestowed upon the regulation of the currency. Kings who wished to be popular turned their attention to this matter. One of the earliest acts of Henry IV was to abolish the ordinance of his predecessor respecting bullion,[1] and Henry V's first Parliament busied itself about the same subject[2]; and even during the brief restoration of Henry VI, in 1470, an indenture was made with Sir Richard Tonstall by which the weight of the coinage was altered.[3] The office of Master of the Mint was frequently bestowed upon prominent public men; Lord Hastings held it for some years, in the reign of Edward IV[4], and Giles, Lord Dawbeney, from 1485 to 1490.[5] The severe treatment of those who tampered with coins is another sign of the value placed upon money; clipping, washing, and filing coins was made treason in 1415,[6] and justices of Assize were empowered to deal with these offences; and counterfeiting foreign coins of gold or silver current in the realm was also declared treason by Henry VII.[7] The underlying reason for all these enactments was the scarcity of the precious metals, and various attempts were made to remedy the evil. Edward IV reduced the weight of gold coins; in 1464 fifty nobles were coined from a pound of bullion, each of which was valued at 8s. 4d., whereas previously a noble had been reckoned as 6s. 8d.[8] In 1465, 45 coins were made from a pound weight of standard gold; these new nobles were called rials, and were worth 10s. each.[9]

Regulations of the currency.

[1] Ruding, *Annals of the Coinage*, I, 249. [2] *Ibid.*, 256. [3] *Ibid.*, 279. [4] *Ibid.*, 33. [5] *Ibid.*, 34. [6] *Ibid.*, 258. [7] *Ibid.*, 294, and 4 *H. VII*, c. 18. [8] Ruding, I, 282. [9] *Ibid.*, 283.

Nor was the regulation of the coinage of silver considered less worthy of attention, and Henry IV introduced considerable changes in its value. 'Since the year 1351, 300 pennies had been struck from the ℔. Tower of silver, and 45 nobles, of 6s 8d each, from the ℔. Tower of gold.' In 1411 it was ordered that 360 pennies were to be struck from the ℔. of silver, and fifty nobles from the ℔. of gold. The penny, which before contained 19⅕ grains of silver, would now contain only 15 grains.[1] The effects of the depreciation of the coinage must sometimes have been very inconvenient. One of the *Early Chancery Proceedings* affords an instance of what might easily happen: John Ferrour borrowed £20 of Thomas Smyth when the noble went for 20 'grotes,' but demanded £25 when he was repaid because the coinage had depreciated.[2] One of the most important expedients adopted to prevent the supply of money in the country running short was the prohibition of the export of 'any gold or silver in money, bullion, plate or vessel by merchants and others.'[3] This veto would have been the death-blow of foreign trade had not the same Act provided a way of escape for merchants. They were permitted to send Letters of Exchange abroad, on condition that they first obtained 'special leave and licence' from the King, 'as well for the Exchangers as for the Persons which ought to make the Payments.' These licences were very explicit: they stated by whom and to whom the Letter of Exchange was sent, and the amount which was to be so exchanged.[4]

[1] Ramsay, *Lancaster and York*, I, 154. [2] *Early Chanc. Proceed.*, 32/402. [3] 5 *R. II*, c. 2. [4] A specimen of a License to draw a Letter of Exchange is printed in *A Formula Book of English Official Historical Documents*, edited by H. Hall, p. 85; in this case it was granted by Letters Close under the Great Seal, p. 80.

The senders were required to swear that they would not 'send beyond the Sea any Manner of Gold nor Silver under the Colour of the same Exchange.'[1] This Act was, however, not found sufficient to stop the depletion of the precious metals, and in 1390, merchants were forced to bind themselves in the Chancery to buy merchandises of the staple or other commodities of the land, to the value of the sum exchanged within three months. The time was too short, and only put a premium on smuggling money out of the country;[2] therefore, in 1421, the term was extended to nine months.[3]

Even these statutes, stringent as they seem, could not stop the export of money, and it was again forbidden in 1423[4] and 1478[5], and at the latter date it was made felony. Nevertheless an Act of Henry VII declared that 'gold and sylver of the coygne of this realm hath and dailly is and ben caried and conveied into Flaundres . . . and othre parties beyond the See.'[6] It therefore made the penalty forfeiture of double the money exported. Another statute of the same reign lamented 'Thenordynat chaungyng & rechaunges' used 'without auctorite gevon of the Kynges gode grace,' and reiterated the command that no man was to make exchange without the King's licence, 'but only such as the kyng shall depute therunto to kepe make and answere such exchaunges and rechaunges.'[7] There were in London, Dover, and Calais, officials called the King's Exchangers. The office was farmed, and the right to issue letters importing licences was conferred on the grantee.[8] This almost wearisome

[1] 5 *Rich. II*, c. 2. [2] Leadam, in *Trans. of the Royal Hist. Soc.* N.S. xix (1905), p. 281, and 9 *H. V*, c. 9. [3] *Ibid.* [4] 2 *H. VI*, c. 6. [5] 17 *Ed. IV*, c. 1. [6] 4 *H. VII*, c. 23. [7] 3 *H. VII*, c. 6. [8] Leadam in *Trans. Royal Hist. Soc.* N.S. xix (1905), pp. 282–3.

repetition of statutes forbidding the export of money shows how exceedingly important the matter was considered, and also how difficult it was to retain restrictions when trade was growing rapidly; but the frequent mention of 'lecters of payment'[1] by the Celys suggests that the regulation of the Exchanges was not quite as futile as the despairing tone of the statutes would make us believe. Parallel to the enactments which forbade the export of the precious metals are the Acts which enjoined the import of bullion. Merchant strangers who bought wools in England and did not sell them at the Staple, were ordered to bring to the Mint, for every sack an ounce of bullion.[2] Merchants of the Staple were commanded to insist upon immediate payment, whereof half was to be in lawful money of England.[3] The Act which regulated the alloy of silver used by goldsmiths for gilding,[4] and another enactment which 'ordeined that no goldsmith or other person melt any Money of Gold or Silver to gild any Vessell, or even Stuffe for Knyghtes apparal,'[5] are proofs that the Government jealously guarded against anything which might cause a drain of money. Less creditable were the attempts to increase the amount of money in the country by means of alchemy. The practice of the craft of the multiplication of gold or silver had been declared felony,[6] yet both Henry VI and Edward IV patronized alchemists. Henry VI granted licences to several persons to transubstantiate inferior metals by their art into gold and silver,[7] and Edward IV sent a Signet Letter to the Mayor

[1] *A.C.*, Vol. 53, No. 99, *Cely Papers*, 18, 159; references to the use of 'letters of exchawnge' also occur in the *Early Chanc. Proceed.*, 34/46, and 29/161. [2] 8 *H. V*, c. 2. [3] 3 *Ed. IV*, c. 1. [4] *Rot. Parl.*, IV, 52. [5] *Ibid.*, VI, 184; a previous Act, 17 *Ed. IV*, c. 1, had permitted the gilding of Knights' apparel. [6] Ruding, I, 63. [7] *Ibid.*, Cf. Syllabus to Rymer's *Fœdera*, II, 683.

of Coventry, ordering him to see that John Frensh, who intended to work at this craft in his city, should be unmolested.[1]

Changes in the theory of prices.

Closer bargaining became possible when prices could be quoted in a money form,[2] and more accurate estimates of the value of goods could be made, and consequently the old ideas which had governed the regulation of prices began to break down. Medieval prices had been regulated by the cost of production, and wages had been a first charge upon them,[3] because it was felt that every man ought to obtain a fair return for his labour. It had been considered wrong to take advantage of a neighbour's weakness or ignorance, but now business men tried to gain as large a return for their money or their stock as they possibly could, and they were not always scrupulous about the means they employed in so doing. The profits of trade seem in some cases to have been enormous. William Lancastre, a hosier's apprentice, states in a Chancery petition, that he made an 'encrese' of £34 on an outlay of £10 in 'thre yere.'[4] In another case we are told that an 'increase' of £259 was made on a sum of 500 marks which was 'occupied in merchandize.'[5] Nevertheless the older views of commercial morality had not entirely lost their force. Prices 'were not yet determined by money considerations pure and simple,' and the economic world was in a curious state of transition between the two conflicting systems of customary and competition prices—a condition of affairs which must have caused a considerable amount of confusion.[6]

[1] *Ibid.*, 64, and Dormer Harris, *Life in an Old English Town*, 288.
[2] Cunningham, *Growth of English Industry and Commerce*, I, 459.
[3] Cunningham, *op. cit.*, I, 461. [4] *Early Chanc. Proceed.*, 9/131.
[5] *Ibid.*, 11/205. [6] Dr. Cunningham says that the results of this state of transition seemed to be complete moral chaos (*op. cit.*, I, 467).

The medieval doctrine of usury.

As trade assumed larger and larger proportions traders found that they needed more and more money to carry it on, and that their own capital was not sufficient for them. They therefore were anxious to borrow, and at the same time, the profits of trade tempted men to lend money. Consequently, one of the most noticeable features of economic life in the fifteenth century is the increased employment of borrowed capital. In the fourteenth century the desire to borrow capital certainly existed, but it has been suggested that lending was partially checked by a fear of the risks of foreign trade; thus the Pepperers, who wished to borrow money, carefully built up a reputation for stability by forbidding their wardens to incur risks beyond the sea;[1] and the Gild of Corpus Christi, Hull, passed an ordinance to somewhat the same effect.[2] In the fifteenth century, even the money of minors was sometimes invested in commercial enterprises. W. Staundon left £100 to William Brook, if he attained the age of twenty-one, the sum to be entrusted to a merchant to trade withal, within the realm of England, and not beyond the sea, the said merchant taking half the profits.[3] This will, which is dated 1409, shows that distrust of foreign trade had not died out, and that the remuneration for services of this kind was large. Nowadays the merchant would be expected to pay for the use of the money. This point of view was, however, quite opposed to medieval thought, which condemned as usury 'taking for the lone any thing more besides or above the money lente,'[4] and which made no distinction between a just and an unjust rate of interest. Economic theory on this subject was embodied in

[1] A. Law in *Trans. Royal Hist. Soc.*, N.S., IX (1895), 70.
[2] *Eng. Gilds*, 161. [3] Sharpe, *Wills*, II, 393. [4] 11 *H. VII*, c. 8.

the Canonist Doctrine,[1] but it was not held by the Church alone ; on the contrary, the civil authorities hated 'l'orrible & abhominable vice de Usure'[2] as much as clerics, 'and restrictions on Usury were so fully indorsed by the public opinion of laymen as to influence legislation long after the ecclesiastical courts had ceased to enforce them.'[3] Practical men like the citizens of London required brokers to swear that they would make no bargain of usury, under pain of paying £100 unto the Chamber, as also of incurring the penalty for usury for brokers which had been previously ordained.[4] But although the theories respecting usury remained unaltered, the exigencies of trade caused many deviations from them in practice. Florentine merchants, writing in 1437 to Henry VI, regret the failure of one of their companies of merchants, mainly on account of the loss sustained by the King's subjects 'qui eidem societati pecunias crediderant sub spe futurae munerationis ac restitutionis.'[5] Some cases occur in the *Chancery Proceedings* in which it is clear that interest was paid for the loan of money,[6] but generally evasions of the Usury laws were justified upon some pretext or another. The debt was purposely not paid punctually, and a greater amount than the original sum was demanded to cover the loss caused by the default.[7] Men entered into partnership, and the stigma of usury was avoided if the lender of the money shared the risk incurred by the transaction.[8] People also fre-

[1] Ashley, *Econ. Hist.*, Part ii, p. 379. [2] *Rot. Parl.*, III, 280. [3] Cunningham, *Christian Opinion on Usury*, Preface. [4] *Liber Albus*, Bk. III, Part ii, p. 315.

[5] Bekynton, *op. cit.*, I, 249. [6] See Appendix B, 1. [7] Ashley, *Econ. Hist.*, Part ii, 399, and he also mentions other evasions of the prohibition of usury, by means of rent-charges (p. 405) and triple contracts (p. 440), but though they were practised abroad, they were not common in England. [8] *Ibid.*, 424–5.

quently gave security for larger sums than they borrowed.[1] Henry VII's second Act against usury acknowledged 'penaltees for nounpament' lawful,[2] which seems like a step towards recognizing the legality of interest; but it was left to a more daring age openly to admit that payment for the mere use of money was not a sin.[3] The admission was only the logical outcome of what had happened in the fifteenth century, but the men of that time were still too much bound by the rigid conservatism of the past to be able to make it for themselves, and probably they did not even realize the difference between their theory and practice.

Some of the subterfuges used to evade the Usury Laws were not so innocent as those described above; Robert Richeman stated that he asked Stephen Brainden to lend him £5, Stephen desired 'vnlawfull gayne for the lone of the forseid £5,' and to 'colour' it, drew up indentures by which it appeared that he lent Robert a hundred sheep for five years, receiving twenty shillings yearly for the same, and also £5 at the end of the term.[4] Oddly enough it was not considered wrong to receive money for the loan of animals, though it was iniquitous to receive it for the loan of money. The Usury Act of 1490 complained of 'bargeynes grounded on usury, colored by the meanes of newe chevaunce or eschaunge,'[5] and probably there were also many transactions which even the modern conscience would condemn as usurious. The *Early Chancery Proceedings* contain complaints of demands for payments for loans which, even allowing for a good

[1] For example, £100 for a debt of a hundred marks (*A. C.*, Vol. XLVI, No. 169), and a hundred marks for eleven marks and forty pence. *Early Chanc. Proceed.*, 44/202. [2] 11 *H. VII*, c. 8. [3] 37 *H. VIII*, c. 9, No. 3, which permitted interest to be paid on loans, provided that it did not exceed ten per cent. [4] *Early Chanc. Proceed.*, 37/38. [5] 11 *H. VII*, c. 8.

deal of exaggeration, were outrageously large. John Seddeley, it is stated, lent John Betson and Edward Ilsley £21, and they agreed to give him 40s. for every fourteen days the money remained unpaid.[1] The unfortunate men who accepted these bargains must have been in great straits for want of money, and those who made them must have been very hardened, for they laid themselves open to the censures of the Church as well as to punishment by the secular arm. The English, said the author of the *Italian Relation*, 'are so diligent in mercantile pursuits that they do not fear to make contracts on usury.'[2]

Revenue.

It is almost impossible to make exact statements regarding the amount of the revenue, because the estimates of historians vary greatly,[3] but it is obvious that the returns to taxation were very much affected by economic conditions. The total revenue appears to have fallen considerably during the century, as may be seen by the subjoined table of the net incomes of successive kings :—

	£
Revenue exclusive of windfalls (20 *Ed. III*)	110,000[4]
Average income of Henry IV..........	106,260[5]
Average income of Henry V............	115,299[6]
Yearly average, Mich. 1422 to Mich. 1428	57,171[7]
,, ,, ,, ,, 1454	69,605[8]
,, ,, ,, 1454 to March 3, 1461	44,005[9]
,, ,, March, 1461–1469	59,295[10]
,, ,, ,, 1472–1483	79,168[11]

[1] *Early Chanc. Proceed.*, 193/36. [2] *Italian Relation*, 23. [3] Bishop Stubbs comments on the discrepancy between the calculations of Sir John Sinclair and Sir James Ramsay, II, 576, note. [4] *Antiquary*, Vol. I, pp. 157–8, Sir James Ramsay thinks this a typical year. [5] Ramsay, *Lanc. and York*, I, 160. [6] *Ibid.*, I, 321. [7] *Ibid.*, II, 266–7. [8] *Ibid.* [9] *Ibid.* [10] *Ibid.*, II, 471. [11] *Ibid.*, II, 472. But Edward IV received £10,000 from the French tribute (1475–8) and £3263 from the Clarence estates (1478–83).

Some reasons for the decrease in the revenue may be gathered from an examination of the yield of some of the sources from which it was obtained. The assessment for lay subsidies (tenths and fifteenths) was fixed in 1334, and in that year they produced £38,000.[1] In 1432 a deduction of £4000 was allowed on the total, and £6000 in 1449; and soon after the middle of the century the tax brought in £31,000, instead of the original amount.[2] The deduction was made 'for the relief of poor towns, cities, and boroughs, desolate, wasted or destroyed, or over greatly impoverished, or else to the said tax over greatly charged.'[3] Amongst those to which partial or entire exemption was granted were Norwich, Lynn, Yarmouth,[4] Truro,[5] Lincoln,[6] and Shrewsbury.[7] In some of these cases the remission was due to special circumstances; for example, Truro had suffered badly from pestilence, and Yarmouth was obliged to spend a great deal of money on keeping its harbour open.[8] A careful study of the assessment of Norfolk has revealed the fact that Lynn and Yarmouth were relieved from the burden of this tax, not because they could not afford to pay it, but because they were being taxed in other ways.[9] It is also evident that this form of taxation had lost a great deal of the importance which it had possessed in 1334, and that indirect taxation was a more profitable form of income. Moreover, an increase of a merchant's stock would not appear at all in the returns when the assessment had been permanently fixed, and therefore a large amount of wealth might accumulate in the

[1] W. Hudson, in *Norfolk Archæl.*, XII, 246–7, and Stubbs, II, 579. [2] Hudson, *Ibid.*, 257. [3] *Ibid.* [4] *Ibid.*, 261. [5] *Rot. Parl.*, III, 638. [6] *Victoria County Hist.*, *Lincolnshire*, II, 320. [7] Campbell, *op. cit.*, I, 213. [8] Hudson, *loc. cit.*, 261. This was also the reason assigned for the reduction of the fee farm of Yarmouth in 1486 (Campbell, I, 326–7). [9] Hudson, 262.

hands of a limited number of merchants without showing itself on the lists.[1] An interesting theory has been advanced that, in some cases at least, towns evaded taxation by entrusting their funds to the Gild Merchant, and then pleading poverty to the Exchequer, so that the demands of the Crown were met with the answer that the town had nothing and the Gild owed nothing.[2] Coventry seems to have adopted this ingenious expedient, and to have disposed of its possessions with so much astuteness, that the Exchequer could obtain nothing from it at a time when the Trinity and Corpus Christi Gilds were both very wealthy.[3] But apparently the funds of the gilds and the town were failing during the last thirty or forty years of the period, so that then, at least, their plea of poverty was not wholly false. While therefore it would be unwise to attach too much weight to the complaints of the towns, they must not be rejected altogether. Yet it must be remembered that if some towns were sinking,[4] others—like Bridport,[5] Rye,[6] Chester,[7] and Plymouth[8]—were rising, and in most cases increasing prosperity was due to the growth of trade. The revenue derived from the Customs was also shrinking, as we have seen, and one cause of its diminution has been suggested[9]; but it was probably due also to smuggling,[10] and to negligence[11] and fraud[12] on the part

[1] *Ibid.*, 261. [2] Mrs. Green, *Town Life*, II, 216. [3] Miss Dormer Harris, *Life in an Old English Town*, 127. [4] There seems no reason to doubt the decline of Norwich (see *Town Life*, II, 397). The raids of the French were a cause of the poverty of some sea-coast towns like Melcombe Regis (Campbell, *op. cit.*, II, 538–9). The Staple had also been removed from Melcombe, which was another reason for its decline (*Victoria County Hist. Dorset*, II, 360). [5] *Town Life*, I, 15, 16. [6] *Ibid.*, 17. [7] and [8] Atton and Holland, *The King's Customs*, 46. [9] That the wool was made into cloth in England instead of being exported. [10] *Rot. Parl.*, III, 510; IV, 454; V, 55. [11] *Ibid.*, III, 439. [12] *Ibid.*, III, 625–6, and IV, 455.

of the collectors. It has been pointed out that the salaries paid to them were very small, and that they were allowed to charge many fees,[1] and it must be borne in mind that, during the continuance of the fee system, no official statement of net revenue could convey even approximate information as to the actual amount extorted from the public.[2] It is therefore probable that the people paid not only in customs, but for other dues as well, far larger sums than ever reached the King's coffers. In the reign of Henry IV it was declared that 'divers of the Sheriffs, Escheators, Aulnagers, Customers, Comptrollers, and other the King's Officers, . . . do defraud and deceive our said Lord the King yearly, in their unlawful and untrue (accompts) concealing and (receiving) to their own Use the greater Part of that which rightfully ought to pertain to the King, to his great damage and loss.'[3] The Requests made by Jack Cade and his followers included the cessation of sundry extortions, such as Estreats of the 'Green Wax'[4] and unlicensed purveyance.[5] An order that no 'bœfs, berbys, porkes, poraill, frument, mieynes, fein, littere ne cariage' should be taken from Christiana de Restwolde, 'contre la bone gree du dite Cristiane,'[6] shows to what exactions the people were subjected if they had no special protection. Loans, including the so-called Benevolences, formed an important item of the Revenue,[7] and they must have been rather a drain upon the lenders, as they received

[1] Atton and Holland, 34–5. [2] *Ibid.*, 35. [3] 6 *H. IV*, c. 3.
[4] i.e. writs issued to enforce payment of Crown dues, which were sealed with a special green wax (Ramsay, *Lanc. and York*, II, 128, note).
[5] Ramsay, *Lanc. and York*, II, 127–8. Statutes against purveyance show the extent of the evil, 2 *H. IV*, c. 14; 1 *H. VI*, c. 2; 20 *H. VI*, c. 8. It seems to have been practised, not only by the King, but by powerful subjects also, 23 *H. VI*, c. 13. [6] *Excheq. Q. R. Wardrobe Accounts*, 406/22. [7] See Appendix D.

no interest on their money, and it was not always repaid promptly, and sometimes not repaid at all.[1] Probably the returns to requests for loans depended partly upon the popularity of the King, and his power of enforcing his demands. The merchants of the Staple advanced large sums of money for the payment of the garrison and other purposes: £4000 in 1407,[2] £4000 in 1423,[3] £2333 in 1430,[4] £10,000 in 1441,[5] 1000 marks in 1450–1,[6] various sums in 1457–8[7] and 1459–60;[8] £10,700,[9] £26,000,[10] and £23,700[11] on other occasions. The citizens of London were also very generous to the King. We find records of debts to them of 7000 marks in 1411,[12] and 10,000 marks the next year.[13] The sum of £2000 lent to Henry V was repaid in 1424,[14] and an assignment was made to them from the tenths and fifteenths, in 1430, on account of a loan of £6666 13s. 4d., which the mayor and commonalty had advanced to the Government[15]; and Edward IV repaid them the large sum of £12,923 9s. 8d.[16] in the eighteenth year of his reign. Nor were the other cities of the kingdom backward in lending money in time of need, though they could not grant as much as London. The men of Norwich, Salisbury, and Winchester were amongst those who offered loans for the expedition to Guienne in 1412.[17] Canterbury provided 100 marks, and Bristol £240 in 1415.[18] Henry VI sent thanks to

[1] Ramsay allows £1500 a year for money borrowed by Henry IV and not repaid, and £5000 a year for that not repaid by Henry V (*Lanc. and York*, II, 261). [2] *Cal. Patent Rolls*, 8 *H. IV*, Part ii, m. 5. [3] *Proceed. Privy Council*, III, 67–8. [4] *Ibid.*, IV, 52. [5] *Ibid.*, V, 167. [6] *Cal. French Rolls*, 1450–1, m. 4. [7] *Ibid.*, 1458–9, ms. 11 and 10. [8] *Ibid.*, 1459–60, m. 16. [9] *Early Chanc. Proceed.*, 22/178. [10] *Rot. Parl.*, V, 297, No. 46. [11] *Ibid.*, VI, 55. [12] *Proceed. Privy Council*, II, 16. [13] *Ibid.*, 32. [14] *Ibid.*, III, 142. [15] Hardy, Syllabus of Rymer's *Fœdera*, II, 649. [16] *Accounts Excheq. Q. R. Misc.*, 516/13. [17] *Proceed. Privy Council*, II, 32. [18] Hardy, Syllabus of Rymer's *Fœdera*, II, 587.

the 'commonaltee of Newcastel' for the loan of 100 marks,[1] in 1443.

The records extant for the city of Coventry are unusually complete and interesting, and it appears that the citizens granted ten loans within the first half of the century, which amounted to the large sum of £1266 13s. 4d.[2] The *Leet Book* enables us to see how the money was raised: collectors were appointed, to whom streets were assigned, and the names of the contributors and the sums they gave were carefully written down. It is quite surprising to find how many persons contributed, and how little some of them lent. For example, in 1430, when £100 was sent to the King, there were 578 contributors, the largest sum given was £1 6s. 8d., and the smallest was 10d.[3] The municipalities were not the only corporations which advanced money to the Government, wealthy religious houses were expected to do their part. Twenty-two abbots, one abbess, and nine priors are amongst those who were asked to lend money in 1403.[4] Some of the counties were also responsible for considerable sums,[5] and rich nobles and churchmen did not escape the burden.[6] Cardinal Beaufort was one of the most frequent of the King's creditors.[7] Thus it will be seen that the loans of the fifteenth century were not raised like those of the fourteenth, by a few wealthy merchants,[8] but by all classes of the community.

[1] *Proceed. Privy Council*, V, 284. [2] There is a receipt for £300 from the mayor, bailiffs, and good men of Coventry (1 and 2 *H. IV*), *Accounts Excheq. Q. R.*, 42/36. The *Coventry Leet Book* notes gifts or loans of £200, £100, and 200 marks (pp. 60–1), £100 (pp. 78–82), 100 marks (p. 84), £100 (p. 124), £100 (p. 159), £66 13s. 4d. (p. 207), £100 (p. 216). [3] *Ibid.*, 125–9. [4] *Proceed. Privy Council*, I, 201–2. [5] *Ibid.*, I, 343–4. Kent 1000 marks, Norfolk and Suffolk between them the same sum, Somerset 500, in 1410. [6] *Ibid.*, IV, 316–29. [7] *Ibid.*, III, 144, IV, 162. [8] Miss Law, in *Trans. Royal Hist. Soc.*, N.S., IX (1895), p. 63.

English financiers.

But Englishmen not only advanced money to the Government, but also frequently acted as bankers to each other, and thus began to oust aliens from a branch of business, which in earlier days they had managed entirely.

In the complaints against money-lenders which have already been quoted it was noticeable that the offenders were Englishmen; and from other sources also we learn that Englishmen acted as bankers and financiers, sometimes only in a private capacity, sometimes on quite a large scale. When Sir William Stonor was in want of money he borrowed from a relative, William Harleston, who in his turn obtained an advance from a friend.[1] In the same way, Elizabeth Clere of Ormesby lent her cousin, William Paston, £40, but she took care to have good security for it in plate.[2] The members of the Gild-Merchant of Lynn, says Mrs. Green, were the bankers and capitalists of the town, and lent money out on usury; in one year, 1408, their loans amounted to £1214.[3] The goldsmiths apparently performed the functions of bankers. Jane Upton delivered to one of them, Robert Bosome, forty marks of money 'savely to kepe,' and to return when required[4]; and Sir John Paston placed sixteen pottingers in pawn with Stephen Kelke, goldsmith of London, and received a loan of forty pounds for it.[5] Other well-to-do traders frequently carried on similar transactions. The Duke of Somerset left 'a panyer of gold with diuers precious stones & other juellez '[6] in pledge, with John Morley, tailor; and Richard Rawlyn, of London, grocer, lent Sir John Paston twenty pounds,

[1] *A. C.*, Vol. XLVI, No. 169.
[2] *Paston Letters*, v, 208.
[3] Mrs. Green, *Town Life*, II, 406.
[4] *Early Chanc. Proceed.*, 9/479.
[5] *Paston Letters*, v. 76.
[6] *Early Chanc. Proceed.*, 24/230.

and held plate as security.[1] Some financial business still remained in the hands of aliens, for example, the chief collectors of Peter's Pence and other papal dues were usually foreigners.[2] There were also many alien brokers in England, but they must have found it difficult to maintain their position, as severe ordinances were passed against them,[3] and they were prosecuted in the law-courts if they dared to break them.[4]

Alien merchants still occasionally provided the King with money,[5] but the amounts they lent were trifling[6] compared with the sums they had granted in earlier days,[7] and were often given very unwillingly. The Privy Council, in one case, offered various Italian merchants the alternative between advancing money or going to prison, and they chose prison; but afterwards they repented and lent the money.[8] Whereas in the fourteenth century it had been a novelty for native merchants to finance the King or to act as bankers, in the fifteenth it was quite usual for them to do so. Englishmen had proved their capacity, and taken their rightful place in this as in all other branches of industry and commerce.

[1] *Paston Letters*, V, 81. [2] O. Jensen, 'The Denarius Sancti Petri,' in *Trans. Royal Hist. Soc.*, N.S., XIX., p. 233. [3] *Rot. Parl.*, III, 554, *Ibid.*, IV, 56, and *Ibid.*, IV, 193. [4] Two law-suits were brought, against Polydore Vergil, early in the sixteenth century for negotiating exchanges without a licence. I. S. Leadam, *Trans. Royal Hist. Soc.*, N.S., XIX, pp. 286–7. Cf. *Chancery Proceedings*, 94/32 and 226/25.

[5 and 6] £200 by the Venetians and 500 marks by the Florentines in 1412, *Proceed. Privy Council*, II, 32; 400 marks by the Florentines, 500 by the Venetians, and 500 by the Genoese in 143[illegible], *Ibid.*, IV, 324; 1000 marks by the Genoese and Florentines, Hardy, Syllabus of Rymer's *Fœdera*, II, 550 and 552; similar sums, *Ibid.*, 587, 589; £5000 by the Medicis and others, *Ibid.*, 707; £1000 by the Albertines, *Cal. Patent Rolls*, 8 *H. IV*, Part ii, m. 5. [7] The Italians offered Edward III £28,000 on an assignment of wool in 1340, *Trans. Royal Hist. Soc.*, N.S., IX., 62. [8] *Proceed. Privy Council*, II, 165-6.

PART II

SOCIAL LIFE

CHAPTER I

THE EFFECTS PRODUCED BY ECONOMIC CHANGES UPON THE STRUCTURE OF SOCIETY

Conflict of medieval and modern ideals.

THE changes which revolutionized trade and industry in the fifteenth century could not fail to produce important effects upon society, because economic and social conditions of life are so closely bound up together that anything which occurs in one sphere inevitably reacts upon the other. Consequently this century witnessed striking social changes; old ties were broken; new ideas became current; and not only were new elements introduced into the fabric of society, but those already in existence entered into new relationships with each other, so that the whole structure was transformed. Changes of such magnitude could only be accomplished gradually; the old order did not yield place to new without many struggles, and therefore this period is one of transition, and exhibits the variety, the many-sidedness, and the inconsistencies which render ages of this kind so difficult to understand. Sometimes the new ideas triumphed, and sometimes the old; and even when the new had really gained the victory, the old forms lingered on;

and thus it is that the changes through which English society passed were not very visible on the surface, though they were great and effectual at heart.[1]

One of the most fundamental economic changes of the fifteenth century was, as we have seen, the increasing employment of capital; and society too began to set a high value upon money. When men saw the numerous uses to which it could be put, and the many things it could obtain for them, they sought it for its purchasing power[2]; money was a convenient representation of all other objects of wealth, and therefore men desired to have as much of it as possible.[3] Once the benefits accruing from the possession of money were realized, it seemed impossible to do without it, and this is perhaps the reason for 'the frenzy of trade'[4] which seized upon all classes of the community. But it was not only that England developed a love of trading, but that the commercial spirit pervaded all departments of life and influenced almost every sentiment. The author of the *Italian Relation* was very much impressed by the Englishman's love of money; he seems to think that anything would be done to gain it.[5] It is curious to find great nobles[6] and ecclesiastics[7] engaged in commerce. Special facilities for exporting wool were granted to Margaret of Anjou[8] and to other members of the Royal family.[9] Popular songs like 'London Lickpenny,'[10] with its refrain 'For lack of money I could not spede,'

[1] Wright, *Hist. of Domestic Manners*, 415. [2 and 3] Cunningham, *Growth of English Industry and Commerce*, I, 465. [4] Atton and Holland, *op. cit.*, 47. [5] *Italian Relation*, pp. 24–6. [6] Ralph, Earl of Westmoreland, *Cal. French Rolls*, 1422–4, m. 12. John, Earl of Shrewsbury, *Ibid.*, 1459–60, m. 23. [7] Lawrence, Bishop of Durham, *Ibid.*, 1459–60, m. 19. [8] *Rot Parl.*, V, 150. [9] Syllabus to Rymer's *Fœdera*, II, 691. Campbell, *op. cit.*, I, 228. [10] Lydgate's *Minor Poems*, 103 and seq.

'Gramercy myn own purse,'[1] and 'A song in praise of Sir Penny,'[2] afford illustrations of the same spirit.

The increase of riches, which trade brought with it, not only enabled men to obtain more material comforts, but also gave them a new chance of rising in the world. It had been practically impossible for a peasant to rise out of his class, except through the Church,[3] or through success on the battle-field, but in the fifteenth century the yeoman could become a gentleman 'by getting into a lord's household, and spending large and plenty'; the squire who would be a knight without bearing arms had only to go to court, with his purse full of money.[4] Whereas in earlier days the possession of land was a man's chief claim to respect, now wealth also bestowed distinctions upon its owner; and even land was desired mainly as a source of wealth.[5] The usher of Humphrey Duke of Gloucester, in estimating the ranks of different classes in society, placed a knight of property and blood above a simple and poor knight, and the wealthy Abbot of Westminster above the 'poor abbot of Tynterne'[6]; and considered the Mayor of London, the representative of the richest city in the kingdom, the equal of viscounts and mitred abbots.[7] Wealth therefore became a means of gratifying the desire for social distinction;[8] and before the recognition of these new qualifications for honours, the old ideas of status and caste broke down, and the futility of attempts to keep the old class divisions may be seen in the failure of the sumptuary laws, which prescribed a certain dress

[1] Ritson, *Ancient Songs and Ballads*, 152. [2] *Ibid.*, 116 and seq. [3] Pollard, *Factors in Mod. Hist.*, 135. [4] Mrs. Green, *Town Life*, II, 10. [5] F. Pollard, *op. cit.*, 139. [6] Russell's *Boke in Manners and Meals int he Olden Times*, 192. [7] *Ibid.*, 188. [8] Cunningham, *op. cit.*, I, 465.

for each grade in society.[1] But even before the old class-distinctions had been wholly swept away new lines of cleavage appeared, and the strife of Capital and Labour began.

How far these changes were due to the worship of money, and how far they indicate admiration for the power and ability which were needed to win it, is impossible to say; but, in any case, they inspired new ambitions. When the barriers between the classes had been destroyed, men were no longer satisfied to stand well in their own grade, but they aspired to rise to others.[2] This aim, and the confusion caused by the loss of the old ideals, engendered a spirit of restlessness, which showed itself in all kinds of people and in all kinds of ways. Sometimes it took the form of a longing for actual physical movement, and led those under its influence to wander from county to county—a tendency which the statutes of Labourers and legislation against vagrancy[3] endeavoured to check. Sometimes it resulted in a revolt against old-established customs and the denial of rights which had existed from time immemorial. Such, for example, was the refusal of the men of Great Yarmouth to allow the barons of the Cinque Ports 'libertees & franchises,' which they had enjoyed (during the fair held in the town) 'de temps dont memorie ne court.'[4] Even the privileges of the Church were not safe from attack. The parson of St. Just in Roseland complained that Alan Bugules and others had forcibly

[1] Statutes of apparel, 1463-4, *Rot. Parl.*, V, 504, repeated 1477, but partially abandoned in 1482; *Rot. Parl.*, VI, 220. [2] Cunningham, I, 465. [3] 12 *Ric. II*, c. 3. [4] *Early Chanc. Proceed.*, 4/153, 6/78, 26/566. The King's tenants in the Forest of Knaresborough obstinately refused to pay tolls to the Archbishop of York during the fairs, and he kept 'Ripon at fair tymes by night, like a towne of warr,' with soldiers; an 'affray' took place between them and the people, and each side blamed the other (*Plumpton Corr.*, liv-lxii).

carried off the mortuaries, the best garment and the second-best beast of certain parishioners, which by custom belonged to the parson.[1] Similarly the Bishop of Chichester laid a petition before the Chancellor, because the Mayor of Chichester had forbidden suitors to sue at the Piepowder Court, a franchise which had always belonged to the Bishops of Chichester.[2] These are examples of revolts against custom on a very small scale; but sometimes popular discontent with existing circumstances showed itself in widespread movements like Jack Cade's rebellion, which, however, was mainly a political rising.

Destruction of Feudalism as the basis of land-tenure.

One of the most practical results of the economic changes of the later Middle Ages was the destruction of Feudalism, and of the substructure upon which it rested, the Manorial System. 'Feudalism,' says Professor Pollard, 'was a rural organization based upon man's relation to the land, and regulated by the conditions of agricultural life.'[3] It could not, therefore, survive changes which altered both 'man's relations to the land' and 'conditions of agricultural life.' The forces which brought about the downfall of Feudalism were active long before the fifteenth century. As soon as economic pressure caused the substitution of hired for compulsory labour, and made the commutation of service for money necessary,[4] the decay of the manorial system began. The economic changes of the fifteenth century increased the power of the forces already at work, and made some addi-

[1] *Early Chanc. Proceed.*, 3/107.

[2] *Ibid.*, 16/20. Some of the tenants of the Prior of St. Martin's, Dover, refused to attend his court (*Ibid.*, 39/110).

[3] Pollard, *Factors in Modern Hist.*, 41.

[4] Trevelyan, *England in the Age of Wycliffe*, 185.

tions to them. Feudalism contemplated only two classes, lords and villeins; the industrial and commercial system of modern history requires two factors which Feudalism did not provide, a middle class and an urban population.[1] The development of both these factors was largely due to the economic conditions of the fifteenth century. To the same cause may be attributed the decrease of serfdom, which was an integral part of the Feudal system. The development of industry, and in particular of the cloth manufacture, provided lucrative employment for capable workmen, and many serfs were tempted by it to withdraw from their lords. In the reigns of Richard II and of Henry IV, the Commons complained that the villeins withdrew every day into the 'veiles marchauntes,' whence it was impossible to reclaim them.[2] A petition presented to Henry VI, in 1447, gives the impression that even the King's serfs were trying to repudiate their obligations; it asked that the 'King's Boundemen within North Wales be bounden and arted[3] to do such labours and services of right, as thei have used to do of olde tyme, notwithstandyng eny Graunte made unto theim, or eny usage used by theyme of late tyme to the contrarie.'[4] The *Early Chancery Proceedings* give some examples of cases in which the lords did not succeed in maintaining their claims to Feudal dues. The prior of Wenlock appealed to the Chancellor against Sir Gilbert Talbot and Richard Walwen because they refused to pay a heriot on behalf of Andrew Walton.[5] Rent was assessed in lieu of customary works, due to the convent of St. Saviour's of Sion, from the

[1] Pollard, *Factors in Modern Hist.*, 41.
[2] Savine in *Trans. Royal Hist. Soc.*, N.S., XVII (1903), p. 259.
[3] Compelled. [4] *Rot. Parl.*, V, 139, No. 23.
[5] *Early Chanc. Proceed.*, 59/46.

manor of Cheltenham.[1] Feudal lords did not, especially in the earlier part of the century, allow their villeins to flee without making efforts to recover them; and in some cases they very unscrupulously claimed freemen as their bondmen. The Rolls of Parliament give an account of the sufferings of 'John Whithorne, gentleman,' who was claimed by Humphrey, Duke of Gloucester, as 'nativum suum'; the unfortunate man was imprisoned and his land seized, and he had the greatest difficulty in obtaining his liberty and the restitution of his property.[2] The *Chancery Proceedings* contain several examples of claims to bondmen, which are said to be quite unjust.[3] In the latter part of the century, when the landowners began to enclose their land for sheep pastures, they did not need so many labourers, and were probably glad if their serfs took to flight, as it left more land for them. We find that in some cases the lord of the manor allowed the serf to pay chevage for licence to remain away from his holding,[4] while sometimes the villein purchased his freedom outright.[5] A careful examination of the history of serfdom in the manor of Forncett, (Norfolk), has shown that a very large number of serfs withdrew from their holdings, and that whereas there were sixteen servile families in 1400, there were only eight in 1500.[6] It has been estimated that by the beginning of the Tudor period only one per cent of the population consisted of bondmen.[7] Possibly we may attribute the decline of

[1] *Ibid.*, 19/66. An entry in one of the Howard Household Books in 1467 gives an account of services due from the tenants of 'Stansted Halle in hervest'; but adds, 'Alle these duetes unpaid of eche of them 5 yere' (*Howard Household Book*, I, p. 396). [2] *Rot. Parl.*, V, 448, No. 35, and Savine, *Trans. Royal Hist. Soc.*, 1903, p. 261. [3] *Early Chanc. Proceed.*, 3/110, 15/159, 16/436, 28/338, 61/397, 233/10. See Appendix B, 4. [4] Davenport, *Trans. Royal Hist. Soc.*, N.S., XIV (1900), 140. [5] *Early Chanc. Proceed.*, 62/260, 20/134. [6] *Trans. Royal Hist. Soc.*, N.S., XIV, p. 131. [7] *Ibid.*, XVII, 248.

serfdom to the fact that the feudal lord no longer cultivated the demesne lands himself; when this happened, the *raison d'être* of serfdom no longer existed, and villeinage became an anachronism.[1] A very interesting point to which Mr. A. Savine has alluded is the change in the nature of servile tenure. Bond tenure, he says, early loses its servile character, and attains the level of 'customary copyhold.' He quotes the case of some copyholders named 'Baroun,' who applied to the Chancellor for assistance, because forcible entry had been made into their copyhold. The land was bond tenancy, but the defendant did not bring forward the exception of villeinage, and his inference is that in the fifteenth century the Chancery drew no distinction between bond and customary tenure.[2] Great changes took place during the fifteenth century and the latter half of the fourteenth, in free tenure as well as in bond. In the fifteenth century leases became more common, and a feature of the period is 'the gradual lengthening of the terms,[3] and gradual change from tenure at terms of years to tenure at a perpetual fixed rent.[4] As an illustration of the comparative rarity of land tenure based on military or other service, at the end of our period, it may be mentioned that out of ninety-six grants of land in the Duchy of Lancaster made by Henry VII in 1486, seventy-six were to be held by the payment of money rent, thirteen by personal service, and seven by yielding both rent and service.[5]

A curious characteristic of the century, which must, one would think, have helped to undermine

[1] Cheyney in *Eng. Hist. Review*, XV, 36–7. [2] Savine in *Eng. Hist. Review*, XVII, 300–1, quoting *Early Chanc. Proceed.*, 16/376. [3] Lease of 66 years, *Early Chanc. Proceed.*, 28/491, Leases of 99 years, *Ibid.*, 12/145, and *Coventry Leet Book, Part I*, 188, 194. [4] Davenport, *Econ. Development of a Norfolk Manor*, p. 76. [5] These figures are extracted from *Materials for the Reign of Henry VII* for 1486.

the Feudal System, was the excessive employment of the 'use' or trust. 'All the land of the kingdom was in the hands of trustees, feoffees, to whom every buyer had his land conveyed, either solely, or jointly with himself, to evade the rights of forfeiture, wardship,' and other claims of feudal lords.[1] The *Chancery Proceedings* contain references to hundreds of such trusts.

Failure of Feudalism as a military system.

Feudalism was not only breaking down as the basis of land tenure, but was also entirely obsolete as a military system. Service in war was no longer rendered as a feudal due, but was merely a matter of contract. Leaders of armies hired soldiers who agreed to fight for them for a specified time at specified wages, which were set forth in an indenture of war. This plan was not a novelty in the fifteenth century, it was used at least as early as the reign of Edward I,[2] but the commercial nature of the bargains is a great contrast to Feudal ideals. Clauses were inserted in the indentures by which it was stipulated that the commander of the army should receive 'the third parte of the wynnynges of werre' of each of the captains serving under him, 'aswele . . . as the thirdde of thirddes wherof eche of his Retinue shalbe answeryng vnto him of their wynnynges of werre.'[3] Ransoms of prisoners were among the most important of these winnings, and there is in the Public Record Office a little bundle of bonds given by various persons to Henry V, promising to pay him his share of the ransoms of their prisoners.[4] Some of the obligations are for quite small sums, for example, 13s. 4d.[5]

[1] Furnivall, *Fifty Early Eng. Wills*, *Forewords*, p. xiii. See Appendix B, 2. [2] *Excheq. Accounts*, *Q. R. Army*, 68/1. [3] *Ibid.*, 72/1, No. 1030. See Appendix E. [4] *Ibid.*, 48/2. [5] *Ibid.*, 48/2, No. 2. Some of the numbers in this bundle are repeated.

and 10s.,[1] but some are for larger amounts, 25 marks in one instance,[2] and £46 13s. 4d.[3] in another. The payment of these thirds was rather a hardship when the soldiers had not received their wages, and in the first year of Henry VI's reign the King was asked to deduct them from the arrears still due from his father.[4] Prisoners of high rank were obliged to pay very large sums of money to obtain their freedom. Louis de Bourbon, Count of Vendôme, agreed to give 100,000 crowns[5] as ransom; and Charles, Duke of Orelans, signed an indenture by which he undertook to pay 40,000 nobles on his liberation, and 80,000 more in six months' time, if by then he had not been able to negotiate a peace between England and France.[6] The money required for ransoms was frequently obtained by commerce, and we have in the *French Rolls* instances of licences granted both to aliens[7] and Englishmen[8] to trade in order to raise their ransoms. And so we have the curious phenomenon of war acting as a direct stimulus to trade, and even in some cases to trade between the belligerents.[9]

The deterioration of Chivalry.

The collapse of the Feudal System brought about the decline of Chivalry, which was closely connected with it. The romantic notions of Chivalry could not stand against the commercial spirit of the age, any more than knights in armour could hold their own against the new methods of warfare. Chivalry, in consequence, lost much of its serious character, although outwardly it was still flourishing; brilliant tournaments were

[1] *Ibid.*, 48/2, No. 13. [2] *Excheq. Accounts, Army, Q.R.*, 48/2, No. 16. [3] *Ibid.*, No. 18. [4] 1 *H. VI*, c. 5. [5] Hardy, Syllabus to Rymer's *Fœdera*, II, 597. [6] *Ibid.*, 667. [7] *Cal. French Rolls*, 1455–6, ms. 33, 29, 26; 1456–7, ms. 24, 15; 1458–9, 18, 12, 9, 5. [8] *Ibid.*, 1455–6, ms. 27, 25, 21, 19, 14, 3; 1456–7, 13, 18 and 3. [9] *Ibid.*, 1422–4, m. 9.

held and were patronized by the Court, like the great tournament at Smithfield in 1406[1]; the nine days of 'jostys of pese' which celebrated the wedding of Margaret, sister of Edward IV, to Charles the Bold of Burgundy[2]; Henry VII's 'justes,'[3] and many others. But these tournaments were held for political purposes,[4] or were merely occasions for pomp and show, and not for real training in arms.

The lawlessness of the age.

The breakdown of Medieval institutions and the failure of Medieval ideals naturally tended to produce confusion and disorder, which were increased by the displacement of labour caused by the economic changes of the century. Lawlessness is therefore one of the most marked characteristics of the period, and official records and private letters are alike full of complaints of outrages of all kinds.[5] Forcible entry into other men's land and the ejection of the rightful owner was a very frequent occurrence[6]; the victims often appealed to the Chancellor for help against their assailants,[7] especially when they could obtain no assistance from any other quarter, on account of the powerfulness of their enemies. The Duke of Suffolk sent three hundred men against John Paston's manor of Hellesdon,[8] and at last took the place and forced the tenants to break down the walls[9]; the Duke of Norfolk attacked Caister Castle in a similar fashion,[10] and Lord Molynes besieged Margaret Paston in her house at Gresham,[11]

[1] Hardy, Syllabus to Rymer's *Fœdera*, II, 556, cf. Strype's *Stow*, I, 718. [2] *Paston Letters*, IV, 298. [3] Campbell, *op. cit.*, I, 232. [4] Strutt, *Sports and Pastimes*, 13. [5] The Commons complained of 'Murdra, Homicidia, Raptus Mulierum, Robberias, Arsuras et alia mala quamplurima' (*Rot. Parl.*, IV, 421). [6] 5 *Ric. II*, st. 1, c. 7; 15 *Ric. II*, c. 2; 4 *H. IV*, c. 8; 8 *H. VI*, c. 9; *Ancient Indictments*, K.B. 8, Bag 1, Nos. 64, 23 and 28. *Rot Parl.*, III, 560. [7] *Early Chanc. Proceed.*, 31/364, 31/465, 32/258, 39/62, 95/28. [8] *Paston Letters*, IV, 160. [9] *Ibid.*, IV, 204–6. [10] *Ibid.*, I, 202; V, 45–6. [11] *Ibid.*, I, 43–4.

carried her out and rifled it, and all this happened to one family. The tenants of landowners suffered many inconveniences when disputes arose as to the possession of the property. Both claimants demanded rent, and the one who did not obtain it frequently distrained the tenants' goods, and perhaps punished them as well for paying his adversary.[1]

Theft was a common offence, and often very serious injuries were inflicted upon the unfortunate persons who were robbed; for example, John Asshewell, of Iseldon, was so badly wounded by Thomas Knyfe that his life was despaired of[2]; and the wife of Robert Netherton was so frightened that she was never again in her 'stedfast mynde.'[3] Sir John Fortescue, when he was singing the praises of England, declared 'there be therfor mo Men hangyd in Englond, in a Yere, for Robberye, and Manslaughter, than ther be hangid in Fraunce, for such Cause of Crime in seven Yers,' and he gives as the reason the superior courage of Englishmen, who will not refrain from taking away other men's riches by might.[4] The fact that the Lord Chief Justice could take pride in crimes of violence committed by his fellow-countrymen is indeed a curious comment upon the condition of society. His opinion is corroborated by the author of the *Italian Relation*[5]; and that it was no idle boast is seen by the records of many criminal proceedings.[6] Many of these were, however, due not to the desire to steal,

[1] *Ibid.*, I, 309-10, and V, 208. [2] *Ancient Indictments*, K.B. 8, Bag 1, No. 50. [3] *Early Chanc. Proceed.*, 66/211. [4] Fortescue, Vol I, *op. cit.*, p. 466. [5] 'There is no country in the world where there are so many thieves and robbers as in England,' *Italian Relation*, 34. [6] *Ancient Indictments*, K.B. 8, Bag 1, Nos. 53, 65, 67, 69, 70, 16, 26, 42; *Coroners' Rolls*, 148, m. 3; and 158; *Early Chanc. Proceed.*, 4/120, 3/92, 3/141, 12/260, 15/207, 17/61, 27/418, 28/475, 31/322.

but to a malicious wish to injure or kill an enemy The *Coroners' Rolls* afford many instances of murderers deliberately lying in wait for their victims,[1] or openly attacking them[2]; sometimes men were assaulted in their own homes and killed[3]; and often quarrels ended in murder.[4] The *Early Chancery Proceedings* also show that assaults of a very brutal kind were quite common; one man declares that he has been assaulted and threatened, so that he dares not go out of his house[5]; on another occasion, fifty armed men made a night attack on the house of Robert Bradshaw and John Worsley of Pollesworth; they brought 'firebrondes and botellys of straw and an axe,' and by threats of setting fire to the house, forced Robert and John to come down to them, and then took them away and imprisoned them for eighteen days.[6] Even churches were not held sacred by some of these lawless ruffians.[7] A striking feature of the period is the contempt shown for legal authority, even sometimes for that of the Chancellor, by some desperate persons: a woman upon whom a writ of subpœna had been served, 'reysyd vpp her neghebors with wepyns drawen forto slee and mordre ye said bryngers of ye writte' . . . 'and compellyd hem forto

[1] *Coroners' Rolls*, 63, m. 1 and 61, m. 8; cf. *Early Chanc. Proceed.*, 4/128, 5/191, 6/216, 10/326, 28/375. [2] *Coroners' Rolls*, 61, m. 4; 63, ms. 3 and 5; 170. [3] *Ibid.*, 60, m. 6. d. [4] *Ibid.*, 61, m. 5; and cf. 63, m. 3. [5] *Early Chanc. Proceed.*, 4/172. See Appendix B, 5. [6] *Early Chanc. Proceed.*, 12/102. [7] Robert Styel, late parson of Lammas (Norfolk), complained to the Chancellor that Roger Dowe and others had made an assault on him in his church, dragged him out and carried him off to Norwich, where they kept him a prisoner until he paid a fine of ten marks, and bound himself in an obligation of twenty pounds not to go to law with them. *Ibid.*, 6/55 and 56, cf. *Paston Letters*, II, p. 12 and *seq.*, which describe how Walter Aslak set up bills on the gates of the priory of Trinity Church, Norwich, threatening to murder Judge Paston, as he had already murdered others. Cf. also the case of a parson imprisoned in his own church, *Early Chanc. Proceed.*, 6/121.

devour the same Writte . . . bothe Wex and parchement.'[1] In some instances, offenders also resisted attempts made to arrest them.[2] Disgraceful scenes sometimes took place at the sessions. Will Pek, who had been assigned to inquire into felonies and insurrections committed in the county of Bedford, was, he told the Council, obliged to adjourn the proceedings, because Lord Grey and Lord Fanhope each came with an assemblage in arms, and he feared a breach of the peace.[3] Outbursts of lawlessness were probably more usual in some parts of the country than in others—for example, in the counties bordering on Wales[4] and on Scotland; but no part of the kingdom was immune.[5] Assaults were even made in Westminster Hall, 'in contempt of the King,'[6] and William Tailboys tried to murder Lord Cromwell there.[7] The sea was no safer than the land, for piracy was more rife than ever before; it was profitable because trade was increasing,[8] and ships were worth robbing. The 'Libelle' deplored it, especially the deprecations of Hankyne Lyons.[9] The ports on the south

[1] *Ibid.*, 15/197 and cf. 3/94 and 6/35. A statute passed in the reign of Henry VI states that 'commandments by writ to appear before the King in his Chancery or Council be and many Times have been disobeyed,' and orders very drastic punishment for defaults in the future, 31 *H. VI*, c. 2. [2] *Ibid.*, 5/106 and 165, and *Coroners' Rolls*, 169, m. 3. [3] *Proceed. of the Privy Council*, V, 35–8. A similar case is reported in the *Chancery Proceedings*, 12/192–3: another Justice of the Peace, Robert Crakanthorp, explained to the Chancellor that he had not been able to hold the sessions, because three hundred persons laid wait to kill him in the forest of Whinfell; and a certificate from Ralph, Earl of Westmoreland accompanied his petition. [4] *A.C.*, LI, 100. *Rot. Parl.*, IV, 421. Complaints against Wales, *Ibid.*, III, 663, IV, 52, V, 53. Statutes, 9 *H. IV*, c. 3; 20 *H. VI*, c. 3. Condition of Shropshire, *Rot. Parl.*, IV, 69. The *Coroners' Rolls* for this county show that a very large number of murders took place, the jury seldom returned a verdict of accidental death, *Rolls* 147–50. Complaints against Northumberland, *Rot. Parl.*, III, 662. [5] See Appendix D, 5. [6] *Early Chanc. Proceed.*, 10/153. [7] *Rot. Parl.*, V, 200. [8] Traill, *Social England*, II, 405. [9] Wright, *op. cit.*, II, 183.

coast seem to have been veritable nests of pirates; the men of Fowey,[1] Dartmouth,[2] Sandwich,[3] Falmouth,[4] and Plymouth[5] were continually seizing vessels. The people of Calais were noted for piracy; a merchant of Brittany appealed to the Chancellor for aid against them because they had captured his ship, and the Chancellor endorsed his petition with an order to the Warden of the Cinque Ports to do him right.[6] The inhabitants of Estergi and Westergi, in Friesland, also asked for aid against Calais, and requested the King to forbid the captain of the town to injure them, as he had in his pay pirates called 'likedelers.'[7] Numerous appeals for the restitution of goods and ships occur in diplomatic documents,[8] and many negotiations were carried on concerning them; the orders for restoration of property, or payment of compensation, prove how often the English were in fault.[9] The reproach hurled by the French Herald at the English, 'Vous appliquez vostre dit navire a faire guerre aux pouvres marchans, piller et rober leur marchandises, et vous faictes pillastres et larrons de mer,'[10] was justified by facts; though we have no reason to think that the English were worse than any other nation. The evil was in part due to the difficulty experienced by merchants in obtaining payment of debts, and to the sanction of the system of reprisal by letters of marque.[11] Rough-and-ready justice

[1] *Early Chanc. Proceed.*, 13/16, 16/30, 16/74, 20/19. [2] *Ibid.*, 6/123, 8/14, 10/37. [3] *Ibid.*, 39/226. [4] *Ibid.*, 11/430-1. [5] *Ibid.*, 9/321, 11/40, 67/172. For illustration see Appendix B, 3. [6] *Early Chanc. Proceed.*, 5/89. [7] Hardy, *op. cit.*, II, 541. [8] Complaints of Hanse merchants, *Ibid.*, II, 545; do. by Teutonic order of St. Mary, *Ibid.*, 600; do. by Flemish merchants, *Gairdner's Letters*, I, 39, and II, 49. Henry VI expressed regret for piracy by Englishmen on a Portuguese noble, Bekynton, *Letters*, I, 190. [9] Hardy, *op. cit.*, II, 553, 572, 717. [10] *Débat des Hérauts*, p. 26. [11] The men of Truro and Fowey arrested ships by reason of letters of mark granted nineteen years before; *Early Chanc. Proceed.*, 20/19.

was the order of the day, and men recouped themselves for their losses; a ship belonging to the Bishop of St. Andrew's was seized by pirates of the West Country,[1] and he in retaliation arrested the goods in the *John* of Calais.[2]

Acts of lawlessness were committed not only by criminals and desperadoes, but by persons of both sexes and of all classes; and perhaps the most frequent offenders were found among the nobility. To take one case out of many, we find that quarrels between the Earl of Devon and William, Lord Bonville kept Cornwall and Devonshire in a state of disorder for many years. The Privy Council made great efforts to bring them to an agreement by peaceful means[3] in 1441, but quite in vain[4]; and fourteen years later it was stated in Parliament 'there ben grete & grevous riotes down in the Weste Countrey, betwene Th' erle of Devonshire, and the Lord Bonevile, by the whiche som Men have be murdred, some robbed, & Children & Wymen taken.'[5] The Earl of Devonshire, it was said, had robbed the 'churche of Excestre, and take the Chanons of the same Churche and put theym to fynaunce.'[7] One of John Paston's correspondents gives a description of an outrage committed by the son of the Earl of Devonshire against a man named Radford; a house was burnt at his gate to force him to open it, and then the assailants rushed into the place, stole all that they could, and carried off Radford and smote him on the head.[6] Some of the *Early Chancery Proceedings* throw more light upon the doings of the Courtenay family. Christian Keynes stated that J. Keylewey, by the 'supporta-

[1] *Ibid.*, 24/3-5. [2] *Ibid.*, 24/261. [3] *Proceed. of the Privy Council*, V, 165. [4] *Ibid.*, 173-5 and 408. [5] *Rot. Parl.*, V, 285, and further complaints, V, 332, No. 8. [6] *Rot. Parl.*, V, 285. [7] *Paston Letters*, III, 49.

cion & mayntenance ' of Thomas, late Earl of Devon, had riotously taken her goods and chattels to the value of £100[1]; and the earl was accused of assisting J. Trelauney to obtain wrongful possession of land, in a similar manner.[2] There are no less than three accusations against Sir Hugh Courtenay for seizing goods from ships at sea, but as there were two persons of the same name, possibly the earlier petition[3] was against the father, and the later against the son.[4] One of them was also accused of carrying off a servant, horses, and goods belonging to Thomas Bodulgate.[5]

Philip Courtenay, too, was rather high-handed in his dealings ; he assaulted an officer of the Exchequer for doing his office.[6] A petition by the grandsons of John Boville the Younger against Edward Courtenay, grandson of the first Sir Hugh, for the possession of some lands, shows that the quarrels of this family were still unended.[7] We have no reason to suppose that the Courtenays were more lawless than others of their class at this time ; on the contrary, they were a most illustrious family, and not only served the King in France,[8] but supplied the nation with an admiral[9] and two bishops[10] in the course of the century. This combination of great ability with an utter disregard for law and

[1] *Early Chanc. Proceed.*, 28/450. [2] 28/298. [3] *Ibid.*, 13/16, date of bundle, 13–21 *H. VI.* [4] 28/476 (38 *H. VI.* to 5 *Ed. IV.*) and 30/60 (3 to 7 *Ed. IV.*). The elder Sir Hugh was the son of Sir Ed. Courtenay, son of Hugh Earl of Devon, who died in 1377 (G. E. C. peerage). [5] *Early Chanc. Proceed.*, 24/223.

[6] 28/440. According to the G. E. C. peerage Sir Philip was the great grandson of Hugh Earl of Devon. [7] *Early Chanc. Proceed.*, 50/313 (date of bundle, 1475–80 and 1483–5). Ed. Courtenay was created Earl of Devon in 1485. [8] Edward Courtenay, Knt., Junior (*Cal. French Rolls*, 1416, m. 31), and Hugh Courtenay, son of Edward, Earl of Devon (*Ibid.*, 1418, m. 2). [9] Edward Courtenay, Admiral of the West (*Rot. Parl.*, III, 152). [10] Richard Courtenay, Bishop of Norwich, and Peter Courtenay, Bishop of Winchester and of Exeter (*Dict. of National Biography*).

order is very characteristic of the age. It was, of course, exceedingly difficult to bring powerful men like the Courtenays to justice, and unfortunately, not content with their own quarrels, they often took part in those of their neighbours and gave them the benefit of their support, and, in consequence, malefactors were often so strong that no one dared to resist them.[1]

One of the chief causes of the lawlessness of the nobility was the 'yevyng of Lyverees and Signes' and the 'Mayntenaunce of Quarels' by powerful men.[2] Great lords kept a large number of retainers, perhaps as substitutes for the feudal vassals who had almost disappeared; and judging from the ordinances made to check the evils of the system, some of these retainers were persons of very bad character. In 1429 it was ordered that no lord of the Council should 'receive, cheryssh, hold in houshold, ne maynteyne Pillours, Robbours, Oppressours of the people, Mansleers, Felons, Outelawes,' and other malefactors.[3] The ordinance gains significance when we remember that the lords of the Council were the foremost men of the realm, and practically the rulers of the kingdom at this time. It was not by any means the first or the last prohibition of livery and maintenance.[4] Henry VII was the first king who succeeded in suppressing it; he required all knights, esquires, yeomen, and

[1] 'A cowper of Geyton slow a tenaunt of Danyell,' but no one dared to indict him, because Tudenham maintained him and Lord Scales apparently maintained Tudenham (*Paston Letters*, II, 214 and seq.).

[2] *Rot. Parl.*, V, 487, No. 39. Instances of outrages said to be due to maintenance, *Early Chanc. Proceed.*, 15/94, 16/100, 16/715, 22/42, 29/521, 31/173, 38/249, 5/106. [3] *Rot. Parl.*, IV, 344.

[4] Enactments regarding Livery and Maintenance, *Rot. Parl.*, III, 23; *Ibid.*, 307, No. 31, and 345, No. 38; *Ibid.*, III, 428, No. 84, 477, No. 110; IV, 348, No. 35; V, 487 and 633. Statutes, 1 *H. IV*, c. 7; 13 *H. IV*, c. 3; 8 *H. VI*, c. 4; and 8 *Ed. IV*, c. 2.

others to take an oath not to break the law against it,[1] and he fined those who disobeyed very heavily.

The use of arbitration in the fifteenth century.

The numerous quarrels which went on in the fifteenth century, and the outrages which so often accompanied them, caused an enormous amount of litigation. Sometimes attempts were made to settle disputes by arbitration. For example, it was ordained by the Privy Council that Lord and Lady Westmoreland should each choose three lords and two justices to 'laboure betwix hem for good accord.'[2] Humfrey Forster writes to Thomas Stonor that 'Heynes . . . is bounde in an obligation of £200 to abide ye rewle' of certain persons in all the matters between him and Fowler[3]; and sometimes persons of superior rank acted as mediators between disputants. Thus a thirteen years' quarrel between the Corporation of Coventry and William Bristowe, concerning the enclosure of the Lammas lands, was finally settled by the arbitration of the Prince of Wales.[4] The respective claims of Sir William Plumpton's son and granddaughters were submitted to the judgment of Richard III, and he made an award in which both sides peaceably acquiesced.[5] The Gilds did their best to prevent lawsuits between their members—'bretheren and sisteren' were ordered to put matters between them to the arbitration of the Master and others[6]; and some ordinances only permitted them to apply to the common law if the master and aldermen had failed to 'accord' them, and then only with the

[1] Campbell, *op. cit.*, Vol. I, 243–4.
[2] *Proceed. Privy Council*, IV, 289.
[3] *A.C.*, Vol. XLVI, No. 47. [4] Dormer Harris, *op. cit.*, 236.
[5] *Plumpton Corr.*, xcv.
[6] T. Smith, *Eng. Gilds*, 21, 55, 76, 96, 271, 279, 280.

consent of the officials of the Gild.[1] The weak points of arbitration were the difficulties of finding impartial arbitrators,[2] and of persuading the parties concerned to carry out the award if they did not like the decision. A dispute between Sir William Plumpton and Ralph, Earl of Westmoreland, was referred to arbitrators, but they did not end it, and a second award was needed.[3] Even Richard III's judgment was set aside early in the sixteenth century.[4] Sometimes disgraceful scenes occurred at 'love-days,' as they were called. Judge Tirwhit came to one, at which Gascoigne was to arbitrate between him and Lord de Roos, with five hundred armed followers, whom he placed in ambush.[5] Under these circumstances it is hardly surprising that many people thought litigation a safer way of setting discord at rest than arbitration, and most of the persons whose letters have come down to us, engaged in numbers of lawsuits. Sir John Fastolf and John Paston were continually at law, and the other members of the Paston family were nearly as bad. 'A register of writs,' belonging apparently to Sir John the Elder, gives some ideas of the legal business in which he was involved. Nine writs are mentioned in this one document, and all of them seem to be dated in the eighth year of Edward IV.[6] Sir William Plumpton was so fond of litigation that it was said that he was suing

The increase of litigation in the fifteenth century.

[1] *Ibid.*, 450–1. Richard Drynkemylk, draper, in a petition to the Chancellor, states that the wardens of his company have caused him to be imprisoned by the Mayor of London, because he sued Richard Odyam in Chancery without their leave (*Early Chanc. Proceed.*, 197/56), and similarly John Paret, of London, mercer, complains that he has been imprisoned at the instance of the wardens of his company for refusal to accept arbitration between himself and his servant (*Early Chanc. Proceed.*, 219/42). [2] *Ibid.*, 29/290, 26/296, 27/34. [3] *Plumpton Corr.*, li. [4] *Ibid.*, ciii. [5] Wylie, *Henry IV*, II, 189–90. [6] *Paston Letters*, V, 97–8.

every true man in the Forest[1] of Knaresborough, where he lived. The *Plumpton Correspondence* also shows that Sir Robert Plumpton was frequently in the law courts; three writs were out against him on February 10th, 1489–90.[2] Reference is made to several other suits in which he was interested in letters addressed to him[3]; and both the Plumptons and the Pastons figure in the *Chancery Proceedings.*[4] Sir John Howard must have given a good deal of occupation to lawyers. On May 8th, 1467, he paid 10s. to 'mastyr Frestone of the Chaunsery for two wryttes'; on the 13th of the same month he obtained a 'wrytte ayens Pryse,' 'a nother wrytte uppon his patent and lyvelode,' and he enrolled two writs, one against 'Sulyard' and the other against himself. His legal expenses that day amounted to 26s. 6d.[5]

It was not, however, only the aristocracy and gentry who indulged in the luxury of going to law; in the flourishing town of Nottingham there were so many suits between the burgesses that in a single year twenty rolls or more were filled with the records of them.[6] Even churches engaged in litigation. We read in the churchwardens' accounts of St. Mary-at-Hill, London, of an action of debt for house-rent,[7] of a suit against a tenant for wrongdoing,[8] and of proceedings against the prioress of St. Helen's regarding a chantry, which cost no less

[1] *Plumpton Correspondence*, p. 23. [2] *Ibid.*, p. 91. [3] *Ibid.*, 112, 130, 132, 133. [4] Petitions against Sir W. Plumpton, *Early Chanc. Proceed.*, 31/330, 31/485, 45/175, 58/327 38/224, 66/77. A great deal of litigation arose out of Sir John Fastolf's will. John Paston petitioned against Yelverton and Jenny for the possession of Caister; William Waynflete, bishop of Winchester, petitioned against Yelverton and William Paston concerning other land with which they had been jointly enfeoffed, 33/214. [5] *Howard Household Book*, I, 402. [6] Mrs. Green, *Town Life*, II, 325. [7] *Medieval Records of a London City Church*, p. 91. [8] *Ibid.*, 111.

than £18 6s. 4½d. in one year.[1] These are not isolated instances,—St. Dunstan's, Canterbury, was engaged in two lawsuits in 1490, one of which was commenced in 1486.[2]

Prosperity of the lawyers.

In consequence of the increased amount of litigation which was carried on in the fifteenth century lawyers were very prosperous, and the legal profession became very popular. It was necessary to provide more accommodation for law-students in London, and Barnard's Inn was handed over to them as early as 1454.[3] Staple Inn was a wool-house in early days, but by 1463 it had yielded up any right it may have possessed to be regarded as a customs-house,[4] and had become an Inn of Chancery. New Inn probably became the habitation of lawyers late in the century; it was a hostel for travellers as late as 1485.[5] In the days of Sir John Fortescue there were four Inns of Court and ten Inns of Chancery; each of the former was frequented by about two hundred students, and each of the latter by a hundred,[6] and they seem to have been very flourishing.

The failure of Medieval ideas and the fall of Medieval institutions ultimately brought about further changes in the structure of society,—men grew tired of lawlessness and litigation, of political strife and private warfare. The 'lack of governance,' which was the chief characteristic of the

[1] *Ibid.*, 179.

[2] *Archæologia Cantiana*, Vol. XVII, p. 146. Yatton church also engaged in a lawsuit and employed three lawyers, Hobhouse, 123.

[3] Douthwaite, *Gray's Inn*, p. 257, and Bellot, *Inner and Middle Temple*, 243.

[4] E. Williams, *Staple Inn*, 99, and Cato Worsfold, *Staple Inn and its Story*, p. 36.

[5] Bellot, *The Inner and Middle Temple*, p. 239.

[6] Fortescue, *op. cit.*, I, 434.

Lancastrian rule in England,[1] aroused a longing for a strong, capable sovereign. Henry VII's determination to keep order, and his enlightened commercial policy, made him acceptable to the nation, and the New Monarchy rose upon the ruins of Feudalism.

[1] Pollard, *Factors in Modern History*, 71–2.

CHAPTER II

THE RISE OF THE MIDDLE CLASS

THE decay of the Feudal System inevitably brought with it a decrease in the importance of the barons, and such power as remained to them was based not on land tenure, as of old, but on the possession of money. Their retainers were not vassals, but hired servants, bound to them not by oaths of fealty, but by the receipt of wages,[1] or by the hope of reward. The Celys called Sir John Weston 'my lord,' and wore his livery, although they held no land of him,[2] and Sir John Paston the Younger was one of the 'ffeede men' of the Duke of Norfolk[3]; but it is obvious that only rich men could afford to have dependents of this kind. The letters of the period are full of requests for patronage,[4] but great men required some return if they granted a favour, and they were not above taking a gift or a loan of money.

Decline of the Baronage.

Richard, Duke of Gloucester, desires a correspondent to lend him a hundred pounds, and adds with his own hand, 'Sir I say I pray that ye fayle me not at this tyme in my grete nede, as ye wule that

[1] An indenture, dated 1471, between Richard Duke of Gloucester and William Burgh stipulates that William shall serve the Duke at all times, in peace and war, for the term of his life, and that he shall take 'yerely for his fee ten marcs sterling' (*Archælogia*, Vol. 47, p. 195).
[2] *Cely Papers*, viii and 55. [3] *Paston Letters*, IV, 200–1. [4] Sir William Stonor is asked to be 'gud maystur' to a poor gentlewoman; Henry Stonor advises his brother to do Lord Fitz Wareyn a service because it would put him 'in suerte to have in tymes to come' if he needed it, 'right good Lordship.' (*A.C.*, XLVI, Nos. 215 and 71.)

I schewe yow my goode lordshype in that matter that ye labure to me for.'[1]

The extravagance of the aristocracy.

How entirely a noble's social position was interwoven with his wealth and the number of his retainers may be seen by the *Liber Niger* of Edward IV, which draws up specimens of the households of different persons of different ranks. A duke should spend £4000 a year and have two hundred and forty attendants [2]; a marquis should spend £3000 and have two hundred attendants[3]; and persons lower down in the social scale should spend proportionately less. The idea that a man's rank should determine the amount of his expenditure was Medieval; but the noble who could not afford to spend as much as his position demanded must have been in a miserable plight; and we have already seen in the *Russell Book* that property had some influence in questions of precedence; moreover, the fashion of raising men to higher ranks because they were rich had begun.[4] The *Liber Niger* also shows that more value was attached to ceremony and outward show than in former days. Edward IV had 'bannerettes or bacheler knights' as his 'kervers or cupberers.' 'In the noble Edwardes' (i.e. Edward III's) 'dayes worshipfull esquires did this servyce but now thus for the more worthy.'[5] Other household books give the same impression; members of the aristocracy could not visit each other without taking a string of servants with them. The *Household Book of Lady Alicia de Brienne* relates that 'Dominus Johannes Howard, "cum vxore, filia

[1] Ellis' *Orig. Letters*, 2nd Series, p. 144, Vol. I. [2] *Ordinances of the Royal Household*, xiii, and 26. [3] *Ibid.*, and p. 27. [4] Michael de la Pole, Earl of Suffolk, in the reign of Richard II, was the first Englishman who owed his peerage to wealth derived from trade (Pollard, *Factors in Modern History*, 40). [5] *Ordinances of the Royal Household*, 33.

ancilla, ij armigeris, ij valectis & iij garconibus," came to see the mistress of the house.'[1] Great nobles entertained most lavishly. On the feast of the Epiphany, three hundred and nineteen strangers dined with the Duke of Buckingham, and two hundred and seventy-nine supped with him.[2] Six oxen were consumed in one meal at the table of the Earl of Warwick, and visitors were allowed to carry off joints.[3] The households of the higher aristocracy were sometimes nearly as magnificent as that of the King. Lord Howard had all kinds of officials—an auditor,[4] a cator,[5] a 'Kowntroller,'[6] a steward, two priests, and two fools, one of whom was called the fool of the kitchen, and who was perhaps kept to amuse the servants.[7] His treasurer was a person of sufficient importance to have a minstrel in his own pay and livery.[8] It is quite possible that the ostentation and extravagance of the English nobles were due to a desire to imitate the Court of Burgundy, which was considered the model of lordly courtesy and high breeding. It was noted for its pomp and magnificence, and for its display of wealth[9]; and England was brought into close connection with it by trade and by political alliances. The expense entailed by such a mode of living was necessarily very great[10]; and therefore, though it gave the aristocracy an appearance of prosperity, it was really suicidal policy, and none but the most wealthy could stand against it. Thus a few great magnates, like the Duke of Buckingham and the Earl of

[1] *Chanc. Misc.*, Bundle 4, No. 8, f. 3. The *Stafford Household Book* speaks of one visitor who had ten attendants and another eight; and the Lady Anne, sister of the lord, had fourteen persons with her on one occasion and fifteen on another (*Archælogia*, Vol. XXV, 321 and 319). [2] *Ibid.*, 325. [3] *Paston Letters*, Introd. I, 328–9. [4] *Howard Household Book*, II, Introd. xxi. [5] *Ibid.*, 141, 190. [6] *Ibid.*, 439. [7] *Ibid.*, xxii. [8] *Ibid.*, xxi. [9] Wright, *Domestic Manners*, 415–16. [10] The household of the Duke of Clarence cost over £4000 a year (*Ordinances of the Royal Household*, 105).

Northumberland, were very powerful, and, indeed, almost overshadowed the throne,[1] but the majority of feudal nobles, impoverished by lavish expenditure, and discredited by the lawlessness of their retainers, declined in social importance. Economic changes co-operated with political causes, such as the Wars of the Roses, in bringing about their downfall.

Inter-marriage between the upper and middle classes.

A method by which needy nobles and gentlemen replenished their empty purses was by marrying the daughters or the widows of rich merchants and traders. 'Marchandes' and 'new Jantylmen' were willing on their side to 'proferr large' for marriages with their superiors.[2] Sir William Plumpton, the grandfather of the Sir William who was the recipient of the earliest letters in the *Plumpton Correspondence*, married the daughter of John Gisburn, a merchant of York,[3] and the widow of George Cely married Sir John Halwell.[4] The wife of Sir Gilbert Talbot had been previously married to a merchant of the Staple.[5] Marriages of this kind were very important because they brought about a fusion of the upper and middle classes.

The rise of the middle class.

The rise of the middle class is the most notable feature in the history of social life in England in the late fourteenth and early fifteenth century, and it was undoubtedly due to the economic changes of the period, and especially to the great industrial revolution, which ended by making England, hitherto a mere producer of raw material, the manufacturer of finished goods in all the chief markets of Europe.[6]

[1] Denton, *England in the Fifteenth Century*, 262. [2] *Paston Letters*, VI, 149. [3] *Plumpton Corr.*, p. xxvii. [4] *Early Chanc. Proceed.*, 196/76. [5] *Ibid.*, 110/30. [6] Vickers, *Humphrey Duke of Gloucester*, 83.

Money gained by successful trade gave importance to the middle class in the fifteenth century, and even kings thought it worth while to bestow favours upon men who could advance loans to them. In 1474 the Prince of Wales was godfather to the child of the Mayor of Coventry; and the Queen sent twelve bucks from Fakenham Forest as a present to the Mayor, his brethren, and their wives.[1] Mr. Vickers has drawn attention to the reliance placed by Humphrey Duke of Gloucester upon the support of the middle classes,[2] and in particular upon the burgesses of London.[3] It is interesting in this connection to remember how impressed the author of the *Italian Relation* was with the 'great riches of London,' which, he says, 'are not occasioned by its inhabitants being noblemen or gentlemen; being all, on the contrary, persons of low degree, & artificers who have congregated there from all parts of the island, and from Flanders, and from every other place. . . . Still,' he adds, 'the citizens of London are thought quite as highly of there, as the Venetian gentlemen are at Venice.'[4] The 'Libelle' reflects national feeling in its praise of

'the sonne
Of marchaundy, Richarde of Whitingdone,
That loode-sterre and chefe chosen floure,
Whate hathe by hym oure England of honoure?[5]

Merchants and artisans often rose to the position of gentry by acquiring landed property. The *Court Rolls* of Tooting Bec Manor show that there were many citizens of London;—butchers,[6] carpenters,[7] and others[8] amongst its tenants. The *Early Chancery Proceedings* also contain numerous allusions

[1] D. Harris, *op. cit.*, p. 191. Cf. Sharpe, *Wills*, II, 555. [2] Vickers, *op. cit.*, 320. [3] *Ibid.*, 415. [4] *Italian Relation*, 43. [5] Wright, *Polit. Songs*, II, 178. [6] Tooting Bec Manor *Court Rolls*, 17 *H. VI*; 1440. [7] *Ibid.*, 1442. [8] 27 *H. VI.*

to land held by tradesmen.[1] John Bristowe gained a livelihood as a draper, and, growing in wealth and influence, he became Mayor, Justice of the Peace, and Master of the Trinity Guild; he purchased an estate at Whitley, and his son spoke of his manor and wrote himself 'gentilman.'[2] One of the correspondents of George Cely gives us an idea of the amount of money made by merchants of the Staple. 'They nede,' he says, 'goo noo farther than the bokes yn the tesery wher they may fynde that yowre sallyz made wtyn lesse than thys zere amountes above ijMⁱ li ster' (£2000).[3] Mr. Malden holds that this would produce an income of £200 a year, which would equal the household expenses of a knight, and double those of a squire, according to the reckoning in the Black Book of Edward IV.[4] The Wills of the period also show that considerable sums of money were made by trade. A mercer of London, John Neve, left more than £840 in cash, as well as a messuage, goods, and chattels.[5] Another mercer bequeathed two thousand marks to charity, two thousand also to his children, a manor to each of his sons, and various lands, rents, and tenements to other persons.[6] Socially, the middle classes seem to have been ranked with squires, and in consequence 'Marchaundes and Franklonz, worshipfulle and honorable, þey may be set semely at a squyers table,'[7] says Russell, and he puts doctors and Serjeants-of-Law and 'riche artyficeris' in the same category.[8] But when members of the middle classes were knighted, they ranked amongst those whom Russell counted as fourth in the order of precedence.[9]

[1] *Early Chanc. Proceed.*, by a draper, 27/99; by a grocer, 27/101; by a goldsmith, 26/427; by a mercer, 39/25. [2] Dormer Harris, *op. cit.*, 206–7. [3] *Cely Papers*, 153. [4] *Ibid.*, Introd., xliv. [5] *Early Chanc. Proceed.*, 67/333. [6] Sharpe, *Wills*, II, 398–9. [7] *Manners and Meals*, 189. [8] *Ibid.*, 187. [9] *Ibid.*, 186.

During the fifteenth century the English yeomanry took root,[1] and its development was assisted by the changes which occurred in land tenure. The *Early Chancery Proceedings* often refer to persons who seem to be small farmers. John Paddon, yeoman, we are told, was possessed of 'a mese and x acres of arable land '[2]; and another yeoman, John Forger, was seised of 'a mes xxij acres of land and iij acres of mede with the appurtenaunces.'[3] Mr. Denton, who takes a most gloomy view of the condition of England in the fifteenth century, says that tenant-farmers were rising into a distinct and important class. He thinks that landlords were willing to let their lands on easy terms, because the old free tenants, who had held land by military tenure, were almost extinct,[4] and the attractions of trade made it difficult to fill their places. Professor Thorold Rogers holds that during the fourteenth century, occupying freeholders possessing eighty acres of land were rare; but in the fifteenth they became sufficiently numerous to form the basis of a new political system.[5] The children of yeomen, especially if their parents managed to educate them, sometimes rose to quite important positions. Henry Chichele, Archbishop of Canterbury, is said to have been the son of a yeoman[6]; and the father of Hugh Latimer was a Leicestershire farmer yeoman.[7] The Church had always provided clever youths with an opportunity of rising in the world, and in the fifteenth century a brilliant career was also open to men of talent in the legal profession.[8] The passion for litigation which distinguished the age created

Growth of the English yeomanry.

[1] T. Rogers, *Work and Wages*, 384. [2] *Early Chanc. Proceed.*, 27/93. [3] *Ibid.*, 28/388. [4] Denton, *op. cit.*, 234-5. [5] *Work and Wages*, 282. [6] *Dict. of National Biography.* [7] *Dict. of National Biography.* [8] Mrs. Green, *Town Life*, II, 263.

a demand for a large number of lawyers, and legal advice was so frequently needed by towns that often the town clerk was a lawyer.[1] An exceptionally clever man might become a judge, and, in any case, an able lawyer could command the market, like Thomas Caxton, the brother of the printer, who went from town to town, wherever he could best sell his services.[2] The history of the Paston family shows what could be done by those who were capable and energetic. Clement Paston lived on his land, and had five or six score acres at the most; he borrowed money and sent his son William to school, and afterwards, with the help of his wife's brother, who was an attorney, to court. William was a 'right cunning' man in the law, and he was made a serjeant and finally a justice.[3] He bought much land, and one of his sons, William, was considered worthy to marry Anne Beaufort, daughter of Edmund Duke of Somerset,[4] and cousin of Margaret Countess of Richmond, mother of Henry VII. Judge Paston's other son, John, also did very well, and two of his sons were knighted. Thus, while the aristocracy was degenerating through its lawlessness and extravagance, the middle class was becoming a more and more important factor in society; and with the victory of Henry VII it came into a position to make its interests dominant.[5]

[1] Mrs. Green, *Town Life*, II, 260–1. [2] *Ibid.*, 261. [3] *Paston Letters*, Vol. I, Introd., pp. 28–9, quoting Yelverton's account of the ancestry of Sir J. Paston. [4] *Ibid.*, Vol. V, 75. [5] Hasbach, *Hist. of the English Agric. Labourer*, p. 33.

CHAPTER III

THE ECONOMIC POSITION OF THE CHURCH

The system of pluralities.

THE secular clergy and the religious orders were considerably affected both by the economic changes of the fifteenth century and by the new ideas engendered by them. They did not escape the love of money, the commercial spirit, and the restlessness which characterized the laity; and their position in society was altered by the changes in the social structure. The love of money showed itself in various ways. Influential men often managed to obtain two or more posts at the same time. A list of wealthy clergy drawn up in 1404 gives some good illustrations of the lengths to which this practice was carried. John Thorp was 'pensionarius in diuersis locis & Rector duarum ecclesiarum parochialium in diocesi Norwicensis'; and this example is by no means exceptional. It was quite common for ecclesiastics to hold three or four appointments, a few possessed five, and one cleric, named 'Nicholas Bubbewyth,' was actually credited with six.[1] Several complaints of the system of pluralities and of the non-residence of the clergy, which necessarily accompanied it, occur in the Rolls of Parliament during the fifteenth century and the last part of the fourteenth.[2] Gascoigne comments very bitterly

[1] *Excheq. K. R. Eccles.*, $\frac{8}{24}$. [2] *Rot. Parl.*, III, 163, 468, 594, 645, and IV, 290, 305. One of the *Early Chancery Proceedings* deals with the payment of a sum of £10, which had been spent on obtaining a Plurality Bull in Rome, and sending it to England (11/328).

upon the non-residency of the Bishops, and declares that when the mob murdered 'Asku, Bishop of Sarum,' they upbraided him with this fault.[1] Churches were farmed and let out on lease as if they were landed property and nothing more; five laymen jointly held to farm the church of St. John in the 'Marresse'[2]; and the lease of the benefice of St. Dunstan's-in-the-East, London, was granted to Thomas Elderton, fishmonger, and afterwards to William Nottyng, clerk, by the factors of Master Adrian Castylyens, the parson of the church.[3] An even more curious arrangement is recorded in which it is asserted that Martyn Jolyff, priest, keeper of the guild of Jesus with St. Paul's, London, 'leet to ferme' 'all the gederingis' . . . 'of Almes of the people of and in fifteen Shires, for a certein Sume of money.' The ecclesiastical authorities said that the agreement was not lawful, and to the damage of the people; but the person to whom it had been granted appealed to the Chancellor against their decision.[4]

Secularity of the clergy.

As a result of the desire to increase their incomes, and possibly also from motives of ambition in some cases, we find clergy of all classes engaged in secular pursuits. Many of the higher clergy were politicians, and too much occupied with affairs of State to devote themselves to their spiritual duties. Bourchier is said to have only officiated once in his cathedral during the ten years that he was bishop of Ely, and that was at his installation.[5] To take one See as an example, amongst the bishops of Exeter in this

[1] Lewis, *Life of Pecock*, pp. 19–21. [2] *Early Chanc. Proceed.*, 100/72, and other cases 17/239 and 41/262, and *Plumpton Corr.*, xxxvii. [3] *Early Chanc. Proceed.*, 216/70, similar cases, 11/8, 11/90, 11/219. [4] *Ibid.*, 66/25, Lease of a Chantry, *Early Chanc. Proceed.*, 10/284. [5] Capes, *English Church*, 202.

century at least five were eminent public men. Edmund Stafford and George Neville were chancellors, and Booth was a statesman who cared little for his diocese[1]; Peter Courtenay took a considerable share in politics, he served both Edward IV and Henry VII, and was made Keeper of the Privy Seal and Commissioner of the Royal Mines by the latter King.[2] Fox, who followed him at Exeter, was one of Henry's chief advisers; his episcopal work was performed by a suffragan, he 'himself for the most part, as it seems, being detained by his public employments about the Court.'[3] Priests in lower positions often acted as secretaries and men of business to their patrons[4]; Sir John Howes made himself very useful to Sir John Fastolf in this way, and he took part in lawsuits, and quarrelled as vigorously as his master. Country parsons sometimes made money by selling their grain,[5] or their malt,[6] and we hear that Sir Thomas Maund, parson of South Tidworth, traded in wool, and did not fulfil his bargain.[7] The parson of Dunster acted as collector of the King's taxes in Somerset,[8] and clergy of all kinds were feoffees to uses.[9]

Incomes of the parish priests.

Dr. Jessop is of the opinion that the incomes of the parish priests had greatly decreased by the fifteenth century through the encroachments of the monasteries, the rivalry of the friars, and other causes.[10] If this statement be true it would be some excuse for their participation in secular employments, and no

[1] Freeman, *Exeter*, pp. 193–4. [2] *Dict. National Biography*, XII, 339–40. [3] *Ibid.*, XX, quoting Fulman. [4] We read that Sir Ralph Kempe, priest, 'was besy abowte ye seruice' of Thomas Charlys, Esq. *Early Chanc. Proceed.*, 9/265. [5] *Early Chanc. Proceed.*, 52/172. *Howard Household Book*, II, 118, and 208–9. [6] *Early Chanc. Proceed.*, 60/2. [7] *Ibid.*, 27/137. [8] *Ibid.*, 11/361. [9] *Ibid.*, 17/94, 18/31, 19/125, 20/17, 21/17, 22/44, 24/48, 25/9, 26/20, and many more; hundreds could be quoted. [10] Jessop, *Parish Life*, 101–4.

doubt some parishes suffered greatly from the appropriation of tithes and other sources of revenue to abbeys and priories. A document in the Public Record Office gives a list of the churches in Kent appropriated to monasteries, and shows how valuable they were. The Abbey of Faversham possessed two churches, which yielded £60 and £30 6s. 8d. respectively; six churches were appropriated to the Abbey of 'Langedon,' and six to the Priory of Dover; and the Priory of St. Gregory, Canterbury, possessed even more.[1] Another document in the Record Office, an inquisition regarding the churches in Bristol, gives the value of eighteen churches in that city or its suburbs; the amounts vary a great deal: two were estimated at £4, and seven were under £10, but two were worth £20 each, and one £25. The average value of the livings was £11 7s.[2] The income of the Rector of Preston, in Kent, was £9 15s. in 1536, and Abbot Gasquet considers that it was ample for those days,[3] so the clergy in Bristol were well off; but possibly this state of affairs was due to the commercial prosperity of the city.

Chaplains, like other wage-earners, demanded higher pay for their services, and refused to take less than twelve marks; consequently, in answer to the petition of the Commons, it was ordered that parochial chaplains should have eight marks, and others seven.[4] It was, however, very difficult to enforce statutes limiting wages. In 1449 the ex-prioress of Rowney, in Hertfordshire, complained that she and her

Wages of chaplains.

[1] *Excheq. K. R. Eccles.*, 1/17. [2] *Lay Subsidies*, $\frac{237}{27}$; one of the figures in this document is faint, so the calculation may not be quite accurate. [3] Gasquet, *Parish Life in Medieval England*, 16. [4] *Rot. Parl.*, IV, 51, and 2 *H. V*, Stat. II, c. 2. In 1362 it was ordered that the wages of chaplains should not exceed five marks.

sisters could have 'noo preste' except a young one, because they asked 'so moche and grete salary.'[1]

Whether we think the secular occupations of the priesthood justified by poverty or not, there seems little doubt that they had a bad effect upon the moral tone of the clergy as a whole. A large number of serious accusations were brought against them during this century, and although it is very unlikely that all the charges were true, a certain proportion must have been, and the fact that they were made shows that the clergy were considered capable of committing crimes. Some of them were charged with wrongfully retaining goods or money belonging to other persons.[2] There are many petitions against them on the ground of assault: William Selby, parson of Denham, is said to have attacked the servant of John Colrede with his fist, an Irish knife, and a staff[3]; William Aufyn of East Barkwith, Lincolnshire, declared that the parson forcibly carried him off from his house.[4] Sometimes the clergy objected to the discipline imposed by their superiors: the Archdeacon of Norfolk complained that when he made a visitation at Cromer the vicar and many armed parishioners assaulted him and his servants in the church and cemetery, and they hardly escaped with their lives.[5] Margaret Paston in one of her letters tells her husband that 'the parson of Snoryng came to Thomas Denys and fetched hym owt of hys hows . . . and hathe a leed hym festhe with hem'[6]; and another priest, named Phylyp, 'com to Haylsdon with a grete nomber of pepell, that ys to say viij^{xx} men and mor in harnysse, and ther toke from the persons plowe ij hors, pris iiij marc and

Deterioration of the clergy.

[1] *Proceed. of Privy Council*, VI, 67. [2] *Early Chanc. Proceed.*, 6/262, 10/97, 17/282, 19/155. [3] *Ibid.*, 28/342. [4] *Ibid.*, 16/65. [5] 16/52. [6] *Paston Letters*, III, 282.

ij hors of Thomas Stermyns plowe, pris, xls.[1] Fabyan says that 'the persone of Wortham in Norfolke . . . haunted Newmarket heth, and there robbyd and spoyled many of ye Kynges subgettes.'[2] Roger Skete accused the vicar of Reigate of carrying off his wife and certain goods[3]; while another petitioner declared that William Roddok, priest, enticed away his daughter[4]; and some dozens of charges of a similar nature were brought against chaplains in the city of London in the time of Henry IV.[5] There are also charges of rioting[6] and of forgery[7] in the *Early Chancery Proceedings*, and numbers of cases in which feoffees were said to have betrayed their trusts.[8]

The first indications of a decline in the social position of the country clergy may be noticed at the end of the fourteenth century,[9] and apparently their numbers were largely recruited from the middle classes and even from serfs, at that time and throughout the fifteenth century.[10] It is possible that the upper classes were not so much tempted to become priests as in former days, because the economic changes of the period had thrown open new careers; and the influx of men of the middle classes into the Church was very characteristic of the condition of society.

Social position of the clergy.

The results of the lower moral tone of the clergy,

[1] *Ibid.*, IV, 137–9. [2] Fabyan, 583. [3] *Early Chanc. Proceed.*, 16/51. [4] *Ibid.*, 28/448. [5] Riley, *Memorials of London*, 566–7, n. [6] *Early Chanc. Proceed.*, 17/257. [7] *Ibid.*, 12/179, and 9/285. [8] *Early Chanc. Proceed.*, 16/378, 17/283, 19/361, 19/211, 26/20, 27/90, 29/482, 33/102, 35/41, 39/101. These are a few examples, but there are many more; it is only fair to remember that no records exist of the cases in which feoffees did their duty, because they did not call for comment. [9] Jessop, *Parish Life*, 105. [10] Gasquet, *Parish Life in Medieval England*, 72. Walter le Hart, Bishop of Norwich (1446–72), was the son of a miller, Gasquet, *Old English Bible*, p. 295.

and perhaps, too, of their lower social position, may be seen in the lower estimation in which some of them were held by the laity. It is not only that satirists scorned 'poopeholy prestis fulle of presomcioun,' who 'Avauncid by symony in cetees and townys,'[1] but the people often treated them with disrespect, and sometimes even with no little roughness. The parson of Snoryng was 'sete' in the stocks,[2] a treatment which he seems to have thoroughly deserved; but he was by no means the only parson who was subjected to this indignity.[3] Many instances of assaults upon the clergy are reported,[4] and some refusals to pay tithes.[5] The comments of the juries dealing with suits in which the clergy were involved also sometimes suggest that they were actuated by bad feeling towards them. Sir Richard Amyson had interfered in a quarrel between two persons concerning a right of way, and the jury promised damages against Amyson 'in such a somm to teche all such prestes to be ware how to medell w[t] any man of the seid Citee.'[6] Yet, on the other hand, the *Churchwardens' Accounts* do not betray any evidence of discord between parsons and their parishioners, and it is probable that the affection felt by the people for their churches was often extended to the priests who ministered in them. Both Abbot Gasquet and Canon Jessop have a very high opinion of the parish priest and of the community of purpose between him and his people.[7]

The economic changes of the fifteenth century produced quite as important effects upon the re-

[1] Wright, *Polit. Songs*, II, 251. [2] *Paston Letters*, III, 290. [3] *Early Chanc. Proceed.*, 31/409 and 61/435. [4] *Ibid.*, 24/35, 31/528, 44/213, 39/175, 64/169, and 216/77. [5] *Ibid.*, 4/73, 11/395, 25/201, and 28/409. [6] *Ibid.*, 60/155. [7] Gasquet, *Parish Life*, 1 and 8; Jessop, *Parish Life*, 107.

ligious orders as upon the secular clergy. The monasteries had undoubtedly performed many useful functions in the early Middle Ages; in the days when the people were ignorant and barbarous they were civilizing agencies. The monks in the scriptoriums had kept a record of passing events, and had taught their younger brethren such knowledge as they themselves possessed. They had entertained travellers,[1] and had endeavoured to cure the sick.[2] They had also done something to relieve poverty by gifts to the poor.[3] But the expansion which had taken place in economic life produced new needs with which they were not adequate to cope, and at the same time it developed the faculties of the laity so that they were able and willing to undertake much that had hitherto been done by the monasteries. Moreover, at the very moment when greater demands were being made upon them, the monks were growing more selfish and less active. By the fifteenth century the literary monk had almost disappeared, and the scriptorium was deserted.[4] The hospitality of many of the great monasteries was dying out, and inns, kept by private individuals, provided accommodation for pilgrims, and for the travellers, whose numbers had increased with the growth of intermunicipal trade. At Abingdon persons of high rank were entertained at the abbot's table, but the hospice for the meaner guests was superseded by a 'new hostelry,' leased out by the convent at a yearly rent as a public inn.[5] At St. Albans, by the end of the century, the nobles were lodged at the 'George.'[6] Even when monas-

Functions of the Monasteries in the Middle Ages.

[1] Thorold Rogers calls the monasteries the 'inns of the Middle Ages,' *Agric. and Prices*, IV, 114. [2] *Ibid.*, and Hobhouse, 249. [3] *Ibid.* [4] Thorold Rogers, *Work and Wages*, 164. [5] Capes, *English Church*, 287. [6] *Ibid.*

teries entertained guests within their own buildings they appear to have received some payment. The Duke of Norfolk paid for some articles of food at Bury St. Edmund's,[1] Thetford,[2] and 'Reygate,'[3] though some things were given to him. The frequent allusions made to inns and taverns in the *Howard Household Books* and other documents show that they must have been numerous in London and other towns.[4] Other duties, besides that of hospitality, were passing away from the monks: rich men and Gilds founded almshouses and hospitals for the sick, and municipal authorities began to organize poor-relief.[5]

Misdeeds of the monks.

The monks of the fifteenth century had ceased to maintain the high standard of morals which had made them an example to the world around them. Many of the larger monasteries were very rich in lands and 'stateli mansiouns,'[6] and costly plate and jewels.[7] They were, according to the *Italian Relation*, 'more like baronial palaces than religious houses,'[8] and wealthy abbots kept large bands of retainers like lay lords. Statutes against livery and maintenance seem to have been aimed as much against spiritual as against temporal lords,[9] and some of them were quite as lawless as any layman. The Abbot of Begham forcibly carried off goods from the abbey of Dereford to the value of £400.[10] He, or another abbot of the same house, brought a false accusation

[1] *Howard Household Book*, II, Introd., xvi, p. 449. [2] *Ibid.*, 434. [3] *Ibid.*, 456–7, 460–2. [4] *Howard Household Book*, I, 151, 265, 485, 487, 500, 504, 530; II, 33, *Early Chanc. Proceed.*, 32/180, 45/11, 11/222, 17/336. [5] To be dealt with in a later chapter. [6] Pecock, *Repressor*, II, 543. [7] *Ibid.*, 344 and Fortescue (*Commodities of England*), I, 552. Seventeen abbots, six priors, and the Masters of the Orders of St. Gilbert of Sempringham and of Burton St. Lazarus are among the wealthy clergy in the list of 1404, *Excheq.*, *K.R.*, *Eccles*, $\frac{8}{24}$. [8] *Italian Relation*, 29. [9] *Rot. Parl.*, V, 487. [10] *Early Chanc. Proceed.*, 6/350.

against Bishop Redman, and was consequently deposed from the post of Commissary-General to the Anglo-Premonstratensian Order, which he had held.[1] Judgment was given against the abbot of St. Augustine's, Canterbury, by the Privy Council for the capture of a ship belonging to Abbeville, Bruges, and Bologne.[2] The abbots of St. Osyth's and of Beaulieu are both said to have received goods taken wrongfully from ships.[3] Sir John Neville was charged in 1443 to bring before the Privy Council 'þe mysdoers þat late have riotted at Fountayns,' also to keep the peace upon pain of £1000 'anenst þ' abbot and convent of Fountayns.'[4] Whether the convent was in this instance more sinned against or sinning is hard to say, but some years later the General Chapter of the Cistercian Order laid a petition before the Chancellor against the abbot of Fountains for resisting by force the reformers of the Cistercian monasteries in the county of York.[5] This same abbot was accused by Margaret, late the wife of Richard Bank of Whixley, of wrongfully seizing her land, whereby she and her seven children were reduced to destitution.[6] The reform of the religious orders in those days seems to have been a work of much difficulty and some danger, and it was not always successfully carried out. In 1441 the abbots appointed for this purpose by the primate of the Cistercians besought the King's 'socour,' because they feared that 'rebelles to religious correccioun' would 'procure resistence and seke mayntenaunce.'[7] When

[1] Gasquet, *Collectanea Anglo-Premonstratensia*, 237 (April 12, 1459); the date of the *Chanc. Proceed.*, 6/350, is not sufficiently definite to make it certain that the two abbots were the same. [2] *Proceed. of the Privy Council*, III, 209. [3] *Early Chanc. Proceed.*, 10/127 and 12/246. [4] *Proceed. Privy Council*, V, 241. [5] *Early Chanc. Proceed.*, 29/159, date of bundle, 38 *H. VI*—5 *Ed. IV*. [6] *Early Chanc. Proceed.*, 28/330. [7] *Proceed. Privy Council*, V, 152.

Redman made a visitation in 1466 he applied to the King for letters of protection, because he was afraid of loss and danger to body and goods from some envious of him, and their accomplices and abettors.[1] The *Collectanea Anglo-Premonstratensia* shows that visitations were frequent, and that severe sentences were pronounced against offenders; but sometimes the punishment seems to have been lightened afterwards to a considerable extent.

The particular evil which the reformers wished to cure in 1441 was the apostacy of the monks and their flight from the monasteries. Their 'speciall labour and intente,' they said, would be to 'reduce to religious observaunce, apostataas disordinate and vagabond persones.'[2] The extent to which this evil had gone is revealed to us by a series of documents kept in the Public Record Office amongst the *Chancery Warrants for Issue*. They are letters from the heads of various religious houses asking the King to grant them letters patent ordering the secular authorities to arrest and hand over to them monks who had fled from their monasteries and were wandering about the country in secular dress. In one case a writ from the King ordering the sheriffs of London to arrest Johannes de Raylegh and hand him over to his prior is still appended to the petition.[3] There is also an order addressed to the Sheriffs of London, commanding them to bring Raylegh before the Chancellor. There are more than three hundred and fifty letters, and Orders of all kinds are represented—Benedictines,[4] Cluniacs and Carthusians,[5] Cistercians,[6] Augustinians,[7] Pre-

[1] Gasquet, *Collectanea Anglo-Premonstratensia*, Part i, 185.
[2] *Proceed. Privy Council*, V, 152. [3] *Chanc. Warrants for Issue*, Ser. I, file 1760, No. 17. [4] *Ibid.*, file 1759. [5] *Ibid.*, file 1760.
[6] *Ibid.*, file 1761. [7] *Ibid.*, file 1762.

monstratensians,[1] monks of the Order of St. Gilbert of Sempringham,[2] Friars Preachers Minor,[3] Carmelites,[4] St. John of Jerusalem and Burton St. Lazarus.[5] Some of the letters complain of the flight of one brother only,[6] but many ask for the arrest of two or more offenders.[7] The evil does not seem to have been confined to any particular locality, but the petitions are from all parts of the country — Glastonbury,[8] Norhampton,[9] Lewis,[10] Herefordshire,[11] the dioceses of Worcester,[12] Lincoln,[13] London,[14] Winchester[15] and Lichfield,[16] Essex,[17] Yorkshire,[18] Bodmin,[19] Norfolk,[20] Somersetshire,[21] the diocese of Canterbury,[22] the diocese of Salisbury,[23] and other places as well. It is interesting to notice that these areas coincide to a certain extent, but not entirely, with districts which Mr. Trevelyan describes as centres of Lollardy; he mentions Gloucester,[24] Salisbury and Reading, the dioceses of Hereford and Worcester,[25] Leicester, Northampton, Nottingham, London, Sussex, Berkshire, Wiltshire,[26] Worcester and Coventry,[27] as especially important in the fourteenth century, and he adds that, in the fifteenth, it grew very strong in the west of England, particularly in Somerset,[28] and in Lincolnshire, Norfolk, Suffolk, Essex, Buckingham, Middlesex and Somerset.[29] There is no suggestion, either in these petitions or in the *Collectanea Anglo-Premonstratensia*, which also mentions vagabond monks,[30] that apostasy was due in these instances

[1] *Ibid.*, file 1763. [2] *Ibid.*, file 1764. [3] *Ibid.*, 1765. [4] *Ibid.*, 1766. [5] *Ibid.*, file 1768. [6] *Ibid.*, file 1759, No. 8. [7] *Ibid.*, No. 53, file 1760, Nos. 13 and 21, file 1761, No. 36, file 1762, 35, 42 and 29. [8] *Ibid.*, file 1759, 16. [9] File 1760, No. 12. [10] *Ibid.*, 11. [11] *Ibid.*, 21. [12] *Ibid.*, No. 24. [13] *Ibid.*, No. 27. [14] *Ibid.*, 17. [15] File 1761, 2. [16] *Ibid.*, 66. [17] *Ibid.*, 50. [18] *Ibid*, file 1762, 14. [19] *Ibid.*, 1. [20] *Ibid.*, 64. [21] *Ibid.*, 68. [22] File 1763, No. 14. [23] File 1769, No. 5. [24] Trevelyan, *England in the Age of Wycliffe*, 322. [25] *Ibid.*, 326. [26] *Ibid.*, 331. [27] *Ibid.*, map, p. 352. [28] *Ibid.*, 340–341. [29] *Ibid.*, map, p. 352. [30] Gasquet, *Coll. Anglo-Premonstratensia*, 158.

to the teaching of the Lollards; it therefore seems wiser to attribute it, not to the spread of any specific doctrines, but to the spirit of unrest and of lawlessness which permeated society, and which could not even be kept out of the cloister. The *Chancery Warrants for Issue* show that some cases of apostasy occurred in the fourteenth century, and earlier still. The appeal to the secular arm for aid is a confession of weakness on the part of the religious bodies, but judging from the repetition of some of the letters, the help of the Government was not very effective. The abbey of the 'Beate Marie de Boclond, Exoniensis,' petitioned no less than seven times, and for seven years, for the arrest of a monk named Thomas Olyver.[1] He forcibly prevented William Breton, who had been appointed abbot, from gaining possession of the abbey, and imprisoned him in it. He himself pretended to be the rightful abbot, and obtained letters patent on his own behalf, by fraud. Finally, the sheriff of Devon was ordered to commit him to gaol.[2] The flight of so many monks from their cells gives the impression that the monastic life was losing its attraction, and that the monasteries were not only failing in their duty towards the outside world, but were ceasing to satisfy any real spiritual need.

From other sources also we learn of laxity of discipline. The *Early Chancery Proceedings* contain many accounts of quarrels between monks,[3] and although we cannot decide on the rights of the

[1] *Chanc. Warrants for Issue*, Ser. I, file 1761, Nos. 8–14. [2] *Cal. Pat. Rolls*, 9 *Ed. IV*, Pt. I, m. 3d.; 49 *H. VI*, m. 13d.; 13 *Ed. IV*, Pt. I, m. 13d.; 13 *Ed. IV*, Pt. II, m. 12d. [3] A monk prevented by force from entering the priory which has been presented to him, *Early Chanc. Proceed.*, 16/92. Other examples, 12/196, 45/389, 47/58, 206/63. Assault by the Prior of St. Peter's, Dunstable, upon the Prior of the Friars Preachers of the same place, 17/279.

cases, we know that they must be discreditable to one party, if not to both. Pecock, in his efforts to defend the 'grete, large, wijde, hiȝe, and stateli mansiouns'[1] within the gates of the monasteries, betrays the worldliness of the motives of the builders; it is beneficial for the monks to have these lordly mansions, he says, because the lords and ladies who lodge within them will be the better 'freendis menteyners and defenders' to the monasteries.[2]

Attacks upon the monks.

It is evident that there was a great deal of ill-feeling against both monks and friars in the fifteenth century. It showed itself not only in the attacks of the Lollards, and in serious poems like 'Jacke Upland,'[3] which accused the friars of all sorts of vices, but also in lighter literature. A little poem called 'The Friar and the Boy'[4] describes with frank enjoyment the troubles of the friar when the boy made him dance in a hedge by playing on a magic pipe. More practical signs of disapproval may be traced in the decrease of bequests to religious bodies. Sharpe's calendar of wills in the Court of Hustings, in London, proves that far fewer legacies were left even to the Mendicants, who had been the most popular of the religious orders; more bequests were made to them in the last half of the fourteenth century than in the whole of the fifteenth; although there were still many endowments for obits.

The foundation of religious houses was an unusual form of benefaction in this period, in spite of the example set by Henry V.[5] Moreover, we have an anticipation of the dissolution of the monasteries in the suppression of alien priories; some of their

[1] Pecock, *Repressor*, II, 543. [2] *Ibid.*, 549. [3] Wright, *Polit. Songs*, II, 16, and seq. [4] *Early English Miscellanies*, edited by Halliwell, 53 and seq. [5] Capes, *op. cit.*, 169.

lands were sold to Chichele and used by him for the benefit of his colleges at Oxford and Higham Ferrers.[1] Waynflete aided his foundation by the suppression of Selborne Priory.[2] Petitions from monasteries to the Chancellor prove that acts of violence against them were not rare.[3]

Part played by the monasteries with respect to inclosures.

The clergy, it has been said, possessed a third of the land of the country,[4] and the monasteries owned more than half of it[5]; they, like other landowners, were affected by the inclosing movement; indeed, their activity in the wool trade gave them a special interest in sheep-raising.[6] Mr. Leadam has compared the methods of lay and ecclesiastical inclosers, and his conclusions are very interesting. He says that they showed almost equal energy, but that, generally speaking, the disturbance of the population was more than ten per cent less on the part of ecclesiastical than of lay lords.[7] With lay lords eviction was comparatively common, and mere displacement from employment rare. In the case of ecclesiastical lords they are nearly balanced.[8] But in Bedfordshire, Leicester, and Warwick the prospects of eviction were practically the same, whether the tenant held of a layman or of an ecclesiastic.[9] In Berkshire, Northampton, and Oxfordshire the ecclesiastical landlord was more ruthless than the lay in his treatment of the tillers of the soil.[10] The Abbot of Peterborough inclosed 998½ acres of land in Northampton, and evicted a hundred persons, who, according to the jury, 'miseri facti sunt.'[11] Proceedings such as this must

[1] T. Rogers, *Agric. and Prices*, IV, 8 9. [2] *Ibid.*, 12. [3] *Early Chanc. Proceed.*, 25/222 and 32/320, 11/106. [4] Dowell, *Hist. of Taxation and Taxes*, I, 97. [5] Hasbach, *Hist. of the English Agric. Labourer*, 36, quoting Gneist, *Englische Verfassungsgeschichte*, p. 488. [6] Leadam, *Domesday of Inclosures*, 323. [7] *Ibid.*, 42. [8] *Ibid.*, 43. [9] *Ibid.*, 48. [10] *Ibid.* [11] *Ibid.*, 263.

have tended to render the monasteries unpopular, and at the same time pasture-farming increased their wealth; and this combination of circumstances was not without elements of danger for the future. Suggestions had already been made that their wealth might be turned to better use,[1] and the richer they became, the more temptation there was to act upon such suggestions.

[1] 'The landed estates of the bishops, abbots, and priors of England, it was said, would suffice to endow 15 earls, 1500 knights, 6200 esquires, and a 100 hospitals.' Oman, *Hist. of England*, 221.

CHAPTER IV

THE LABOUR PROBLEM

THE increasing demand for labour caused by the growth of industry and commerce in the fifteenth century should, it may be thought, have made this period one of great prosperity for the working-classes. Some writers, indeed, have told us that it was the golden age of the labourer.[1] Unfortunately the frequent complaints of lack of work[2] made by artisans do not bear out this statement. The reason given by them is the employment of aliens,[3] and this was probably one very important factor in the situation, but it was by no means the only cause of the trouble. Curiously enough, while the workmen complained that they could not 'have ther labour for ther levyng,' the masters declared that they suffered because their servants departed from their service without leave or licence;[4] and the laws were modified because they could not get workmen enough.[5] The breakdown of the Manorial System had set many labourers free from the land; they flocked into the towns to take up trades, and formed a distinct wage-earning class with interests and objects apart from those of their employers.[6]

This class of workers probably existed long before the fifteenth century,[7] but it grew in numbers at

[1] T. Rogers, *Work and Wages*, 326, and Hyndman, *Hist. Basis of Socialism*, I. [2] Cunningham, *op. cit.*, I, 442; *Rot. Parl.*, V, 325, 506–7. [3] *Ibid.*, V, 567; Bickley, *Little Red Book of Bristol*, II, 128, 159, 177. [4] *Ibid.*, 108. [5] Mrs. Green, *op. cit.*, II, 86. [6] Hunt, *Bristol*, 79. [7] Mrs. Green, II, 101.

this time; and one great reason for its growth was the change in the spirit and organization of the Gilds. These associations, in their earlier days, had sought to benefit all their members—masters, journeymen, and apprentices—alike; but when money became such a source of influence and such an object of desire, the richer members gained the predominance, and they tried to obtain for themselves a larger share of the privileges and profits than their poorer brethren enjoyed.[1] The change which had taken place showed itself in the differentiation of classes within the gilds. There were three distinct grades amongst the Tailors of Exeter: those who had goods to the value of £20, who were of the Master's 'ffeleschippe and cloþynge,' and who paid a silver spoon as entrance fee, xijd. and an offering at midsummer, and the price of the clothing; 'euery yowte Brodere that ys nott preuelage of the forsayde ffraternyte' who paid sixpence a year; and 'euery seruant that ys of the forsayd crafte, that takyt wagys to the waylor of xxs.' who paid twenty pence to be a 'ffre sawere.'[2] In several companies there was, Professor Ashley tells us, a select body (such as the 'Livery,' and the Court of Assistants in the great companies in London[3]), which took the direction of affairs out of the hands of the general assembly. The Drapers numbered two hundred and twenty-nine full members in 1493; of these, one hundred and fourteen constituted 'the craft in the clothing,' and one hundred and fifteen the 'brotherhood out of the clothing.'[4] In early days liveries

Change in the spirit of the Gilds.

[1] Brentano says that 'as trade advanced . . . it afforded greater opportunities for the employment of capital . . . the Craft-Gild changed from a society for the protection of labour into an opportunity for the investment of capital' (*Eng. Gilds*, cxxxvii). This is, perhaps an overstatement of the case, but it contains an element of truth.
[2] *English Gilds*, 313–14. [3] Ashley, *Econ. Hist.*, II, 125. [4] *Ibid.*, 131.

had been worn as a means of binding the members of the Gilds more closely together, and each member had provided his own; but with the increasing extravagance of clothing in the fifteenth century, and the growing wealth of the more influential craftsmen, expensive liveries came to be ordained, which were beyond the means of the poorer freemen,[1] and so they became the outward symbols of the plutocratic government of the Gilds. The ruling class in the Gilds was not content with social pre-eminence, but it also tried to keep for itself the greater share of the profits of trade, by checking the admission of new members,[2] by limiting the number of workmen and apprentices existing masters might employ,[3] and by preventing journeymen from becoming masters. Journeymen were, as far as possible, deprived of the power of influencing the policy of the Gilds, lest they should alter the ordinances in their own interests; the Weavers of Hull decreed that 'no journeyman shall at the eleccon day gyff any voyce to the chesyng of any Alderman or other officer.'[4] The journeymen were not inclined to submit to curtailment of their powers, and many quarrels arose between them and the masters.[5] Gilds of 'yeomen,' or journeymen, seem to have been fairly common at this time,[6] and union increased the strength of the men. The journeymen Weavers of Coventry were so persistent that they three times formed a Gild, which was each time suppressed.[7] They had a most serious disagreement with the masters in 1424, and they not only refused

Struggles between masters and journeymen.

[1] *Ibid.*, 130. [2] T. Smith, *op. cit.*, 317, and D. Harris, *op. cit.*, 272–3. [3] *Ibid.*, 271, and T. Smith, 315. [4] Lambert, *Gild Life*, 205. [5] *Little Red Book of Bristol*, II, 151. [6] D. Harris, *op. cit.*, 276, and Prof. Ashley gives instances of journeymen Gilds in London, *Econ. Hist.*, Part ii, 123–4. [7] D. Harris, *op. cit.*, 276–7.

to work themselves, but hindered others also. The Corporation took the matter in hand, and settled it by arbitration[1], and the judgment appears to have effected a compromise between the two parties. The history of the Journeymen Tailors in London is somewhat similar; in 1415 it was intimated to the Mayor that 'some serving-men and journeymen of the tailors . . .' called 'yomen taillours,' dwelling with one another in companies by themselves, did hold and inhabit divers dwelling-houses in the City against the will of their superiors and the masters of the trade. They oftentimes assembled in great numbers, and had held assemblies and conventicles in various places; they had wounded, beaten, and maltreated one of the masters of the trade and many others. The Mayor summoned the journeymen before him and forbade them to do any of these things, or to wear a livery of their own, and ordered them to submit to the governance and rule of the Masters and Wardens of the trade, the same as other serving-men.[2] It seems, therefore, that in London, and probably elsewhere, the power of the Masters, supported by that of the Corporation, was too strong for the Journeymen, even when an appeal was not made to the Crown, as at Coventry.[3] An act was passed in the reign of Henry VI to check the aggressions of the Gilds; it states that 'the Masters, Wardens, and People of (the) Guilds, . . . make themselves many unlawful and unreasonable Ordinances, as well of (many) such Things, whereof the Cognisance Punishment and Correction all only pertaineth to the King, Lords

[1] *Ibid.*, 278, and *Coventry Leet Book*, 92–4. [2] Riley, *Memorials of London*, pp. 609–12. [3] Assemblies of Masons, whereby the Statute of Labourers was violated, were strictly forbidden, and those who attended them declared felons (3 *H. VI*, c. 1). Hardy, *op. cit.*, II, 578, and D. Harris, *op. cit.*, 276.

of Franchises, and other Persons, whereby our Sovereign Lord the King and other be disherited of their Profits and Franchises, as of Things, which (oftentimes in Confederacy is made) for their singular Profit, and common Damage to the People.' The Gilds were consequently ordered to register their charters before the Justices of the Peace, or before the Chief Governors of Cities, and they were forbidden to make new ordinances unless they were first approved by these persons.[1] The statute is a striking comment upon the selfish policy of those who ruled the Gilds, but it is doubtful whether the journeymen gained much from it, because the 'Chief Governors of Cities,' whose authority was made paramount, were often traders and merchants themselves,[2] and they favoured the masters rather than the men. So the unions of journeymen were, for the most part, crushed by the Gilds and the towns,[3] and they went to swell the number of hired wage-earners. It is little wonder that, smarting under a sense of grievance, they were embittered against their masters.

Treatment of apprentices by their masters.

Masters often forced apprentices on entering their service to take an oath not to set up in business for themselves when their period of apprenticeship was over.[4] Among the *Chancery Proceedings* is a petition from John Kelet, servant to Richard Harpham of London, girdler, who has brought an action against him to prevent him opening a shop of his own.[5] There are also several petitions made by apprentices against

[1] 15 *H. VI*, c. 6. [2] For a hundred years Coventry was celebrated for clothmaking, and the sellers of cloth were the richest men in the city, and more frequently in office than those of any other occupation (D. Harris, *op. cit.*, 241, cf. 259 and 270). Mrs. Green expresses the opinion that power in the towns was in the hands of merchants and thriving traders (*Town Life*, II, 251–2). [3] *Ibid.*, II, 129. [4] D. Harris, *op. cit.*, 272 n. [5] *Early Chanc. Proceed.*, 67/169.

their masters, complaining of bad food and clothing,[1] insufficient teaching,[2] and ill-treatment of various kinds.[3] The term of service was sometimes very long, as much as eight or nine years in some cases,[4] though seven years was probably a more usual period.[5] Occasionally masters applied to the Chancellor for aid in recovering fugitive apprentices,[6] and it is evident that there was a good deal of ill-feeling between masters and servants, and that there were faults on both sides. One petition declares that William Ingland sold John Calker 'oon Richard Dugdale . . . for terme of ten years to do hym seruice in his craft '[7]; this appears to be a very extraordinary arrangement, but it is not the only instance of the sale of workmen of which we have knowledge. It is said that the Weavers of Bristol received and 'put in occupacion of the seid Crafte, Straungiers, Allions,' and others 'people of divers Countrees not born vndir the Kynges obeisaunce but rebellious,' brought by 'divers marchauntz' to whom they had been sold.[8] Such degradation of the workmen is, however, extremely rare.

The wages question.

The chief point in dispute between employers and employees was the amount of wages to be paid. This question had nominally been settled by Parliament,[9] but legislation on it does not seem to have been effectual in the fifteenth century.[10] Scarcity of labourers was caused

[1] *Ibid.*, 10/68 and 11/367. [2] *Ibid.*, 106/8 and 186/105. [3] *Ibid.*, 17/50, 28/171, 64/110, 66/236. [4] Eight years, *Ibid.*, 28/171, 38/40; nine years, 15/165, and 94/22 and 108/42. [5] 'Ordinances of Worcester,' in T. Smith, *Eng. Gilds*, p. 390. [6] *Early Chanc. Proceed.*, 6/7 and 19/349. [7] *Ibid.*, 10/124. [8] This complaint was directed principally against the employment of Irish workmen, *Little Red Book of Bristol*, II, 123 and 128. [9] *Rot. Parl.*, II, 234 and seq., V, 112, and 11 *H. VII*, c. 22. [10] Hasbach, *The Eng. Agric. Labourer*, 24. Miss Putnam thinks it was effective from 1349 to 1359. (*The Enforcement of the Statutes of Labourers*, 149.)

in the first place by the ravages of the Black Death ; and from that time onwards workmen were dissatisfied with the wages fixed by statute. Attempts were made to meet the difficulty by directing the Justices of the Peace to assess wages in accordance with the prices of victuals[1]; but this arrangement does not appear to have worked well. Dr. Hasbach suggests that it would not necessarily mean that the position of the labourer was improved, because the Justices of the Peace belonged to the landlord class, and the legislature united them into a kind of employers' association, which could set the price of labour.[2] Petitions were frequently laid before the King in Parliament, stating that the men would not work for the legal wages and that masters were forced to give them more[3]; and it was also said that the labourers fled from one county to another to escape the operation of the Acts.[4] Penalties were imposed upon both the givers and the receivers of excess wages,[5] and labourers were forbidden to leave the Hundreds in which they lived without Letters 'Patent' containing the cause of their going.[6] The punishment for disobeying this prohibition, and for refusing to serve according to the Statute of Labourers, was, in 1444, made imprisonment without the option of bail.[7] Whether the objections of the labourers to the rate of wages were reasonable or not is difficult to decide. Thorold Rogers says emphatically that they were well paid[8]; but his average of sixpence a day for artisans and fourpence a day for labourers is perhaps a little high, and was not the recognized rate until the end

[1] *Rot. Parl.*, III, 269, 330 and 352.
[2] Hasbach, *op. cit.*, 25.
[3] *Rot. Parl.*, IV, 330–1.
[4] 2 *H. V*, c. 4.
[5] *Rot. Parl.*, IV, 258, 330–1, 352.
[6] 12 *Ric. II*, c. 3, and 2 *H. V*, c. 4.
[7] *Rot. Parl.*, V, 110 and seq.
[8] *Work and Wages*, 326.

of the century.[1] He does not take sufficient notice of the reduction of wages by frequent recurrence of holidays and half-holidays[2]; and he seems to underestimate the hours of work when he speaks of eight hours a day. From the middle of March to the middle of September the men worked from five o'clock in the morning till eight o'clock at night, with intervals which never exceeded two hours; and during the other months of the year they worked from the springing of day till night.[3] The fact that wages were raised twice during the century,[4] and that finally the statutes regulating them were repealed, seems to show that these acts were not altogether wise. On the other hand, the sumptuary laws prove that workmen could afford better food and clothing in the fifteenth century than they had in the fourteenth.

Uncovenanted labour.

There was, at least in Norwich, and probably elsewhere, an increasing number of labourers who worked at a subsistence wage of a penny a day.[5] Their condition must have been wretched in the extreme, and their existence must have complicated the labour question; but they were useful to the employers on account of their helplessness, and it was the policy of the masters to foster this class of uncovenanted labour while they limited the number of privileged serving-men.[6]

Agricultural labourers.

Agricultural labourers, like other workmen, obtained a rise of wages in the course of the century, but they were subjected to some disadvantages which did not affect artisans. They were forbidden to change their occupation if they had followed it up to the age of

[1] 11 *H. VII*, c. 22; but in 1444 freemasons and master carpenters were paid 4d. and food, or 5½d. without food, from Easter to Michaelmas, and other labourers in proportion (*Rot. Parl.*, V, 112). [2] 4 *H. IV*, c. 14 forbade payment for holy-days. [3] 11 *H. VII*, c. 22. [4] In 1444 and 1495; repealed by 12 *H. VII*, c. 3. [5] Mrs. Green, *op. cit.*, II, 101. [6] *Ibid.*, 102.

twelve years,[1] and they were more in the power of their masters than those who could find other means of livelihood. The enclosing movement, which decreased the demand for their labour, must have pressed hardly upon them. Perhaps they themselves were partly to blame for these misfortunes, as the movement was encouraged by the difficulty of finding labourers who would work at the old wages. The conditions of their lives must also have been considerably altered by the substitution of leasing for manorial administration,[2] whether the new landlords were peasant freeholders,[3] as Dr. Hasbach thinks, or rich merchants as Prof. Pollard suggests.[4] Both classes of men would regard their lands as a source of income; the former because they needed to make money, the latter because it was the habit of their lives.[5] Neither of them would have the same interest in the welfare of their dependents as the feudal lord who had needed men more than money.[6]

The unemployed.

The breakdown of the Manorial System, though it improved the status of the labourer, and was beneficial to him in the long run, did not always bring him immediate material advantages. The serf tied to the soil was at least sure of a dwelling, and of some kind of food to eat; but emancipated villeins sometimes found that they had gained freedom to starve, and wandered about the country, vainly seeking work. Some of those who had run away from their lords, and 'waived their lands, to try their fortunes in' the 'lottery of trade,'[7] discovered that they were totally unfit for the new life when it was too late to return to the old. Moreover, as we have seen, even skilled artisans sometimes had a hard struggle

[1] 12 *Ric. II*, c. 5. [2] Hasbach, *op. cit.*, 39. [3] *Ibid.*, 38.
[4] [5] [6] Pollard, *op. cit.*, p. 138. [7] Eden, *State of the Poor*, I, 57.

to earn a living[1] when competition had become keen, and every one seemed in a hurry to grow rich. The eviction of tenants by owners who wished to enclose their land increased the proletariat[2]; and although much of the labour set free from the land was finally absorbed in commercial and industrial pursuits, the transference was neither easy nor rapid, and the workers suffered much misery in the transition. The long war with France and heavy taxation were additional causes of poverty: 'The Kyng goth so nere us in this cuntre, both to pooer and ryche, that I wote not how we shall lyff, but yff the world amend,' wrote Margaret Paston to her son.[3] Soldiers, engaged by lords to assist them in fighting the country's battles and their own, were often turned out of door when they were maimed, sick, or aged,[4] and they were not only unemployed, but unemployable.

Increase of vagrancy.

Thus the era which witnessed the growth of industry, the expansion of commerce, and the development of a prosperous middle class, witnessed also the growth of the pauper class and an increase in vagrancy. The relief of the impotent poor and the punishment of sturdy beggars became such serious questions that Parliament was frequently forced to turn its attention to them, and the number of ordinances and statutes passed concerning them gives the measure of their importance.[5] A careful distinction

[1] Mrs. Green attributes much of the poverty of this period to the policy of the Gilds. 'The triumphant gild system,' she says, 'developed throughout the country a formless and incoherent multitude of hired labourers, who could not rise to positions of independence, and had no means of association in self-defence, the weaker members of this class sank into utter penury' (*Town Life*, II, 108). [2] Hasbach, *op. cit.*, 38. [3] *Paston Letters*, V, 233. [4] Gairdner, *Letters of Ric. III and H. VII*, Vol. II, lx. [5] *Rot. Parl.*, II, 332, 340; III, 65, 158; V, 113; VI, 198, 278.

was drawn between those who were unable to work and those who were merely idle; the latter were punished like run-away labourers,[1] the former were, under certain circumstances, licenced to beg. The *Chancery Proceedings* afford one or two examples of persons petitioning the Chancellor to grant them letters patent to gather alms.[2] John of Burton tapicer, who had fallen on evil days through 'infortune,' asked for 'letters of Pardon' to give to any one who bestowed alms upon him.[3]

Poor relief.

The increase of pauperism led to the employment of new agencies for its alleviation, and laymen to a great extent took the place of ecclesiastics. The relief of the poor was one of the recognized functions of the parish priests,[4] but we learn, from complaints made in Parliament, that it was neglected through the non-residence of the clergy.[5] The parish priests lost revenues, part of which should have been devoted to charity, when their tithes were appropriated to monasteries; and although pious individuals sometimes left money for 'almesse dedys to be do amonge the pore parysshyns,'[6] these, after all, only supplied a precarious source of income. Nor did the monasteries take a very large share in assisting the poor; a statute passed in the reign of Richard II, and repeated in the time of Henry IV, reserved for them a share of the tithes which the monasteries received, instead of the rectors,[7] but it does not follow that the abbots obeyed the statutes. On

[1] 12 *Ric. II*, c. 7 and *Rot. Parl.*, V, 110. [2] *Early Chanc. Proceed.*, 16/389, 19/500, 19/499, 28/420. [3] *Ibid.*, 32/57. [4] Gasquet, *Parish Life*, 9. [5] *Rot. Parl.*, III, 293, and IV, 290. [6] *Early Chanc. Proceed.*, 16/325; Sharpe, *Wills*, II, 412, 465, 543. Bequests were often made to the poor in connection with chantries and obits (*Medieval Records of a London City Church*, 11–12, 190). [7] 15 *Ric. II*, c. 6, and 4 *H. IV*, c. 12, quoted by Miss Leonard, *Early Hist. of English Poor Relief*, 7.

the contrary, they were admonished by Parliament for not doing their duty,[1] and this may have been one reason why they had so much trouble in collecting their tithes.[2] Prof. Ashley thinks that the aid given by the monasteries, for at least two centuries before their dissolution, did but little for the relief of honest poverty.[3] There is no doubt that their method of indiscriminate almsgiving at the door was not wise, and it may, indeed, have tended to foster the very evil that Parliament was trying to cure, as the vagrant would be helped on his way by it; at the best it was fluctuating and arbitrary.[4]

While the Church was thus failing to meet the needs of the time, the laity was willing and able to do its part. Civic governors and gilds began to manage charitable endowments.[5] At Sandwich the burgesses controlled two hospitals and contributed to their support[6]; at Rye payments were made to the poor from municipal funds[7]; and the steward's book at Southampton states that the town gave weekly to the poor the sum of £4 2s. 1d., which would relieve about a hundred and fifty people.[8] The *Coventry Leet Book* records a grant of a bed in gaol, 'ȝeue on almes,' for the use of those who could not afford to pay for one,[9] and also mentions £3 spent in paying poor men's fines in the Court of King's Bench.[10] A regular sum appears in the accounts of the Corpus Christi Gild as paid to mendicants every year; and in 1492, 25s. 4d. was given to beggars; and the Master also asked allowance for £17 6s. due to diminution of the gild rental, and for 'allowances for the mendyaunts of the said

[1] Cunningham, *op. cit.*, I, 377. [2] Complaints of detention of tithes by religious houses (*Early Chanc. Proceed.*, 4/99, 75/101, 9/304). [3] Ashley, *Econ. Hist.*, II, 312. [4] Hobhouse, 249. [5] Miss Leonard, *op. cit.*, 7. [6] *Ibid.*, 7–8, quoting Boys, Sandwich. [7] *Ibid.*, 8, quoting *Hist. Mans. Com.* [8] *Ibid.*, 9, quoting Davies, Southampton. [9] *Coventry Leet Book*, I, 130. [10] *Ibid.*, I, 121.

gilde.'[1] Stephen Brown, grocer, in 1439, when corn was very scarce in England, sent to Prussia and bought a large quantity, which he sold very cheaply in London.[2] Simon Eyre, upholsterer and draper, built a common granary in London[3] (1419). London made arrangements for a constant supply of corn, in order that there might not be famines in times of dearth; but the public store was not a permanent institution until the sixteenth century.[4] A favourite form of charity in the fifteenth century was the foundation of almshouses.[5] This was often the work of the gilds; for example, the Gild of Holy Trinity, Hull, started one for poor and infirm seamen.[6] Sometimes almshouses owed their existence to the munificence of private persons; Elias Dawy, mercer, left his servant the next vacancy in his almshouse[7]; and Thomas Beaumond, salter, left six mansions, in which six members of his art were to be maintained, each receiving sevenpence a week.[8] Lady Stonor possessed an almshouse with a priest and poor men belonging to it.[9] Members of gilds also often left money to poor brothers and sisters of their fraternities,[10] and in these instances probably the bequests were administered by the officials of the gilds. Household Books show that rich men gave a good deal to the poor, both in money[11] and food; they had almoners, whose business it was to collect 'broken mete' 'to dele to pore men at þe ȝate.'[12] The Ordinances for the household of the Duke of Clarence provide that

[1] Dormer Harris, *op. cit.*, 313. [2] Strype's *Stow*, I, 310. [3] *Ibid.*, I, 415. [4] Leonard, *op. cit.*, 23-4. [5] Ashley, *Econ. Hist.*, II, 326. [6] Lambert, *Gild Life*, 127.

[7] Sharpe's *Wills*, II, 548. [8] *Ibid.*, II, 534. Edward Rich, Mercer of London, also founded almshouses (Strype's *Stow*, I, 311). [9] *A.C.*, Vol. 46, No. 241. [10] Sharpe, II, 526, 528. [11] 'A woman for almys,' 8d. (*Howard Household Book*, II, 167); 'To porefolke at the gate,' 8d. (*Ibid.*, 223); 'To fryeres to disposse in almes,' 10/- (*Ibid.*, 447). [12] *Russell Boke* in *Manners and Meals*, p. 324.

'the Duke's Awmener have, for every daye xiid, . . . to distrybute and dispose in almes, to poure people by his discression. . . . And the seid Almonere, at every dynner & souper, wayte uppon the seid Duke's table, and there take uppe every dishe when the seid Duke hathe sette it from hym, and thereof to make sufficyently the almes-disshe, to be gyven to the moste needy man or woman by his discression.'[1] This kind of charity is picturesque, and gives evidence of good-nature and kindheartedness; but it is of the same type as the doles bestowed by monasteries, and likely to increase rather than to cure pauperism. Moreover, rich men were, even in the fifteenth century, not very numerous, and the part played by them in relieving poverty cannot compare either in method or in degree with that played by towns and the gilds. There seems no question that the most valuable work in this respect was done by the municipal authorities and the traders.

[1] *Ordinances of the Royal Household*, p. 89. The amount expended by the Duke of Clarence upon 'almesse' during a year appears to have been £18 5s. od., and his total expenses were £4505 15s. 10½d. (*Ibid.*, 104, 105). The *Stafford Household Book* mentions that two loaves were given in alms on Christmas Day; *Archælogia*, XXV, p. 319.

CHAPTER

THE INDUSTRIAL POSITION OF WOMEN AND CHILDREN

Employment of women in agriculture and industry.

THE majority of English women, says Miss Dixon in her interesting article on 'Craftswomen, in the *Livre des Métiers*,' were, prior to the introduction of machinery, unpaid domestic workers rather than wage-earners. This proposition she brings forward as a possible explanation of the unlimited freedom of competition left to women by the Act of 1363, which restricted the occupations of men by ordering them to keep to one trade.[1] This statement, however true it may be of women in the early Middle Ages, does not hold good in the fifteenth century, probably because the growth of industry increased the demand for labour and led to the employment of women. Moreover, then as now, women worked for a smaller wage than men, and it was cheaper to employ them. The Act quoted by Miss Dixon mentions several kinds of women artificers — 'Braceresces, Pesteresces, Tisteresces, Fileresces, and Oevresces si bien de Leine come de Liegne Toile & de Soie, Broudesters, Kardesters, Pyneresces de Leine, & toutes autres que usent & oeverent Overaignes manueles.'[2] The two important statutes which regulated the conditions of labour apply equally to men and women. 'He or she,' says the first of the two, 'which use to labour

[1] *Economic Journal*, Vol. V, 225. [2] *Rot. Parl.*, II, 278.

at the plough '[1]; while the other decrees 'no Man or Woman . . . shall put their Son or Daughter to serve as Apprentice, to no Craft nor other Labour within any City or Borough of the Realm, except he have Land or Rent to the value of twenty shillings by the year.'[2] The ordinances of London also allude to the training of women for industrial occupations. In 1413, when the Corporation wanted to raise money for the new work at the Guildhall, it ordered that every apprentice, male and female, should pay certain fees at the beginning and end of the period of apprenticeship.[3]

There were in addition, in London, rules regarding the apprenticeship of 'femmenis' by 'lez femmes couverts qe usent certeyns craftis deinz la citee par eux mesmes saunz loure barouns.'[4] Not in London only, but in several towns, ordinances were passed respecting the position of the woman as a trader. In certain boroughs she could, even though married, plead and be impleaded alone,[5] and in many cases her husband was freed from responsibility concerning her trade debts.[6] The *Chancery Proceedings* afford some examples of suits brought against women on the ground that they were sole merchants.[7] In most of these instances the women declared that the debts were incurred by their husbands; and in one petition the husband is said to have absconded.[8] In Lincoln, it was the rule that if a plea of trespass were brought against husband and

The position of the woman trader.

[1] 12 *Ric. II*, c. 5. [2] 7 *H. IV*, c. 17. The Petition of the Artificers also mentions women as well as men. *Rot. Parl.*, V, 506. See Appendix A. [3] Riley, *Memorials of London*, 590. [4] Bateson, *Borough Customs*, I, 229. [5] *Ibid.*, II, cxii, Worcester, Winchelsea, Lincoln, I, 227, Hastings, I, 228. In London, actions could be taken 'devers une femme sole et devers enfauntz dedincz age, s'ils soient marchauntz' (*Liber Albus*, 1419. *Borough Customs*, I, 227). [6] Worcester, *Ibid.*, I, 227, and Fordwich, I, 228. [7] *Early Chanc. Proceed.*, 64/607, 64/883, 110/125, 201/32. [8] *Ibid.*, 66/229.

wife, and the husband absconded, the wife was treated as sole.[1] Some of the earlier borough customs, on the other hand, made the husband answerable for the wife,[2] and although there is a good deal of variety in the ordinances of different towns, there seems to have been a tendency to give the wife more independence in her business dealings in the later period than she had hitherto possessed, perhaps because she more often engaged in trade. The *Fordwich Customs* speak of the possibility of a woman being a professional trader in fish, fruit, cloth, or the like, and a fair number of trades appear to have been open to her. Miss Toulmin Smith says that nearly all gilds were formed equally of men and women, and that women had many of the same claims and duties as men.[3] Brentano agrees that women might become members of gilds, but thinks they were admitted because they were the wives or daughters of gild-brothers, and that they were seldom free of the gild in their own right,[4] and that though they shared in the advantages and burdens of the association, they took no part in its administration or councils.[5] We find frequent allusions to sisters as well as brothers of fraternities, and sometimes with reference to gilds where their presence is rather surprising. For example, there were women amongst the Tailors and Armourers of Linen Armour of St. John the Baptist,[6] and amongst the Tailors of Salisbury,[7] and amongst the yeomen tailors of London.[8] Women might join the Merchant Gild at Totnes,[9] and both men and women

[1] *Borough Customs*, I, 226. [2] Salford, about 1270 (*Ibid.*, I, 223); but there were exceptions. Ipswich, a husband was responsible for debts incurred by his wife both before and after marriage, but not when she became a pledge for a debt (*Ibid.*, I, 224). [3] T. Smith, *English Gilds*, Introd., xxx. [4] *Ibid.*, civ. [5] *Ibid.* [6] Sharpe, *op. cit.*, II, 526. [7] *Early Chanc. Proceed.*, 108/14. [8] Riley, *op. cit.*, 653. [9] Mrs. Green, *op. cit.*, II, 33 n.

belonged to the Gild Merchant of Lynn.[1] Women are mentioned in the ordinances of the Dyers of Bristol,[2] and in the charter of the Drapers o London.[3] Bishop Hobhouse gives cases of gilds of 'Maidens' and 'Wives,' amongst the contributors to the funds of Croscombe Church.[4]

The occupations open to women.

These references to women as members of crafts, and the regulations with regard to their rights and responsibilities as traders, prove that they were too important to be ignored, and that they had a recognized position in the industrial world. Entries in Household Books of payments to them, and descriptions of work done by them give us further information upon the subject. They were sometimes clothmakers,[5] and often cloth-workers.[6] Metyngham College paid a woman named Bonde 'pro pano textando,'[7] and 'pro lana facienda in filo'[8]; and we have, in one of the *Howard Household Books*, a memorandum that 'Alys Haweryng hat spowne and cardyd and twystyd tweyntey pownde of zerne for the aras man, for everey pownde howeyng 2d.'[9] Wright tells us that 'a pair of card' is stated in the 'Promptorium parvulorum' to be especially a 'wommanys instrument.'[10] The *Howard Household Books* also contain entries of payments of £22 to 'Kateryne Hache of Stoke, for clothe,' and of 45s. 5d. to 'Rechard Snappes wyfe for 1 brode clothe of plonkett,'[11] and to other women for cloth of various kinds.[12] In the *Paston Letters* we have an allusion to 'Hayis wyf,' who sold 'frise' 'best

[1] *Ibid.*, II, 404–5. [2] Bickley, *Little Red Book of Bristol*, II, 83.
[3] Hazlitt, *Livery Companies of London*, 200. [4] Hobhouse, p. 1.
[5] 'every Man and Woman being Clothmakers' (4 *Ed. IV*, c. 1).
[6] 'women Kembers, Carders, and Spynners' (*Rot. Parl.*, V, 150).
[7] Add. MSS., 33, 985, 9, dorso. [8] *Ibid.*, 11 d. [9] *Howard Household Book*, I, 551. [10] Wright, *Hist. of Domestic Manners*, p. 426.
[11] *Howard Household Book*, I, 330. [12] *Ibid.*, II, 164, 293, 327.

chepe '[1]; and in the ordinances regulating the sale of cloth in Coventry, 'women sellyng dosens in hir armes' are mentioned.[2] In the *Patent Rolls* reference is made to the men and women weavers of linen of the city of London[3]; and in the *Chancery Proceedings* it is stated that Isabel Hale, widow, sold linen cloth[4]; and that Catherine Thorneton of London, 'wedowe,' was a draper.[5]

The silk trade was mainly in the hands of women,[6] and 'silkewymmen' and 'throwestres' of London petitioned the Crown, in 1455, that the importation of wrought silk goods might be stopped. Their words give some idea of the extent of the industry, though they may have exaggerated a little: 'And where upon the same Craftes,' they say, 'before this tyme, many a wurshipfull woman within the seid citee have lyved full honourably, and therwith many good housholdes kept, and many gentilwymmen and other in grete noumbre like as there nowe be moo than a thousand, have be drawen under theym in lernyng the same craftes and occupation.'[7] The silk-women numbered even kings among their customers: Anne Claver made tassels and lace for Edward IV's books,[8] and Cecyly Walcot supplied fringe of gold and silk for a canopy for Henry VII.[9] Wright reproduces, in his *History of Domestic Manners*, a picture of a lady mercer, taken from a poem called 'The Pilgrim,' which has been ascribed to Lydgate.[10]

[1] *Paston Letters*, II, 102. [2] *Coventry Leet Book*, Part i, 104. [3] *Cal. Patent Rolls*, 1440, Part iii, m. 19 d. [4] *Early Chanc. Proceed.*, 30/47. [5] *Ibid.*, 67/351–4. [6] Miss Dixon thinks that women were much more unequivocally employed on a regular industrial basis in this craft than in any other (*Econ. Journal*, V, 225). [7] *Rot. Parl.*, V, 325. [8] Nicholas, *Wardrobe Accounts of Edward IV*, p. 125. [9] Campbell, *op. cit.*, II, 12. A merchant of Genoa brought an action for debt against this woman (*Early Chanc. Proceed.*, 110/125). Other silkwomen are mentioned (Campbell, II, 13, 15, 491, 493). [10] Wright, *Domestic Manners*, 412.

Women sometimes dealt in general merchandise, like Julian Mermean, who sent 'diuerses wares' to Sir John Lane at Wells,[1] and Anneys Marchaunt, who sold malt and merchandise ware.[2] Sometimes they sent their goods to be sold at fairs,[3] and one woman declared that she was 'seased in and of 18 bothes in Sterebriggez Fair.'[4] Three women are described as chapmen in the pleas of the market of St. Ives, held on March 5th, 1429.[5]

They did not confine themselves to trade in England, but sometimes took part in foreign commerce. A licence was granted to Alice Mengeham to export corn to Rouen,[6] and another to merchants of Bayonne acting on behalf of Petronilla, widow of Bertram seigneur de Montferrat, who had been imprisoned for loyalty to the English.[7] For the same reason Isabella Chernok was allowed to trade from France to England to compensate her for the losses sustained by her husband and herself during the war.[8] Margaret Cokkes, widow, of Calais, was permitted by Henry VII to ship, from London and Southampton, forty-one sacks of wool and five hundred skins with the wool on them,[9] so her business must have been on a fairly large scale. Margery, late the wife of John Russell, of Coventry, and her son petitioned the Chancellor, the Bishop of Winchester, to grant them a letter of marque and reprisal against the merchants of certain places in the Kingdom of Castille and Leon, until they were compensated for the sum of twelve hundred marks, of which she had been robbed by men of 'S. Andier en Espaigne'; Henry, 'nadgaire Roy

[1] *Early Chanc. Proceed.*, 15/85. [2] *Ibid.*, 45/306. [3] *Ibid.*, 100/73. [4] *Ibid.*, 65/166. [5] C. Gross, *Law Merchant*, Vol. I, 121. [6] *Cal. French Rolls*, 1421, m. 13. [7] *Ibid.*, 1455–6, ms 6 and 1. [8] *Ibid.*, 1456–7, m. 24. [9] *Materials for a History of the Reign of Henry VII*, I, 223.

Dengleterre,' had already granted her one, she said.[1] She apparently obtained the letter, and used it effectively, for Peter Gunsales petitioned the Chancellor for the restitution of a Spanish balinger and wines taken by virtue of a letter of marque, granted to 'Margery de Coventre,' by the 'Roy Dengleterre & le Roy Despaigne,' against the men of Santander.[2]

Women also engaged in humbler occupations; many of them kept inns and taverns.[3] We hear of 'the gode wif of the Taberd in Grasechurche strete,[4] the good wife of the 'Belle in Bryge Stret,'[5] and of many others. The *Howard Household Books* contain many payments to women for beer and ale[6]; and we know that they often made the beer as well as selling it. Maud Cranesby of London is described as a brewer, in a petition lodged in the Court of Chancery against her[7]; and Margery Clerk of Ramsey was said to be in the occupation of brewing.[8] This business was, indeed, 'almost wholly in the hands of females,'[9] not only in the fifteenth century, but also in earlier days. Women also earned money by selling poultry[10] and game[11] and even cattle.[12] Metyngham College paid 'Alicia Gyrlyng' thirty shillings for '2 vactas, 2 jumentas, & 2 boviculos.'[13] Sir John Howard had quite extensive dealings with a woman named 'Mawt Clerke,' apparently one of his tenants. He gave her, on one occasion, 33s. 4d. for a ram and nineteen ewes, 5s. for five lambs, 26s. for 'alle her

[1] *A.P.*, 306/15259.
[2] *Early Chanc. Proceed.*, 6/120; another case of a letter of marque granted to a woman, 6/247. [3] *Ibid.*, 11/222, 61/379, 67/146. [4] *Howard Household Book*, I, 530. [5] *Ibid.*, 578. [6] *Ibid.*, 504, 511, and II, 163, 357. [7] *Early Chanc. Proceed.*, 66/251. [8] *Ibid.*, 234/43, cf. *Howard Household Book*, II, 163. [9] *Liber Albus*, Introd., lx. [10] Add. MSS., 34, 213, f. 22; *Ibid.*, 33, 986, f. 135, d.; *Howard Household Book*, I, 313. [11] Riley, *op. cit.*, 643. [12] *Howard Household Book*, I, 282. [13] Add. MSS., 33, 986, f. 65 d.

corne as it growethe on the grownde,' 5s. for seven 'yonge shotes,' 2s. for a sow, 4s. for geese, and 12d. for a cider press.[1] Dame Katherine Chiderok seems to have been a sheep-farmer, as her landlord stocked her land with sheep.[2] Sir John Howard numbered several women among his tenants; there were at least three in the 'manere of Estwynche'[3]; and the Metyngham College accounts from Michaelmas to Easter, 4 Edward IV, show that nearly all the money received from 'Boylound in Howe,' during that term, was paid by Margareta Kent.[4] Women must have been frequently employed in husbandry, as their wages were determined by statute.[5] In an entry recording payment for haymaking, among the Duke of Norfolk's accounts, more women than men are mentioned.[6] Yelming, or laying the straw for the thatcher, was woman's work.[7] Women were, as might be expected, laundresses,[8] sempstresses,[9] and domestic servants[10]; even the daughters of men of good position, like the Pastons, were put 'to hard service in the houses of other people.'[11] Margaret Paston wrote of her daughter Elizabeth, 'she must use hyr selfe to werke redyly, as other jentylwomen done, and sumwhat to helpe hyr selfe ther with.'[12] These seem to have been the usual occupations of women, but they occasionally took part in others. We hear of 'the herynge wyffe,'[13] and there is a case in the *Chancery Proceedings* of a man being bound apprentice to a

[1] *Howard Household Book*, I, 296. [2] *Early Chanc. Proceed.*, 27/61. [3] *Howard Household Book*, I, 542–3. [4] Add. MSS., 33, 987, f. 59.
[5] *Rot. Parl.*, V, 112, and 11 *H. VII*, c. 22. [6] *Howard Household Book*, II, 119. [7] Wylie, *op. cit.*, II, 467. [8] *Early Chanc. Proceed.*, 76/65, and Hobhouse, 183. [9] Nicolas, *op. cit.*, 121. [10] *Early Chanc. Proceed.*, 28/179, 66/264, 28/519. [11] *Italian Relation*, 24. [12] *Paston Letters*, III, 123. [13] *Howard Household Book*, II, 121, and payments for fish to women, *Ibid.*, I, 334 and 528.

woman, 'in the crafte and occupacoun off fflerchers'[1] (arrow-makers). There was a rather odd case of a woman barber at Coventry[2]; and more curious still, the butlership of Glastonbury Abbey was once vested in a girl.[3]

In every trade woman's wage was much below man's; even in work for which she was especially suited, such as embroidery, a woman earned 4¼d., 5¼d., and 6¼d. a day, when a man earned 9¼d. and 10¼d.[4] Mr. Lapsley has published 'The Account Roll of a fifteenth century Iron Master' (Langley, Bishop of Durham). He says that two women were employed for various miscellaneous tasks, breaking up iron-stone, blowing the bellows, or helping their husbands, and their wages were 'determined by nothing short of caprice.'[5] In 1444 a common servant in husbandry, if a man, received 15s. and 40d. for clothing a year, but if a woman, only 10s. and 4s. for clothing.[6] This amount was, however, a good deal more than had been granted to women working in the field or dairy, by the Statute of Cambridge.[7] Mr. Wylie is of the opinion that women were rapidly gaining on men.[8] It is noticeable, however, that the wages of women-servants in husbandry were not, like men's, raised at the end of the fifteenth century.[9] In 1449 the Coventry Leet was obliged to pass an ordinance that no person should deliver wool to spinners under the specified weight,[10] and two years later the ordinance was repeated with the addition: 'þat no man delyuer no werk but be weyghtes ensealed and that þe

The wages of women.

[1] *Early Chanc. Proceed.*, 107/27. [2] *Coventry Leet Book*, I, 238.
[3] Capes, *op. cit.*, 291. [4] Wylie, *Henry IV*, Vol. II, 467.
[5] *Eng. Hist. Review*, Vol. XIV, 511. [6] *Rot. Parl.*, V, 112.
[7] Wylie, *op. cit.*, II, 465. [8] *Ibid.*, II, 467. [9] 11 *H. VII*, c. 22.
[10] *Coventry Leet Book*, I, 243.

officers take no more for sealyng of a wyght and dimidium wyght but ob. (i.e. ½d.) and no more.' 'The sweating of women workers in industrial life,' says Miss Dormer Harris, commenting on this passage, 'is ancient.'[1] Mrs. Green holds that the employment of women and cheap workers was one of the causes of the labour disputes of this period.[2] Evidence of disapproval of woman's work can be seen in the ordinances of two Gilds of Weavers. At Bristol, in 1461, weavers were forbidden to 'putt or hire' . . . 'wyfe, doughter or maide' . . . to the occupation of weaving, because by it 'many and divers of the Kynges liege people likkely men to do the Kyng seruis in his warris and in the defence of this his lond, . . . gothe vagaraunt & vnoccupied.'[3] The Weavers of Hull were as much opposed to the employment of women, and ordered that 'ther shall no woman worke in any warke concernyng this occupacon within the town of Hull, uppon payn of xls.'[4]

Assistance rendered by women to their husbands.

Women not only traded independently, as we have seen, but some of them gave valuable assistance to their husbands in the management of their affairs. No reader of the *Paston Letters* could fail to be struck by the ability of Margaret Paston. She carried on all kinds of business for her husband; she collected his rents[5]; she kept accounts for him[6]; and when the Duke of Suffolk claimed Drayton, she attempted to hold a court there. Her men were seized by the Duke's, but she spoke with the judges in the presence of the bailiff of Cossey and the whole of the Duke's council, with the result that her men were released and his

[1] *Ibid.*, 255. [2] Mrs. Green, *Town Life*, II, 88. [3] *Little Red Book of Bristol*, II, 127. [4] Lambert, *Gild Life*, 206. [5] *Paston Letters*, I, 218. [6] *Ibid.*, IV, 66.

were censured.[1] It is no wonder that John Paston writes admiringly: 'And in god feyth ye aquyt yow ryght wel and discretly and hertyly to yowr wurchep and myn, and to the shame of your adversarijs.'[2] She seems, indeed, to have been more than a match for his enemies, in many cases. 'Ther was grete labours made by the bayly of Coshay and other,' she writes to him, 'for to have endytyd your men both at Dyrham and at Walsyngham, but I purvayd a mene that her purpose was lettyd at thos ij tymes.'[3] Merchants of the Staple, and others whose trade required their presence abroad, often depended a great deal upon the co-operation of their wives. Thomas Kesteven informs George Cely that he has written to his wife to take actions for the recovery of sums of money owing to him[4]; and we find other women also taking actions of debt in the absence of their husbands.[5] Elizabeth Stonor shows an intelligent interest in her husband's commercial dealings,[6] and has a good deal of correspondence with him, and with a man named Thomas Betson on business matters.[7] She tells William Stonor that she has housed his wool,[8] and once she writes to him: 'send me a answere of the mater that I wrote to yow for the lumbarde,'[9] which gives the impression that she was carrying on some financial business for him. An example of the assistance which a wife might render to her husband is given in one of the Chancery Petitions. William Warner of Boston, trading in Selond, states that he sent home to his wife 'Islond stockffish' and other goods, that 'she shulde putte the marchaundise to sale as she dydde other marchaundise.'[10]

[1] *Ibid.*, I, 226–7. [2] *Ibid.*, IV, 164 (1465.) [3] *Ibid.*, IV, 179. [4] *A.C.*, Vol. LIII, Letter 6. [5] *Early Chanc. Proceed.*, 94/12 [6] *A.C.*, Vol. XLVI, Letter 116. [7] *Ibid.*, Letter 234. [8] *Ibid.*, Letter 120. [9] *A.C.*, Vol. XLVI, Letter 213. [10] *Early Chanc. Proceed.*, 12/118.

Signs of business capacity in women.

Evidence of the confidence felt in the administrative capacity of women may be seen in the large number of cases in which they were appointed executrices,[1] and not by their husbands alone, but by all kinds of people.[2] Women were also made feoffees to uses[3]; they themselves were often possessed of property,[4] bestowed upon them by their fathers or their husbands on their marriage, and the care of it gave them some training in the management of land. Occasionally we hear of women being free of the City of London[5]; and Henry IV granted Isabel de S. Simphorin, lady of Landiras, the privileges of a burgess of Bourdeaux.[6] Women were considered capable of taking part in parish affairs; not only had they a voice in the choice of churchwardens at the annual election,[7] but they sometimes served in this office themselves.[8] This was no light matter in those days when the functions of wardens were so varied. They had to manage farming, trading, the sale of gifts in kind, housing corn, selling beef when a bull was killed, furnishing the church-house, overseeing its brewery, bakehouse, and entertainments, and making presentments at the Archdeacon's court of delinquen-

[1] *Ibid.*, 8/25, 9/56, 11/343, 12/57, 14/39, 15/90, 16/11, 17/190, 18/92, 19/247, 20/133, 21/19, 22/64, 24/52, 25/171, 26/113, 27/164, 28/55, 29/185, 30/45, 31/527, 33/48, 35/8, 36/1, and many more; Furnivall, *Early Eng. Wills*, 'Ione my wyff . . . myn Executorice Cheff, pp. 17, 24, 28, 29, 88, 90, etc. [2] *Ibid.*, 51, 66; *Early Chanc. Proceed.*, 15/107, 15/286, 16/1, 18/193, 19/396, 26/26, 26/113, 27/385, 28/390. [3] 29/183, 16/374, 18/162, 20/15, 22/121, 22/139, 24/119, 24/123, 26/281, 27/80, 28/219, 29/71, 30/15, 31/360, 35/31, 40/232, 41/127, etc. [4] Petitions of women regarding their property are numerous; *Early Chanc. Proceed.*, 40/116, 41/6, 41/117, 42/32, 44/90, 45/298, 47/148, 53/19, 58/101, 60/80, 100/51, 107/86, 109/27, 183/15, 185/28, 192/2, 194/54, 195/36, and many more. [5] Sharpe, *Wills*, II, 381, 520, 590, 602, and 604. [6] Hardy, II, *op. cit.*, 563. [7] Gasquet, *Parish Life in Medieval England*, 104 and 102, and Hobhouse, xi. [8] Gasquet, *op. cit.*, 106, at St. Petrock's, Exeter; Hobhouse, 120, at Yatton.

cies of the rector or the parishioners.[1] Nor were women entirely excluded from public duties, although they might not sit in Parliament.[2] The Duchess of Suffolk was Constable of the Castle of Wallingford, where the Duke of Exeter was confined[3]; and Dame Agnes Foster had Lord 'Gravyle' and 'Sir Cardot Malorte,' prisoners, in her 'warde and rule.'[4] The Countess of Hereford was associated with the Bishops of London and Ely and the Sire de Burnell for the collection of a loan in Essex, Hertford, Cambridge, and Huntingdon,[5] and similarly Lady Abergavenny was among those who were appointed to treat with lenders concerning a loan to the King in 1430.[6] The Duchess of Burgundy carried on negotiations between that country and England concerning commercial intercourse and other matters.

The employment of child-labour.

It would be very interesting to know how the economic changes of the fifteenth century affected the employment of child-labour; unforfunately we have not very much information upon this subject, but one point at least seems clear—children began to work at a very early age. The statute concerning servants in husbandry speaks of those 'which use to labour at the plough . . . till they be of the Age of Twelve,'[7] so it was evidently customary to employ young children in agriculture. The *Chancery Proceedings* contain an instance of a child who, it was said, was put to the plough at the age of eight.[8] The order that they should 'abide at the same Labour,' if they had followed it up to this

[1] Hobhouse, xiv. [2] 'Margaret . . . Countess of Northfolk, to whom no place in Parlement myght apperteyne, by cause she was a woman'; *Rot. Parl.*, IV, 270. [3] In 1455, *Proceed. Privy Council*, VI, 245–6. [4] *Early Chanc. Proceed.*, 31/446. [5] *Proceed. Privy Council*, I, 343. [6] *Coventry Leet Book*, I, 123. [7] 12 *Ric. II*, c. 5. [8] *Early Chanc. Proceed.*, 28/471

age, encouraged parents to apprentice their children to trades before they reached it, and another Act was passed to check this evil[1]; not, however, because it was bad for the children, but because husbandry suffered. Nevertheless, children continued to start their careers very early in life. In one of the *Chancery Proceedings* it is said that John Hyll, draper, of London, enrolled one of his apprentices at the age of eleven, although the ordinance of the City said the person enrolled must be between thirteen and fourteen at the least.[2] From this it appears that the municipal authorities tried to stop the apprenticing of very young children. Yet in London it was recognized that 'enfauntz dedincz age' could be 'marchauntz' or 'tiegnent comunes shopes de mesteer et des merchaundises'; and ordinances were made concerning them.[3] The weavers of Bristol speak of the employment of children,[4] so it was not confined to London. Children earned money also by helping their parents. Sir John Howard paid a gunner 'for him and his child 6 days . . . 2s. 4d.'[5] In one of the *Coroners' Rolls* for Leicester we read that while Margaret Roost, aged eleven, was driving her mother's cart, she jumped off to put the harness of one of the horses right, fell on her head, and broke her neck.[6]

Children were included in the households of great nobles; there were four 'chylder' of the 'stabyllys'[7] and four 'chelderne of the Kechyn'[8] in the Duke of Norfolk's establishment. There were also 'chylderne of owir Lady chappell,'[9] but they were in a much higher position. Boys, who were paid fourpence a day, were amongst the twelve persons

[1] 7 *H. IV*, c. 17. [2] *Early Chanc. Proceed.*, 19/466. [3] Miss Bateson, *op. cit.*, I, 227. [4] *Little Red Book of Bristol*, II, 123–4. [5] *Howard Household Book*, I, 309. [6] *Coroners' Rolls*, No. 61, m. 10. [7] *Howard Household Book*, II, 426. [8] *Ibid.*, 439. [9] *Ibid.*, 438.

in attendance on Eleanor Cobham, when she was in the charge of Lord de Sudeley.[1] Pages were numerous in the Royal Household, and were allowed to do more responsible work than in earlier times. 'In noble Edwards[2] household, pages were none officers, nor yet long sene, beryng no charge nor sworn in the countyng-house; but now they be permytted for an ayde of every office, chosen oftyn tymes by the maysters of offices, as for labours, so by theyre vertuous disposition may grow, and by succession to be preferred to hygher servyse.'[3] There was a regular gradation of offices in the Household, and they might rise to be grooms, and then yeomen, and then sergeants, and finally clerks in various departments. So even in the Royal Household we have an illustration of the increased employment of children.

The idea of setting young children to arduous work is repugnant to the modern conscience; but before passing judgment upon the men of the fifteenth century we ought to remember that probably the average duration of life was shorter in those days, because so little was known of the laws of health. Consequently they reached maturity then sooner than we do now; a child in the language of the *Statute Book* seems to have been a person under fourteen.[4] The four Orders of Friars were forbidden to receive any 'infant' under this age[5]; and women heiresses were allowed to have 'livery of their lands and tenements' when they were fourteen years old.[6] Nevertheless, even when every excuse has been made, the fact remains that chil-

[1] *English Chronicle*, 190. [2] e.g. Edward III. [3] *Liber Niger* of Edward IV, in *Ordinances of the Royal Household*, p. 39. [4] Wages are ordained for 'a child under fourteen,' *Rot. Parl.*, V, 112. [5] 4 *H. IV*, c. 17. [6] 39 *H. VI*, c. 2. As an illustration of the rapid development of men in the fifteenth century the precocity of the sons of Henry IV might be noticed. Henry was

dren often began to work before they were fit for it. Contemporary writers do not assign any reason for this characteristic of the period, except in the case of evasions of the law of 1388; but we should probably not go far wrong if we attributed it, like the employment of women, to the increased demand for labour caused by the growth of industry, and possibly also to the difficulties caused by the insistence of workmen upon higher wages and the desire of the masters for cheap labour.

Viceroy of Wales, Thomas Viceroy of Ireland, and John shared the command on the Scottish Marches with the Earl of Westmoreland, in 1406, when their respective ages were nineteen, eighteen, and seventeen (Ramsay, *Lancaster and York*, I, 105–6). The Prince of Wales commanded half his father's army at the battle of Shrewsbury when he was only fifteen (*Ibid.*, I, 60).

CHAPTER VI

THE STANDARD OF LIVING

Standard of living in the fifteenth century.

THE economic changes of the fifteenth century not only considerably modified the structure of society, but also produced important effects upon the material conditions of existence. The expansion of commerce and industry revealed to men new objects of desire, and at the same time provided the means of obtaining them. Consequently there are signs of increasing luxury in food, clothing, and housing. The development of sea fishing certainly added greatly to the quantity, and possibly also to the variety of fish available for food, and this must have been no slight advantage in the days when it was a religious duty to abstain from meat during certain seasons of the year. Household Books show how frequently fish was eaten, and the numbers of different kinds used. One entry in the accounts of Anne, Duchess of Buckingham, includes cod, 'thornbakkis,' plaice, soles, haddocks, 'gurnard,' and crabbs[1]; and there were many others — 'mackerell,'[2] 'bret,'[3] 'sturgion,'[4] 'conger,' 'rochett,'[5] 'crevissh,'[6] 'molett,'[7] 'breym marin '[8] (sea-bream), oysters,[9] prawns,[10] tench,[11]

Increasing luxury in food.

[1] Add. MSS. 34,213, p. 11. [2] *Ibid.*, 16 d. [3] *Ibid.*, 18.
[4] *Ibid.*, 19 d. [5] *Ibid.*, 20 d. [6] *Ibid.*, 21.
[7] *Ibid.*, 23. [8] *Ibid.*, 30 d. [9] *Ibid.*, 33.
[10] *Ibid.*, 35 d. [11] *Ibid.*, 48.

halibut,[1] lampreys,[2] whiting, flounders, eels, dog-fish,[3] sprats,[4] minnows, porpoise,[5] doree,[6] shrimps and whelks.[7] The fisheries for 'oystres, musklys, cockles . . . & autre pessen esshelez,' off the Ore, were so valuable that the Mayor of London laid a petition before the Chancellor, when the Abbot of Faversham imposed a duty upon them.[8] We know that a great quantity of stockfish was brought from Iceland. They were apparently not dear, although they came from such a distance, on one occasion three hundred only cost £3, while a freight of '600 grene heed ffishes' cost £23[9]; but the comparison is not wholly satisfactory, because we do not know the weight of the fish in either case. For the same reason no accurate estimate of the price of fish can be given from Household Books. Salmon is mentioned in most Household Books; sometimes it was salted and sometimes fresh.[10] 'Salmon recens' was one of the items of a dinner given by the Duke of Buckingham on January 6th.[11] Herrings formed a staple article of food in Lent,[12] a convoy taking them to the besieged town of Orleans, in February, 1429, was attacked by the French, and they gave their name to the battle which followed.[13] Considerable skill was expended in curing herrings in the fifteenth century: some were salted and smoked, and these were called red herrings; but others were pickled without being smoked, and they were known as white herrings.[14] And salt fish of all kinds was

[1] *Ibid.*, 110 d. [2] *Ibid.*, 119 d. [3] *Stafford Household Book*, in *Archælogia*, XXV, 327. [4] *Ordinances of the Royal Household*, 102. [5] *Manners and Meals*, 166–7. [6] *Ibid.*, 167. [7] *Ibid.*, 168. [8] *Early Chanc. Proceed.*, 6/241. [9] *Early Chanc. Proceed.*, 19/480. [10] *Ordinances of the Royal Household*, p. 102; *Stafford Household Book*, *Archælogia*, XXV, 341; Add. MSS. 34, 213, 8 d. [11] *Archælogia*, XXV, 326. [12] *Ordinances of the Royal Household*, 102. [13] Ramsay, *Lancaster and York*, I, 385. [14] T. Rogers, *Work and Wages*, 240.

largely used, as Household Books show. Besides these, the preservation of fresh-water fish, as of old in 'stews' was continued, and before long, trout were added, as a delicacy, to the pike, bream, and roach of early inventories.

The spices which Italian merchants brought to England were much appreciated. A payment of £9 11s. 6d. for various kinds of condiments occurs in the *Household Book of the Duchess of Buckingham*,[1] and George Duke of Clarence spent £72 6s. 8d. on them in a year.[2] Pepper cost 12d. a pound, cinnamon 14d., cloves 2s. 6d., and mace 2s. 8d.,[3] and these seem large sums when we remember that a lamb could be bought for 1s. 1d.,[4] and a shoulder and breast of mutton for 5d.[5] Sugar cost about 10d. a pound[6]; it was, Mr. Beazley tells us, imported from Madeira.[7] The effects of foreign trade may also be traced in purchases of salt,[8] of Gascon,[9] and Spanish wine,[10] of malmsey,[11] and claret.[12] The municipal authorities of Coventry fixed the price of Gascon wine in that town at 8d. a gallon, malmsey at 6d., and that of Rochelle at 16d.; and they ordered that 'no Osey ne algarbe . . . be sold until the mayor and his peers have seen it and set a price on it.'[13] The result of the development of the coal trade can be seen in the use of coal and charcoal as well as wood for fuel.[14] In 1405 a proclamation was issued in London regulating the prices of charcoal and faggots.[15] Coal is sometimes

[1 and 3] Add. MSS. 34, 213; 86. [2] *Ordinances of the Royal Household*, 103. [4] Add. MSS. 34, 213, p. 9. [5] *Howard Household Book*, I, 435. [6] Add. MSS. 34, 213, 86. [7] C. R. Beazley, *Prince Henry the Navigator*, 166. [8] Add. MSS. 34, 213, p. 21. [9] *Howard Household Book*, I, 153, and *Archælogia*, XXV, 329. [10] *Howard Household Book*, I, 153. [11] *A.C.*, Vol. XLVI, Letter 172. [12] *Ibid.*, Letter 218. [13] *Coventry Leet Book*, Part i, p. 24. [14] *Archælogia*, XXV, 321, 'woode and coole,' *Ordinances of the Royal Household*, 104. 'Carbon siluestre,' Add. MSS. 34, 213, 48 d, 54, 60, 74 d, and 'focal,' 31 d. [15] Riley, *Memorials*, 560.

mentioned in bequests to the poor.[1] Evidence of the care bestowed upon the preparation of food may be seen in the receipts for cookery which have come down to us, such as those bound up with the *Ordinances of the Royal Household*,[2] and those printed in *Manners and Meals in the Olden Times*.[3] The menus also to be found in the latter book afford practical illustrations of the elaborate dinners of 'flesche' or fish [4] enjoyed by the rich.

Extravagance in dress in the fifteenth century.

The repeated complaints of the Commons in Parliament that 'as well men as women, have used, and daily usen, excessive & inordynat arayes,'[5] and the failure of statutes and ordinances[6] to stop it, point to increased extravagance in dress. It is interesting to notice that all classes in the community were included in the condemnation of the Commons, so apparently all shared in the rise of the standard of comfort, in this respect at least. Even labourers, who in 1363 might use no 'Draps sinoun Blanket & Russet, L'aune de douse deniers,'[7] were allowed, in 1463–4, to wear cloth of which the price did not exceed two shillings a yard.[8] The comments of the writers of the period create the same impression as legislation. Lydgate wrote, *A litelle short ditey agayne hornes*, which was a protest against women's head-dresses with trimming like a pair of cow's horns. Occleve, in the *De Regimine Principum*, says that tailors will have to go into the fields to shape and spread and fold, as their boards will be too narrow for the cloth that shall be worked into a gown; the skinner, too, will have to go into the fields, his house being too

[1] *Early Eng. Wills*, 101; Sharpe, *op. cit.*, II, 478, and II, 417.
[2] Printed for the Soc. of Antiquaries. [3] *Early Eng. Text Soc.*, Orig. Series, No. 32. [4] *Ibid.*, 164–8. [5 and 8] *Rot. Parl.*, V, 504.
[6] *Ibid.*, III, 506; 37 *Ed. III*, cs. 8–14; 38 *Ed. III*, c. 2; 3 *Ed. IV*, c. 5; 22 *Ed. IV*, c. 1. [7] *Rot. Parl.*, III, 281–2.

small for his trade.[1] A writer *On the Corruption of Public Manners*, makes a bitter attack upon 'prowd galonttes hertlesse,' with 'hyght cappis witlesse,' and 'schort gownys thriftlesse,' and 'longe peked schone.'[2] An incident which happened in Canterbury Cathedral shows the capaciousness of the sleeves which were then worn: a fugitive, who had escaped from prison, took refuge within the rails of Archbishop Chichele's monument, but the mob thrust their arms between the bars, and beat him with sticks, which they had hitherto concealed in their sleeves.[3] The prices found in records give us some idea of the amount of money which must have been spent on clothes and jewels: martin fur for a gown was valued at £17[4]; 'Harry, Duke of Warwick, bought cloth of gold and other stuff for £455 19s. 10d.[5]; two ouches of gold, with a ruby and certain diamonds in each, were said to be the equivalent of £200, and a bishop's mitre worth £100.[6] A petition was made for the possession of a girdle harnessed with silver and overgilt, and it was valued at £4.[7] The Privy Council ordered that £24 should be given to James I of Scotland to purchase cloth of gold for his marriage.[8] 'Riche crymsin clothe of golde' sometimes cost as much as £8 a yard, and 'purpull velvet' forty shillings.[9] The Mayor of Bristol was allowed £8 for twelve yards of scarlet and ten marks for his fur; and out of a total of £93 9s. 4d. paid yearly to the city officers, the sum of £37 6s. 8d. was expended on clothing.[10]

[1] Morley, *English Writers*, VI, 126. [2] Wright, *Polit. Songs*, II, 251. [3] *Hist. MSS. Commission*, Report IX, Appendix on Register S. of Christ Church, Canterbury. [4] *Early Chanc. Proceed.*, 97/44. [5] *Ibid.*, 22/117. [6] *Ibid.*, 29/467. [7] *Ibid.*, 186/22. [8] *Proceed. Privy Council*, III, 133. [9] *Materials for the Reign of Henry VII*, Vol. II, 6. [10] Ricart, *The Maire of Bristowe is Kalendar*, pp. 81–2. See also Appendix C 1c.

The number of garments possessed by men and women of good position must have been very large. Sir John Fastolf had clothes made of cloth of gold, satin, fugre (figured satin), velvet, leather, cloth, fustian, and damask.[1] The wills of all kinds of people are full of legacies of articles of dress: Richard Dixton, Esq., left gowns of 'blake furred with ficheux,' 'grene damaske lyned,' 'Russet furred with blak,' 'rede damaske,' 'Russet medley,' 'a scarlet gowne furred with foynes,' 'a gowne of scarlet with slyt slyues y-furred,' and many others,[2] including a 'gowne of Goldsmythes werk.'[3] Even armour, which we should expect to be made for use and not show, became elaborate and ornamental. John Payn, Fastolf's servant, was robbed by Cade's followers of 'one peyr of Bregandyrns[4] kevert with blew fellewet and gilt naile, with legharneyse, the vallew of the gown and the bregardyns viii li.'[5] Large prices seem to have been given sometimes for armour, Sir John Paston gave £20 for 'an harneys' for himself.[6] At a tournament held at Westminster, before Henry VII, we are told of the combatants: 'Allsoo their hors harneys was of blake velvet, bordred and losenged of goldsmythis werke, and on every corner of the said losenges a rounde silver bell, and in the myddys rosses, oon red, a nothre whit, and oon every roos a waffir gilt.'[7] Armour and the richer materials, such as satin and velvet, were, as we know, imported,[8] but woollen stuffs were the products of English looms.

A rise in the standard of living can also be seen in the construction and furnishing of the houses of

[1] *Paston Letters*, III, 174 and seq. [2] Furnivall, *Early Eng. Wills*, 110–11. [3] *Ibid.*, 109. [4] A coat of leather or quilted linen, with small iron plates sewed on to it; the back and breast were sometimes made separately and called a pair. [5] *Paston Letters*, II, 155. [6] *Paston Letters*, V, 7–8. [7] Gairdner, *Letters of Richard III and Henry VII*, Vol. I, 396. [8] See p. 36, *supra*.

this period. They were larger and better arranged than they had been in earlier times. In the fourteenth century they were usually not more than two stories high,[1] even in towns; but in the fifteenth, prosperous merchants often had vast cellars for merchandise below their houses, a warehouse and two or more shops on the ground-floor, and above them a parlour and bed-rooms, the whole being three stories high; and there were, in addition, attics in the sharply-pitched gables, and a lofty hall behind the other buildings.[2] Mr. Pryce's description of a house and furniture shows us how Bristol merchants lived,[3] and we had, until quite recently, in London, an even better illustration of a 'mansion' of the reign of Edward IV in Crosby Hall. Stow describes the Goldsmiths' Row, in the Cheap, London, as 'the most beautiful Frame and Front of Fair Houses & Shops, that were within all the Walls of London or elsewhere in England.' It was built by Thomas Wood, goldsmith, in 1491, and contained 'ten fair Dwelling-houses and fourteen shops, all in one Frame, uniformly built four stories high, beautified towards the street with the Goldsmiths Arms, the Likeness of Wood-men, in Memory of his Name, riding on monstrous Beasts. All which is cast in Lead & richly painted over & gilt.'[4] There seems to have been a tendency to increase the number of rooms contained by houses. In Sir John Fastolf's castle, at Caister, there were no less than twenty-six chambers besides the public room, chapel, and offices.[5] He was, it is true, an exceptionally wealthy man, but the same feature appears, though in a

Improvements in houses.

[1] Turner and Parker, *Domestic Architecture*, II, 187. [2] Hunt, *Bristol*, 108. [3] Pryce, *Memorials of the Canynges' Family*, 116–21. [4] Strype's *Stow*, I, 686. [5] *Paston Letters*, I, 119 (Introd.), quoting Dawson Turner, *Hist. Sketch of Caister Castle*, 4.

less marked degree, in houses of smaller size. The house of Richard Merlawe, 'iremonger,' consisted of a hall, parlour, chamber, butlery, pantry, and kitchen[1]; and the care taken by testators to specify which chambers they wished to bequeath to their friends shows that they possessed several. Richard Gosselyn, 'iremonger,' left a large painted chamber, with panelled ceiling, and a small chamber[2]; and William Hobbys, 'medicus et sirurgicus' to the Duke of York, gave his sister Katherine the best chamber with all its hangings, or the hangings of the parlour.[3] Permanent offices, such as the kitchen, pantry, and butlery, and outbuildings of stone, were not general before the fifteenth century,[4] but they were very important adjuncts to houses in our period, perhaps because so much attention was devoted to eating and drinking. Additional sitting-rooms were needed, because the master and mistress of the house desired more privacy, and no longer dined in the hall with their dependents, but were served apart in the great chamber or parlour.[5] By the *Stafford Household Book* we see that 'messes' were served separately in 'the chamber of the Lord and Lady,' the great chamber and the hall.[6] The ladies of the family also seem to have had their own reception-room. More bedrooms were required, because the hall was no longer used as a general sleeping chamber, and this change certainly indicates a considerable advance in the social condition of the nation.[7] As a consequence of the decreasing use

[1] Sharpe, *Wills*, II, 428. [2] *Ibid.*, II, 464. [3] *Ibid.*, 591.
[4] Turner and Parker, *op. cit.*, II, 12.
[5] *Archæologia*, XXV, 321 and 315. Turner and Parker, *op. cit.*, III, 76. [6] *Archæologia*, XXV, 323. [7] Turner and Parker, III, 18. Sir John Howard, when he wants some measurements for hangings, mentions the 'al' (hall), 'parlor,' 'chawember hover the parlor,' 'the chaumber wer that I lay in,' and the 'chawember over the pantery and the botery' (*Howard Household Book*, I, 557).

made of the hall, it declined in size at this time, and it is perhaps not altogether fanciful to trace in its waning importance the decline of the system under which it had played so prominent a part.

Another outward and visible sign of the fall of Feudalism is the fact that the type of the castle was gently dying out, and the type of the domestic house breaking forth into existence.[1] A comparison of the numbers of licences to crenellate granted in the fourteenth and fifteenth centuries is most striking: whereas over one hundred and seventy were issued in the reign of Edward III, and more than fifty in that of Richard II, only twenty were granted between the years 1399 and 1483.[2] Manor houses were sometimes fortified to a certain extent, in order that they might be able to resist sudden attacks of marauders, but they were not intended for serious warfare.[3]

In regard to the material used for building, it is probable that men took whatever was ready at hand, and did not spend money in bringing anything from a distance, except in very special cases[4]; so stone was used in Somerset, Wiltshire, and Gloucestershire, and brick in the eastern counties, where no stone was found.[5] The improvements in brick-making introduced by the Flemings were therefore especially valued in this part of the country. Timber was still frequently employed for building purposes,[6] and 'estrich' boards (that is, Estland boards) were bought from Norway and Sweden,[7] though 'goode trewe hert of oke' was

[1] Turner and Parker, III, 5. [2] Lists of the licences to crenellate are given in Turner and Parker, *op. cit.*, for the reign of Edward III, Part ii, pp. 408–17, and 422; Richard II, Part ii, 418–20; 1399–1483, *Ibid.*, 421–22, and III, 261. [3] *Ibid.*, 10–11.
[4] Stone was brought from Caen for Westminster Abbey, *Cal. French Rolls*, 1456–7, m. 2. [5] Turner and Parker, *op. cit.*, III, 22.
[6] Timber houses in London, *Early Chanc. Proceed.*, 56/93 and 63/213.
[7] Addy, *Evolution of the House*, 109n.

also greatly valued.[1] There was, however, a growing dislike to timber chimneys and thatched roofs, perhaps from fear of fire, and both were forbidden in Worcester[2] and other towns.

The glazing of windows, not only of ecclesiastical[3] and municipal buildings,[4] but also of dwelling houses, grew more common. Thomas Maykyn, who was building a chamber for William Marchall, Clerk of the Chancery, informed him that 'There are goodly windows, in the fronte a wyndowe of iiij dayes, and in euery syde a goodely wyndowe of ij dayes.'[5] By the custom of London, windows could be removed by the person to whom they belonged, so a petition was laid before the Chancellor by a tenant who was not allowed to take them with him when he left the house.[6] A will enrolled in the Court of the Hustings, by John Herst, skinner, directs that the glass windows should not be removed from a tenement, but should be left in it, when it was let.[7] Another will gives us an idea of what were then considered the necessaries of a tenement; they included cisterns, glasses, standards, presses, 'warbordes,' 'dressours,' shelves, 'crestes,' and benches.[8] The price of glass was about fivepence a foot. Sir John Howard paid 'to the glacyer of Yipswyche for 9 fote of glasse to the new closet, 3s. 9d.'[9]

Among the most important pieces of furniture in a house were the beds, and their costliness and magnificence are signs of the growing luxury of

[1] *A.C.*, Vol. XLVI, Letter 263. See also the description of Waynflete's School; it was to have 'a flore with a Rofe of Tymber of good herte of ooke' (Chandler, *Life of William of Waynflete*, p. 369). [2] T. Smith, *Eng. Gilds*, p. 386. [3] *Paston Letters*, III, 135, glazing the chapel at Mauteby, 10/-; repairing and glazing the vestry of St. Michael's, Queenhithe, Sharpe, II, 561. [4] Glazing the Guildhall, London, Strype's *Stow*, I, 559. [5] *A.C.*, Vol. XLVI, Letter 263. [6] *Early Chanc. Proceed.*, 64/234. [7] Sharpe's *Wills*, II, 546. [8] *Ibid.*, 587. [9] *Howard Household Book*, I, 511.

the age. A bed of arras of hawking left to Thomas, Duke of Exeter, by Henry V, was valued at £139 11s. 8d.[1] The description of a bed belonging to Edward IV shows that comfort was considered as well as ornamentation. He had 'a grete large federbedd and the bolster therunto stuffed with downe; & tapettes[2] of verdours with crownes and roses paled blue & crymysyn; a sperver[3] of ray velvet of the colours grene, rede and white, conteignyng testour, celour[4] and valance of the same suyt, lined with busk[5] and frenged with frenge of divers colours, with ij syde curtyns and a fote curtyn of sarcinet chaungeable.'[6] Making the royal bed was quite a solemn function.[7] Beds, like gowns, were often left by will to friends and relatives. Nicholas Sturgeon, priest, bequeathed a 'bed of grene sylke, wiþ the testour and Canape ther-to, palid tartyn white and rede,' to a cousin, and 'a blew bed with the lyoun Curteynes, Couverled, blankettis, a peyre of shetis and a gowne' to a servant.[8] The hangings of chambers, such as tapestry for the walls and coverings for the benches, were also very elaborate. The indenture of the goods of Henry V mentions '1 autre pece d'Arras d'or, que comence en l'estorie, Ycy comence pur une message, contenant xxxv vergées de longure, & v vergées demi de large, en tout c $\overset{xx}{iiii}$ xii vergés demi, pris le vergé xs . . . cxv li. xs.'[9] Carpets seem to have been just coming into use.[10]

Furniture.

[1] *Proceed. Privy Council*, III, 58-9. [2] Costers, the sides of a bed (*Wardrobe Accounts of Edward IV*, Glossary). [3] The canopy of a bed (*Ibid.*). [4] Ceiling of the bed (*Ibid.*). [5] A sort of linen cloth (*Ibid.*). [6] *Ibid.*, p. 143. [7] *Ordinances of the Royal Household*, 122. There is a similar description of bedmaking in *Manners and Meals*, 313-14. [8] Furnivall, *Early Eng. Wills*, 133; cf. pp. 19 and 36. [9] *Rot. Parl.*, IV, p. 232. [10] *Ordinances of the Royal Household*, 121, 125, 126, 128, and Turner and Parker, *op. cit.*, III, 110.

The rest of the household furniture was, as a rule, simple, though considerable sums of money were spent on plate. Lord Howard paid £12 for a silver hot-water dish.[1] Rich men showed their wealth by a display of plate, which was often set out on a buffet,[2] and this was carried to such an extent that it became necessary to forbid goldsmiths to melt money of gold or silver 'to make any vessel or other thing thereof,' or to gild anything with the same.[3] The author of the *Italian Relation* was immensely impressed with the 'wonderful quantity of wrought silver' he saw in London, not only in private houses, but also in goldsmiths' shops and inns.[4] 'The riches of England,' he says, 'are greater than those of any other country in Europe.'[5]

The share of the lower classes in the rise of the standard of living.

Taking all these circumstances into consideration, it is clear that there was a rise in the standard of living in the fifteenth century, and that it was mainly due to economic changes, being directly caused by the increased production and importation of articles of luxury, and indirectly by the growth of wealth through successful trading. It is not, however, equally clear, except in the case of clothing, that all classes in the community benefited by it. Unfortunately the Household Books which we possess deal only with the expenditure of the rich, and few contemporary authorities tell us how the poor lived. The writer of the *Italian Relation* comments upon the 'immense profusion of every comestible animal'[6] in England,

[1] *Howard Household Book*, II, 138. [2] The plate cupboard of a rich merchant must have been a fair ornament to his hall; Thomas Baker, grocer, left 350 oz. of silver to his children, in bowls, cups, salt-sellers, and spoons (Hunt, *Bristol*, 108; see also Appendix B, 6). [3] *Rot. Parl.*, VI, 184. [4] *Italian Relation*, 42 and 29. [5] *Ibid.*, 28. [6] *Ibid.*, 10.

but there may have been many persons too poor to buy them. Fortescue declares the 'comune peple of thys londe, the beste fedde and also the best cledde of any natyon crystyn or hethen[1]; but the years he spent in France, where the condition of the people was very bad, had perhaps lowered his ideas of comfort. The *Russell Boke* gives a menu for 'A Fest for a franklen,' by which it appears that he fared very well—

> 'beef or moton stewed seruysable,
> boyled Chykon or capon agreable
> . . . .
> Rosted goose & pygge fulle profitable.'

were some of the items of his first course, and they were to be followed by 'veel, lambe, kyd, or cony' and many other dishes.[2] The standard of living of the classes below the franklin is a much more difficult question. The *Chancery Proceedings* give us, incidentally, some information as to the resources of artisans and others. We read that John Stok, carpenter, of London, took a lease of ground, with old buildings on it, for thirty years, at a rent of fifty shillings, and spent a hundred marks in building on it.[3] Thomas Wrottyng, mason, in the county of Essex, left £40 to his two grandsons.[4] Twenty acres of land in Sevenoaks were purchased by Richard Stretend, smith, of John Matan, carpenter.[5] A saucemaker of York left his two sons £58 15s. 4¾d. and £40 respectively.[6] William Milbourn, painter, sold lands for £80.[7] William Crosby of York, dyer, bought lands and tenements to the yearly value of ten marks.[8] Cases of this kind (and

[1] *Works of Sir J. Fortescue*, Vol. I, 552. [2] *Manners and Meals*, 170. [3] *Early Chanc. Proceed.*, 15/273. [4] *Ibid.*, 16/494. [5] *Ibid.*, 17/169. [6] *Ibid.*, 27/372. [7] *Ibid.*, 31/236. [8] *Ibid.*, 41/203.

there are many more) show, at least, that it was possible for artisans to save money.

Some idea of the resources of workmen (and others) may be gathered from the rents they were able to pay. The *Churchwardens' Accounts* of St. Mary-at-Hill, London, enable us to gain information about some of their tenants. An 'yremonger' paid £6 13s. 4d. a year; a 'Poyntemaker,' £1 6s. 8d.; a capper the same; an organ maker, £1 6s.; a 'Patynmaker,' 13s. 4d.; and a 'taillor,' £4 13s. 4d.[1] The rent of a chamber described as a 'kechen' was 6s. 8d.[2] A grocer's shop, in Cheapside, with 'a place above it,' let for £4 6s. 8d. a year in 1482.[3] These seem very large sums, and it is surprising that the tenants could afford to pay them; but possibly they were master craftsmen,[4] and even if they were journeymen, they would be earning more money than the average artisan, because the rate of wages was higher in London than elsewhere.[5] Nevertheless, when due allowance has been made for this circumstance, the impression remains that London artisans were able to live comfortably. Probably the conditions of life varied very much in different parts of the country. We read in the Accounts of St. Dunstan's, Canterbury, that in 1492 three acres of land were let for 1½d. a year, and that 'Mr Fenex paid sixpence for a tenement'; and, in spite of the lowness of the rents in this district, many of the tenants were in arrears with them.[6] The prosperity of the London workmen may be fairly attributed to the high place which the city held in the commercial and industrial world.

[1] *Medieval Records of a London City Church*, 125. [2] *Ibid.*, 112. [3] *Howard Household Book*, II, xxv, note. [4] This remark applies equally well to the instances quoted from the *Chancery Proceedings* on the last page. [5] T. Rogers, *Work and Wages*, 327. [6] *Archæologia Cantiana*, Vol. XVI, p. 304.

An indenture for building a house, preserved in the Record Office, enables us to see what the houses of Londoners of the middle class were like. It was to be situated at Charing Cross, and to 'conteyn in length from the olde halle there x fote of Assise, with a Chambre aboue the same Getteyd xij fete and a halfe of assise in hight, and [he] shuld make vppon the seid grounde A gate hous crosse the seid Chambre, the which gate house shuld conteyn in Wydnesse ix fete of Assise, and xviij fete of Assise in length, and xij fete of Assise in heght, with a Garet in the same and Gates.' Another house was to be built also, and they were both to be 'of newe, able and sufficient Tymbur of Oke' . . . 'fully garnysshed with dores, steyres, Wyndowes, benches, Speres and all other thyngis belongyng to the crafte of Carpyntry,' . . . 'togedir with a bey Wyndowe in the loft of the forseid gatehouse.' The rent of the two houses for two years was to have been twenty marks.[1]

The house of the agricultural labourer could not possibly have been nearly as grand as these. We are told that it was merely a covered shed without floor, ceiling, or chimney,[2] that his food was very poor, and that meat was only occasionally within his reach.[3] Thorold Rogers, on the other hand, says that the labourer could live comfortably upon his income; he estimates that the cost of living for a family of four persons would be £3 4s. 9d., and that out of this, £1 3s. 6d. would be spent on wheat; 7s. 7d. on beer; 16s. 8d. on meat; and 17s. on clothing.[4] It has been pointed out that Thorold Rogers has reckoned that the man would work on three hundred days of the year, but that in reality there were only two hundred and sixty working-

[1] *Early Chanc. Proceed.*, 63/213.
[2] Denton, *op. cit.*, p. 197.
[3] *Ibid.*, 206.
[4] *Agric. and Prices*, IV, 759.

days, because holy days were so numerous.[1] It is certainly open to doubt whether Thorold Rogers has rightly interpreted his figures.[2]

A rise of prices, such as might be occasioned by a bad harvest, must have pressed very heavily upon a man with a small income. An entry in the *English Chronicle*, under the date 1434–5, states that 'the nexte yeer aftir began the grete derthe of corn in this land, the whiche endurid ij yeer, so that a busshelle of whete was sold for xld., & the poer peple in dyuers partieȝ of the Northcuntre eet breed maad of farn rotes.'[3] Similar tales are told of the famine of 1438–9,[4] but these two calamities seem to have been the only times of very great scarcity, although there are a few complaints of poverty caused by the 'Chierte des Blees,'[5] and there were probably local famines,[6] as, for example, one which occurred in Cornwall in 1437–8, when the people were allowed to trade with Ushant.[7] But even when corn was at its normal price, the labourer must have found it difficult to save enough money to provide for his family when he was out of work, if he had nothing but his wages to depend upon. It is, however, possible that labourers sometimes had some land of their own, and that would enable them to keep poultry or pigs, or perhaps raise a little corn. There are in the *Chancery Proceedings* quite a fair number of references to land in the possession of husbandmen; the amounts vary greatly. John Smith, of Wells by the sea, was

[1] *Social England*, II, 530. A few prices are given in Appendix C 1 *d*, to show how much the labourer could buy with his wages.

[2] Cunningham, *Growth of Industry and Commerce*, I, 372.

[3] *English Chronicle*, Camden Soc. O.S., 64, p. 55.

[4] Chronicle of Croyland quoted by Creighton, *Hist. of Epidemics*, 223.

[5] *Rot. Parl.*, III, 645 (1410); *Ibid.*, V, 31 (1438–9); *English Chronicle* for 1400–1, p. 23.

[6] *Work and Wages*, 62.

[7] *Cal. French Rolls*, 1437–8, m. 11.

'seised of a messuage and ten acres of land '[1]; while John Pentecost, husbandman, of Buxted, Sussex, had 'ij meses lx acres of londe, xx acres of pasture and xx acres of mede.'[2] Men who had as much land as this could live upon it, but those who had only a few acres would be obliged to work for hire as well. The rent of land was low, in some parts of the country at least, for William Heneworth, of Mickleham, only paid three shillings a year for 'iij mesys, l acres of land, x acres of mede, & iij acres of wode' in Hellingly and Hailsham.[3]

One or two other petitions presented to the Chancellor throw a little light on the position of the husbandman. John Ledale, of Cherhill, Wiltshire, complained that he had been robbed of forty-one marks of money and goods (woollen cloth, napery, and bedding) to the value of £10.[4] William Hunte tells a pathetic tale. He says he 'hath ben all his lyf a laborer with dyverse husbondez gaderyng in ye mene tyme by his sore labor to haue levid with in his age.' He sealed a document empowering, as he thought, Thomas Hamond to collect his debts, but it was really a 'dede of gyft of all his goodes,' and by virtue of it Thomas took away his sheep, 'catall' and goods to the value of £10.[5] The value of the goods stolen may, of course, be exaggerated by the petitioners; the fact that they could save even a little money is not without significance. In another case a husbandman in the county of Kent left his daughter 36s. 8d. and six quarters of barley-malt.[6] These petitions give us a more favourable impression of the lot of the husbandman than the Statute Book would have led us to expect; but it must be remembered that the *Chancery Proceedings*

[1] *Early Chanc. Proceed.*, 26/495.
[2] *Ibid.*, 30/53.
[3] *Ibid.*, 27/173.
[4] *Ibid.*, 27/387.
[5] *Ibid.*, 28/280.
[6] *Ibid.*, 27/337.

would not be likely to include those who owned no property, so that we only have one view of the matter presented to us here. Nevertheless, it is satisfactory to find that so many were in possession of land,[1] but the Inclosing movement, in so far as it tended to displace the labourer, or the peasant proprietor, from his holding, must have materially altered his position for the worse.

Condition of public health in the fifteenth century.

A study of the material conditions of life in the fifteenth century would be incomplete without some mention of the state of public health. The rise in the standard of living was accompanied by an improvement in health in one respect; leprosy, although it is mentioned occasionally,[2] had almost died out.[3] On the other hand, the testimony of chroniclers,[4] the Rolls of Parliament,[5] and private letters[6] concur in showing that outbreaks of pestilence were frequent.

Pestilence in the fifteenth century.

Dr. Creighton, who made a special study of the subject, records more than twenty instances of its appearance,[7] and he has made some very interesting comments upon what he calls the change in the habits of the plague between the time of the Black Death and the reign of Edward IV. In the earlier part of this period, he says, plagues were general throughout England, but were on a small scale;

[1] Some other instances of husbandmen holding land, 19/235, 26/129, 26/161, 27/263, 36/3, 9/26, 35/71, 53/8, 53/15, 54/193, 90/60, 186/50.
[2] One of the duties of the King's 'Doctoure of Physyque' was 'to espie if any of the Courte be infected with leperiz or pestylence' (*Liber Niger* in *Ordinances of the Royal Household*, p. 43). Some few bequests were made to lepers (Sharpe, *Wills*, II, 351, 509, 518, 578, and 589).
[3] Creighton, *Hist. of Epidemics*, I, 224.
[4] Annalist of St. Albans quoted by Creighton, *op. cit.*, I, 220 and 225, and Walsingham, *Ibid.*, 221.
[5] *Rot. Parl.*, III, 619 (1407); III, 638 (1410); IV, 143 (1421); III, 503 (1402); V, 238 (1453).
[6] *Paston Letters*, No. 260 (1454); IV, 180 (1465); V, 119 (1471); V, 137 (1472); VI, 148 (1493).
[7] Creighton, I, 282-3 and seq.

for example, the epidemic of 1407 was 'universal and in the homes of the peasantry' as well as those of other classes[1]; but later in the century pestilence was 'a disease of towns,'[2] and it was usual to flee from the towns to the country in order to avoid it.[3] According to Sir John Paston, no 'Borow town in Ingelonde' escaped 'the most unyversall dethe' of 1471.[4] Parliament was adjourned several times on account of pestilence in London,[5] and sometimes even the Justices postponed their business.[6] 'The sekenese,' writes Richard Cely to his son in May, 1479, 'ys sore yn London werefor meche pepyll of the sete ys yn to the contre for fere of the sekenese.'[7] Towards the end of the century a new disease, called the Sweating Sickness, made its appearance in England. Dr. Creighton is of the opinion that the foreign soldiers who helped Henry VII to win the throne in 1485 brought it from Normandy.[8] It chiefly attacked the upper classes, whereas the plague had fallen most heavily on the poorer people, the worst fed, the worst housed, and those most hardly pressed by poverty.[9] It is not possible to estimate accurately the ravages of the plague; it seems to have grown more severe during the latter part of Edward IV's reign; but the apparent increase of mortality may be due to the greater number of the records which exist for that period.[10] It often carried off two or three members of a household at the same time. Thomas Pole, of Staunton, we read, died of pestilence, and 'he and

[1] and [3] Creighton, I, 233. (The *Rolls of Parliament* speak of the pestilence of 1439 as universal, V, 31). [2] Creighton, I, 226. [4] *Paston Letters*, V, 110. [5] *Rolls of Parl.*, IV, 420 (1433); V, 67 (1444); V, 143 (1449); V, 618 (1467–8); VI, 99 (1474). [6] Campbell, *Materials for Hist. of the Reign of Henry VII*, II, 136 (1487); *Proceed. of the Privy Council*, IV, 282 (1434). [7] *Cely Papers*, p. 16. [8] Creighton, *op. cit.*, 269–270. [9] *Ibid.*, 268–9. [10] *Ibid.*, 233.

ij of his children were buryed in oon pytte.'[1] An entry in the Accounts of St. Mary-at-Hill, London, acknowledges payment for the burial of John Clark's three children and himself in 1487–8.[2] Other similar entries occur, but no comment is made upon any of them, and they are treated quite as a matter of course.

Sanitary condition of towns.

One great reason for the frequent recurrence of the plague was the insanitary condition of the towns, and especially the pollution of the water supply. The law of the land and ordinances of cities alike forbade any one to throw 'fimos, exitus, intestina bestiarum, nec alia sordida, in fossatis, ripariis, aquis, aut aliis locis infra civitates, burgos, seu villas '[3]; but the almost wearisome repetition of the ordinances by municipal authorities show how ineffectual they were.[4] Complaints of their neglect are also frequent.[5] The Fleet Ditch, which was only cleansed occasionally, must have been a special source of danger to London.[6] The author of the *Italian Relation* makes the remarkable statement that there was a penalty for destroying ravens, because they, it was said, kept the streets free from filth; and for the same reason kites were so tame that they would eat bread out of the hands of children.[7] It is no wonder that the air of cities was noisome and infected.[8] Nor were the personal habits of the

[1] *Early Chanc. Proceed.*, 22/191 (31–2 *H. VI*) in the county of Shropshire. [2] *Medieval Records of a London City Church*, 128. [3] *Rot. Parl.*, III, Appendix, p. 669, No. 4. [4] Ordinances concerning the cleansing of streets or ditches or the river (*Coventry Leet Book*, Part i, pp. 21, 23, 30, 31, 91, 100, 107, 118, 119, 130, 190, 208, 227, 231, 254). [5] Riley's *Memorials of London*, p. 616; *Early Chanc. Proceed.*, 4/176; and 4 *H. VII*, c 3.

[6] Strype's *Stow*, I, 25. [7] *Italian Relation*, 11. [8] Creighton, *op. cit.*, 282–3; D. Harris, *Life in an Old English Town*, 290–2; Strype's *Stow*, I, 308; and the *Rolls of Parl.* concerning London, already quoted.

English at this time very conducive to health, judging from the exceedingly elementary advice on the subject of cleanliness given to the children of the nobility in the 'Babees Book.'[1] Moreover, even when food was plentiful it was not always wholesome. Household Books show how small the consumption of fruit and vegetables was in comparison with that of meat.[2] Russell tells his readers to 'beware of saladis, grene metis, & of frutes rawe.'[3] In addition to this, they were obliged to live mainly on salted meat for part of the year, because, in the absence of root crops, they had not enough food for their cattle to keep them alive during the winter; and consequently a great slaughter of cattle took place at Martinmas.[4] Much of their fish was also cured.

Medical science in the fifteenth century.

Much danger to life and limb must also have been occasioned by lack of knowledge on the part of many who called themselves surgeons and doctors. A complaint laid before the Mayor of London declares that some barbers of the said city, who are inexperienced in the art of surgery, do oftentimes take under their care many sick and maimed persons . . . and by reason of their inexperience such persons are oftentimes maimed. Two masters were appointed to oversee the barbers, and a penalty of six shillings and eightpence was imposed for refusal to be amenable to their supervision.[5] The physicians also complained that 'many unconnyng

[1] *Manners and Meals*, 134–5 and lxii–iv; cf. Thorold Rogers, *Agric. and Prices*, IV, 105.

[2] *The Household Book of Ann, Duchess of Buckingham* (Add. MSS., 34, 213), which gives the expenditure day by day, shows this very clearly, and the lists of food in the *Stafford Household Book* (*Archæologia*, XXV, 319 and seq) give the same impression.

[3] *Manners and Meals*, 124. [4] *Cely Papers*, xii.

[5] Riley, *op. cit.*, 608–9.

an unapproved in the forsayd Science practiseth, and specialy in Fysyk, . . . to grete harm and slaughtre of many men.' They therefore prayed that no man or woman should be allowed to practise, 'bot he have long tyme y used the Scoles of Fisyk withynne som Universitee, & be graduated in the same '[1]; but this evil was not restrained by law until the reign of Henry VIII.[2] Results of the doctors' want of ability may perhaps be traced in numbers of deaths attributed to injuries apparently not bad enough to cause death. Men who broke or wounded their legs languished and died,[3] and we hear of persons dying through the bites of swine.[4] In one instance the coroner's jury swore that death was caused by the cutting of a 'wenne' from the patient's neck by the doctor.[5] Medical knowledge does not seem to have been very highly esteemed or rewarded. William Bradewardyn agreed to serve Henry V, during the war with France, with nine 'hommes de son mestier'; he was to be paid twelve pence a day, but they were only to have sixpence,[6] that is to say, no more than a private soldier or a carpenter. Doctors were often promised a certain sum of money on the condition of effecting a cure; but they sometimes had a good deal of trouble in obtaining it,[7] and if they did not succeed in their treatment of the case, enraged relatives of the patients might bring actions of

[1] *Rot. Parl.*, IV, 158. [2] 3 *H. VIII*, c. 11.

[3] *Coroners' Rolls*, 60/5, 61, ms. 4, 6, and 7.

[4] *Ibid.*, 61, m. 6; 145, m. 8. [5] *Ibid.*, 61, m. 8.

[6] *Accounts Excheq. Q. R. Army*, 48/3; a similar sum was paid to four surgeons who were to reside in the King's household, as assistants to William Stalworth (Syllabus to Rymer's *Fœdera*, II, 648); but one of Henry's VII's physicians, Benedict Frutze, received £40 a year (Campbell, *op. cit.*, I, 67), and that was apparently the usual salary of the King's chief doctors. See also *Proceed. of the Privy Council*, III, 282–3.

[7] *Early Chanc. Proceed.*, 12/248 and 42/108.

trespass against them.[1] References to the denization of the King's physicians, and the employment of alien doctors occur in Rymer's *Fœdera* and elsewhere,[2] so possibly the English were more backward than other nations in medical science.

[1] *Ibid.*, 187/89, and *Plumpton Corr.* p. 78.

[2] Syllabus to Rymer's *Fœdera*, II, 566, 570, 662, 671; *Patent Rolls*, 6 *H. IV*, Part ii, m. 20; *Cal. French Rolls*, 1426–7, m. 9.

CHAPTER VII

THE EFFECTS PRODUCED BY ECONOMIC CHANGES UPON EVERYDAY LIFE IN THE FIFTEENTH CENTURY

THE commercial spirit and the love of money, which seized upon all classes of society, were not without effects upon family life. We cannot help being struck by the extremely business-like view which was taken of marriage; it was an arrangement made in order to obtain material advantages for the contracting parties, but with comparatively little regard to mutual affection or compatibility of temper. Discussions in letters regarding the suitability of possible brides always contain an account of their property and prospects; sometimes a description of their dispositions and personal appearance is added,[1] but the amount of the dowry was evidently the chief point. Geffrey Ikelyngton, we read in the *Chancery Proceedings*, promised his cousin Isabell ten marks of money on her marriage, whereupon William Bewell married her.[2] Women were apparently as mercenary as men; one who thought of marrying George Cely made careful inquiries as to his income[3]; and Thomas Mull confided to William Stonor that a lady whom he had approached on the subject repulsed him by saying: 'Sir, I may haue ccc marcs in ioyntur and I to take þe lesse wher I may haue

Family life.

[1] *A.C.*, Vol. XLVI, Letter 62; *Cely Papers*, pp. 59 and 102–3.
[2] *Early Chanc. Proceed.*, 10/268.
[3] *Cely Papers*, 153.

þe more my ffrendes wolde þenke me not wyse.'[1] But human nature could not be entirely eradicated, and Thomas Mull in this case was very hurt and quite sentimental about the matter.[2] Margery Brews, too, was determined to marry John Paston the Youngest, even with half the 'livelode' he possessed, and gave her mother no peace till the affair was settled.[3] Men and women seem to have had (under these conditions) a little more chance of consulting their own inclinations than under the Feudal régime, which placed the wardship and marriage of heirs at the disposal of the superior lord, who made them a matter of sale and bargain[4]; so that 'only men of humble birth were at liberty to choose their own wives.'[5] There were still, however, many cases in which the decision was in the hands of the lord or his deputy[6]; but economic changes, so far as they tended to break down the Feudal System, tended also to make the growth of more rational ideas of marriage possible. There are many examples of marriage contracts[7] amongst the *Chancery Proceedings.* The terms were often set forth in an indenture,[8] and to make the bargain safer, those concerned sometimes bound themselves by an obligation to carry out the agreement.[9] Nevertheless there are several complaints of breaches of promise of marriage,[10] and many of the non-fulfilment of settlements.[11] The care taken by

[1] *A.C.*, Vol. XLVI, Letter 105.
[2] There is not the apparent want of feeling in *The Stonor Papers* which Dr. Gairdner noticed in the *Paston Letters.*
[3] *Paston Letters*, Introd., I, 300 and 302, and V, 267.
[4] *Paston Letters*, Introd., I, 325. [5] Gairdner, *Letters of Richard III and Henry VII*, Preface, II, xxvii; Feudal lords were entitled to the marriage of minors who held lands from them by military service. Pollock and Maitland, *Hist. of Eng. Law*, I, 319. [6] *Early Chanc. Proceed.*, 15/335, 18/183, 27/193. [7] *Ibid.*, 15/340, 16/314, 19/38, 29/74.
[8] *Ibid.*, 40/144, and *Plumpton Corr.*, lxx–lxxii.
[9] *Early Chanc. Proceed.*, 18/102. [10] *Ibid.*, 9/396, 27/406, 20/4.
[11] *Ibid.*, 16/334, 9/448, 16/343, 16/386, 28/52.

parents to provide dowries for their daughters[1] shows how difficult it was for women to marry if they had no property, and it was considered essential for them to marry. A little poem, published by Dr. Furnivall in *Manners and Meals*, called 'How the Good Wijf tauȝte hir Douȝtir,' impresses upon the mother the necessity of finding husbands for her daughters as soon as possible.[2] The petitions brought before both the King and the Chancellor against men who had forcibly carried off heiresses, in order to obtain possession of their property, show the wisdom of this advice and that women needed protectors in those lawless times.[3] It was considered a meritorious act to leave money to enable poor girls to marry. John atte Bergh ordered a 'mees and xiij acres of lande' to be sold and the proceeds to be distributed 'to pouer maydens and wedows in mariage and in diuerse other werkes of charite' for the 'wele of his soule.'[4]

Wright tells us that there was a separation of the sexes after marriage, and that husbands and wives sought amusement apart from each other. He bases his opinion on the pictures of domestic life given in the mysteries and morality plays, which portray women as excessively overbearing and quarrelsome.[5] The glimpses we have of the married life of real men and women in the letters of the Pastons, the Celys, and the Stonors do not confirm this impression. Margaret Paston shows great affection for her husband—in her anxiety about his health, her desire to have him with her[6] and to hear

[1] Sir W. Drury left 200 marks to be used to promote the marriages of his two daughters (*Early Chanc. Proceed.*, 27/153); Judge Paston left £200 to his daughter, ad Maritagium suum (*Paston Letters*, VI, 198). [2] *Manners and Meals*, p. 46. [3] *Rot. Parl.*, IV, 498, V, 15, 269 and seq.; *Early Chanc. Proceed.*, 5/41, 5/45; the offence was made felony (3 *H. VII*, c. 3). [4] *Early Chanc. Proceed.*, 18/62. [5] Wright, *Domestic Manners*, 420. [6] *Paston Letters*, II, 55–6.

from him,[1] and her constant readiness to serve him. She was most distressed when he was annoyed with her on one occasion: 'Be my trowth,' she says, 'it is not my will nother to do ne sey that shuld cawse yow for to be displeasid; and if I have do, I am sory thereof, and will amend itt. Wherefor I beseche yow to forgeve me. . . .'[2] She always treats him with great respect and addresses him as 'ryth reverent and worsepful husbon,'[3] or by some other equally polite title. He on his side, though not as a rule demonstrative, seems to have been fond of her.[4] The relations between Elizabeth Stonor and her husband were apparently very harmonious; she took the greatest interest in his affairs,[5] would not act without his concurrence concerning her daughter,[6] and when he is in an infected atmosphere and in danger of catching the 'poxes,' she was willing to put herself 'in jubardy' to come to him.[7] He, on reading her letter, longed to have her with him.[8] Amongst the unpublished *Cely Papers* there is a letter from George Cely's wife to him; it is very short, but is couched in the same tone of affection as those of Margaret Paston.[9] In none of the three sets of letters is there any mention of quarrels between husbands and wives. The wills of the period also show how much confidence was placed by husbands in their wives. John Rogerysson writes in a codicil, 'dere and trusty wyf . . . I pray ȝow, as my trust es hely in ȝow, ouer alle oþere creatures, þat this last will be fulfyllet.'[10] Walter Newent left all his goods to his wife, with the condition, 'she for to do me like as she wolde I dede for her in þe same cas.'[11] The 'Boke of Curtasye'

[1] *Ibid.*, II, 282. [2] *Ibid.*, II, 228. [3] *Ibid.*, 49 and 55. [4] *Ibid.*, IV, 188; III, 223–4. [5] *A.C.*, Vol. XLVI, Letter 116. [6] *Ibid.*, Letter 119. [7] *Ibid.*, Letter 115. [8] *Ibid.*, 120. [9] *Ibid.*, Vol. LIII, Letter 133; cf. Letter 146. [10] *Early Eng. Wills*, p. 41. [11] *Ibid.*, 83.

expresses the ideas of the age when it urges the wife 'To worschyp hyr husbonde bothe day and nyȝt

'To his byddyng be obediente.'[1]

Another poem, called 'How the Wise man tauȝht His Son,' tells the husband his duty to his wife, and exhorts him not to burden her too much or to displease her.[2] Husbands sometimes claimed a good deal of control over their wives. A very odd case is recorded, — Thomas Botiller states that Isabel Frensshe bought ale of his wife and resorted to his house for it, and when he asked her husband to pay for it, Simon Frensshe brought an action of trespass against him because 'he receyued bothe his wife and his godes in his house withoute his licence.'[3] In London a wife was not allowed to make a will, even though her husband consented; but the custom was different in other towns. In Lincoln her devise held good without his consent, and coverture did not prevent her making a will.[4] She also had some privileges, of which not the least was her right to a third,[5] or in some cases half[6] of her husband's property, as dower, after his death.

The relations of parents and children were by no means as satisfactory as those of husbands and wives. Children were brought up very strictly; if they rebel, says the 'Good Wife' to her daughter, 'But take a smert rodde & bete hem on a rowe.'[7] Parents, too, often looked upon their children as a source of income. Wyndham sold the marriage of his son to obtain money to bring about a marriage for himself.[8] John Paston was very angry with

[1] *Manners and Meals*, 307. [2] *Ibid.*, 50–1. [3] *Early Chanc. Proceed.*, 27/398. [4] Miss Bateson, *Borough Customs*, II, civ. [5] *Ibid.*, 121 n. [6] Miss Bateson, *op. cit.*, 125–6. [7] *Manners and Meals*, p. 46. [8] *Paston Letters*, II, 283.

his eldest son because he was no use to him. 'Every pore man,' he grumbles, 'that hath browt up his chylder to the age of xij yer waytyth than to be holp and profited be hes chylder, and every gentilman that hath discrecion waytith that his ken and servantis that levith be hym and at his coste shuld help hym forthward.'[1] Mothers, judging by the Pastons, were anxious to rid themselves of their daughters, who were sent away from home, and acted as servants or ladies-in-waiting to the persons in whose houses they lived. Sometimes their parents paid for them, but sometimes they were expected to help themselves.[2] Margaret Paston, writing to her son, asks him to find a place for his sister, and adds, 'I wull help to her fyndyng, for we be eyther of us werye of other.'[3] She was very displeased at the idea of having her daughter Anne home, and said, 'with me shall she but lese her tyme, and with ought she will be the better occupied she shall oftyn tymes meve me, and put me in gret inquietenesse.'[4] When Elizabeth Paston, the daughter of Agnes and Judge Paston, objected to marrying the husband chosen for her by her mother, she was 'betyn onys in the weke or twyes, . . . and hir hed broken in to or thre places.'[5]

The number of accidents which happened to children make us doubt if very great care was bestowed upon them. An infant was burnt in its cradle in the absence of the mother,[6] we learn from the *Coroners' Rolls ;* another child, aged two, fell into a pit full of water, and was drowned[7]; and another was accidentally shot by a man who was practising archery.[8] Three children were found

[1] *Ibid.*, IV, 157. [2] *Ibid.*, III, 123. [3] *Ibid.*, V, 16. [4] *Ibid.*, V, 93. [5] *Ibid.*, II, 110. [6] *Coroners' Rolls*, 60, m. 4 d., and similar cases, m. 5 and 61, ms. 10 and 11.

[7] *Coroners' Rolls*, 61, m. 9. [8] *Ibid.*, 61, 6.

drowned in the diocese of Canterbury, and the coroners imposed fines on their careless parents; but the Church disputed the sentence, and said it was a moral offence.[1] The perils to which wards were exposed at the hands of unscrupulous guardians have already been mentioned, and the *Chancery Proceedings* afford illustrations of the ill-treatment of both boys and girls.[2] Children of citizens were probably much better off in this respect than those of a higher class, for their guardians were obliged to give 'suffycyentt suerte afore the meyer and Aldermen of the cite,'[3] to treat them well during their minority, and in many towns a record was kept in a book of orphans. Children paid a great deal of deference to their parents, and addressed them very humbly. 'My ryght reuerent and wurshypfull fadyr I recomaund me vn to your good fadyrhod jn the most vmbylle wyse that I kan or may, mekely besechyng your good fadyrhod of your dayly blessyng,' writes William Stonor.[4] In spite of this reverential tone, in many cases there seems to have been little real affection between parents and children, and the *Chancery Proceedings* contain a number of petitions in which the parents complain not only of the seizure of their property,[5] but also of personal injuries at the hands of their children.[6] The motive of the children in most of these cases seems to have been to secure for themselves goods and chattels, or land.

One of the most interesting features in the social life of the fifteenth century is the growing desire for education evinced by the lower and middle

[1] *Hist. MSS. Comm.*, Ninth Report, Appendix, p. 117. [2] *Early Chanc. Proceed.*, 7/70, 19/152, 20/154, 28/271. [3] *Medieval Records of a London City Church*, p. 18; *Little Red Book of Bristol*, I, 181–5 (1422–47). [4] *A.C.*, Vol. XLVI, Letter 74. [5] *Early Chanc. Proceed.*, 11/539, 16/262, 33/7. [6] *Ibid.*, 6/185, 6/294, 10/313, 28/333.

classes, a feature which may reasonably be ascribed to the stimulating effects of industrial expansion, because it is found in the most marked degree amongst the classes, and in the places most influenced by the economic changes of the period. In the closing years of the fourteenth century the Commons prayed the King that no neif or villein of a bishop or other religious person might put his children to school.[1] But in the reign of Henry IV it was enacted that any man or woman might send his or her son or daughter to any school in the kingdom.[2] Occasionally it appears that masters undertook to provide their apprentices with a certain amount of education. Thomas Bodyn was apprenticed to Robert Churche, haberdasher, of London, for twelve years, on the agreement that Churche should find him to school for two years—for the first year and a half he was to 'lerne gramere,' 'and the residue of the seid two yere . . . to lerne to wryte.'[3] In a petition brought against William Trypp of Taunton, weaver, on behalf of two of his apprentices, it was stated that during their term of service with him they were to learn, amongst other things, the language of Brittany.[4] The wish for knowledge of this kind was directly due to the growth of foreign trade, and skill in languages seems to have been valued highly. When John Paston was recommending a clerk of the kitchen to Lord Hastings, he said, 'He is well spokyn in Inglyshe, metly well in Frenshe, and verry perfite in Flemyshe. He can wryght and reed.'[5] The estimation in which education was held by men who wished to improve their position

The value set upon education.

[1] *Rot. Parl.*, III, 294. [2] *Ibid.*, III, 602, and 7 *H. IV*, c. 17. [3] *Early Chanc. Proceed.*, 19/491. [4] *Ibid.*, 108/42. Another case in which the master agreed 'to find' an apprentice 'to scole' occurs in the *Early Chanc. Proceed.*, 47/52. [5] *Paston Letters*, V, 253.

is shown by the trouble they took to secure it for themselves and their sons. Judge Paston left careful instructions in his will to ensure that his sons Edmund, William, and Clement should be properly educated.[1] John Paston thought it of sufficient importance to send two of his sons to school in London,[2] and another to Eton.[3] John Paston himself seems to have gone to Cambridge, after he was married, for his wife writes to him 'abidyng at Petyrhous in Cambrigg[4]; and two other members of the Paston family also went to college.[5] Further proof of the value set upon education is seen in the number of bequests made for the maintenance of scholars and schools. Bartholomew Seman, 'goldbetere,' left a tenement and rents to the master and scholars of the House of St. Michael,[6] Cambridge, on condition that they should receive two poor scholars[7] into their house. Nicholas Sturgeon, priest, left twenty-four shillings to find his cousin William to scole for four years[8]; and there are many similar bequests.[9] Henry Frowyk, mercer, left money to the master of the Hospital of St. Thomas the Martyr de Acon, so that he might maintain and educate two boys as choristers.[10] An item in the Accounts of St. Mary-at-Hill mentions money 'spent vppon Bower at his scole,' and it is amongst the 'costes of ij children,' who were choir boys[11]; so possibly some churches paid partially, or wholly, for the education of the children who sang for them. Rich men sometimes sent poor children to school or college; Sir John Howard seems to have provided for more than one child in

[1] *Paston Letters*, App., Vol. VI, 192–3. [2] *Ibid.*, II, 330. [3] *Ibid.*, VI, 8 and 11. [4] *Ibid.*, II, 49. [5] *Ibid.*, V, 320, and VI, 157. [6] The House of St. Michael developed into Trinity College in later days (Sharpe, *Wills*, II, 459). [7] *Ibid.*, II, 459–60. [8] *Early Eng. Wills*, 133. [9] Sharpe, II, 525, 534, 599, 600. [10] *Ibid.*, II, 542. [11] *Medieval Records of a London City Church*, 148.

this way,[1] and among Sir William Stonor's correspondence is a letter signed by 'your scoler Edmunde.'[2]

Ancient schools.

A considerable number of schools were in existence before the fifteenth century; 'every large monastery, hospital, cathedral, and college had long had its room where choristers and novices were taught by the resident rector or master.'[3] The monastic schools, however, taught mainly those boys whom the monks hoped would join their communities,[4] and they did not do much to assist popular education.[5] Moreover, by this time the monks had ceased to take much interest in learning,[6] and the visitations of the monasteries show that they were neglecting their duty in this respect.[7] The cathedral schools were also very ancient; Mr. Leach mentions several that were of pre-Norman origin[8]; these schools formed an integral part of the foundation of collegiate churches of secular canons. There were generally two schools—a grammar school under the schoolmaster, and the song school under the music or song master.[9] The song schoolmaster taught singing, reading, and we may suppose writing. Grammar, Dr. Furnivall says, quoting Wright, usually means Latin.[10] Sometimes the two schools were joined.[11] In addition to these schools, Chantry priests sometimes devoted part of their time to teaching the children of the neighbourhood. John Stafford left his Chantry priest 33s. 4d. a year for instructing boys in singing and grammar, and ordered him to teach poor children gratuitously.[12]

[1] *Howard Household Book*, II, 214 and 468. [2] *A.C.*, Vol. XLVI, Letter 150. [3] Wylie, *Henry IV*, Vol. II, 485. [4] *Manners and Meals*, xliv, cf. Capes, *English Church*, 330. [5] Hobhouse, 249. [6] Gasquet, *Collect. Anglo-Premonstratensia*, xxxv. [7] Capes, 330. [8] Leach, *Early Yorkshire Schools*, vii. [9] *Ibid.*, *History of Warwick School*, 71. [10] *Manners and Meals*, xi, note. [11] *History of Warwick School*, 72. [12] Sharpe, *Wills*, II, 507.

Foundation of new schools.

The opportunities for education provided by these means were not sufficient to satisfy the growing desire for knowledge shown by the people in the latter part of the fourteenth century and in the fifteenth, and new schools were opened in various parts of the country; and whereas in earlier days education had been entirely in the hands of the clergy, now laymen began to do their part, both in founding schools and in teaching the children. Some of the gilds maintained free schools; for example, the Gild of St. Nicholas, Worcester,[1] the Gild of the Palmers in Ludlow,[2] and the Gild of the Kalenders in Bristol.[3] At Barnard's Castle, the Gild of the Holy Trinity paid a priest to keep a free grammar school and a song school for all the children of the town.[4] The municipal authorities did their best to encourage education. An entry in the *Coventry Leet Book* says that John Barton may come to the town, if he knows well how to teach children, and will keep a grammar school.[5] A few years later another 'skolemayster of Grammar' is mentioned.[6] The presence of these teachers in Coventry seems to have caused friction with the Prior, who also kept a school, and in 1439 the Corporation deputed the Mayor and six of his council to go and commune with him upon the matter, 'wyllyng hym to occupye a skole of Gramer, yffe he like to teche hys Brederon and Childerun off the aumbry, and that he wol-not gruche ne meve the contrari, but that euery mon off this Cite be at hys ffre chosse to sette hys chylde to skole to what techer off Gramer that he likyth, as reson askyth.'[7] In Ipswich a grammar school was founded

[1] *English Gilds*, edited by T. Smith, 203–5.
[2] *Ibid.*, 198.
[3] *Ibid.*, 288.
[4] Gasquet, *Medieval Parish*, 142.
[5] *Coventry Leet Book*, I, 101.
[6] *Ibid.*, 118.
[7] *Ibid.*, 190.

by the burgesses,[1] and in Plymouth by the Corporation.[2] Several schools were also endowed by rich traders, and others. Sir Edmund Shaa, goldsmith, of London, established a school at Stockport.[3] The master was to receive a salary of £10 a year, and to teach all who came to him freely.[4] Grantham Grammar School was re-founded by Henry Curteys, alderman and merchant of Grantham.[5] A school at Ewelme was endowed by the Duke of Suffolk in the reign of Henry VI, and this was, like Shaa's, a free school.[6] Davy Holbeche, a lawyer, steward of the town and lordship of Oswestry, founded a school in that place in the reign of Henry IV.[7] Lands and tenements were left by a grocer to provide a teacher for the poor children of Sevenoaks, with the express stipulation that he should not be in holy orders.[8] Not one of the three schoolmasters in St. Peter's School, York, were priests at this time. Mr. Leach thinks that it was probably the rule for the masters to be laymen in the largest grammar schools[9]; he cites as an instance a man named Harding,—a master in Beverley School from 1436 to 1456, who constantly served on the Corporation of the town.[10] At Bridgenorth, in 1503, an ordinance was passed that no priest should keep a school.[11]

It must not, however, be thought that the clergy did nothing to aid education ; schools at Acaster,[12] Rotherham,[13] and Wainfleet,[14] and colleges at Wye, near Ashford, Kent,[15] and Higham Ferrars,[16]

[1] Redstone in *Trans. Royal Hist. Soc.*, N.S. XVI, p. 166.
[2] Carlisle, *Endowed Grammar Schools*, I, 335. [3] Mrs. Green, *op. cit.*, II, 16. [4] Carlisle, *op cit.* I, 125. [5] Leach in *Victoria County Hist.*, *Lincolnshire*, II, 479. [6] Carlisle, II, 301. [7] *Ibid.*, 365. [8] Sharpe, *Wills*, II, 484. [9 and 10] Leach, *Early Yorks. Schools*, I, xxviii. [11] Mrs. Green, II, 18. [12 and 13] Leach, *Early Yorkshire Schools*, Vol. II, xxi. [14] *Ibid.* in *V.C.H.*, *Lincolnshire*, II, 484. [15] Carlisle, I, 633. [16] *Ibid.*, II, 209.

all owed their origin to eminent ecclesiastics. Nor did the Church tamely submit to the curtailment of its powers. In 1393–4 the Archbishop of Canterbury, the Bishop of London, the Dean of the free chapel of 'St. Martin le Grant,' and the Chancellor of the Church of St. Paul's complained to the King that whereas they had always had in the past the 'prescript, l'ordenance, disposicion, et examinacion' of the masters of grammar in the city of London, 'nientmains ore tard ascuns estrangers lour feynantz mestres de gramer, nient apris' suffisaument en mesme la facultee, sanz assent, scien, ou volunte des avant ditz Ercevesque, Evesque, Dean, et Chanceller . . . tiegnent escoles generales de Gramer en votre dite citee.' They went on to say that the three masters of the schools of St. Paul's, of St. Martin, and of the Arches had proceeded against the strange masters, in the Courts Christian, in defence of their own rights of teaching; but the strange masters had applied to the secular courts against the suit of the three masters; they therefore begged the King to grant them letters of Privy Seal ordering the Mayor and Aldermen of London not to interfere in the matter, which belonged to the jurisdiction of the Church.[1] A petition presented to the King by the Prince of Wales (7 *and* 8 *H. IV*) drew attention to the propagation of teaching against the temporal possessions of the clergy, in 'lieux secretes appellez escoles,' and prayed that no man or woman might 'exercize ascuns escoles d'ascun secte ou doctrine desore en avaunt encountre les suis ditz Foye Catholike, & Sacramentz de seinte Esglise.'[2] It was perhaps in consequence of the severe treatment of all teachers suspected of Lollardy that there was a dearth of schools in London in 1447,[3] and of school-

[1] *Rot. Parl.*, III, 324. [2] *Ibid.*, III, 584. [3] *Ibid.*, V, 137.

masters in the eastern counties[1]; but there may have been other causes at work, too, such as the suppression of the alien Priories near London,[2] an increase in the number of persons who came to the city to be educated,[3] and the lack of encouragement given to the study of grammar in the Universities.[1] In London the evil was remedied by the foundation of four schools by the four parsons who had petitioned the King on the subject,[4] and of five others, by the care of the Archbishop of Canterbury and the Bishop of London.[5] The persons who benefited most by the creation of new schools in the fifteenth century were undoubtedly the children of citizens and tradesmen.[6] We have already noticed that several of the grammar schools were free, and Dr. Furnivall mentions others of the same kind in his list of endowed schools in *Manners and Meals.*[7] As he very truly says, the progress of education was from below upwards.[8]

Education of the nobility.

The children of the nobility occasionally received tuition in monasteries, or in the abbot's house.[9] Warton tells us that Lydgate opened a school in his monastery for them.[10] Payment to the schoolmaster of the sons of Sir John Howard is recorded in one of his *Household Books*,[11] so possibly they had a private tutor. More often, however, boys of this class were trained in the houses of great nobles. The *Liber Niger* gives us some idea of what they learnt. It was the duty of the master of the henchmen 'to shew the schooles of urbanitie and nourture of Englond, to lerne them to ryde clenely and surely; to drawe

[1] Petition of W. Byngham, parson of St. John Zachary, London, quoted in Willis, *Architectural History of Cambridge*, Introd., lvi. [2] Strype, *Stow*, I, 128. [3] *Rot. Parl.*, V, 137. [4] and [5] Strype's *Stow*, I, 182. [6] *Manners and Meals*, lii. [7] *Ibid.*, liii. [8] *Ibid.*, lxii. [9] *Ibid.*, xviii. [10] Warton, *Hist. of Eng. Poetry*, II, 270 (ed. 1840). [11] *Howard Household Book*, I, 269.

them also to justes; to lerne them were theyre harneys; to have all curtesy in wordes, deeds, and degrees, dilygently to kepe them in rules of goynges and sittinges, after they be of honour. Moreover, to teche them sondry languages, and othyr lerninges vertuous, to harping, to pype, sing, daunce;'[1] and there was also a 'Maistyr of Gramer,' who taught them 'quem necessarium est in poetica atque in regulis positionis gramatice.'[2] It is evident that courtly manners and knightly accomplishments were considered the most important part of their education, and it was perhaps in consequence of the care bestowed upon this part of their training that the author of the *Italian Relation* was so impressed with the courtesy of Englishmen.[3]

Education of women.

We have very little information respecting the education of girls; in the Act which gave every man the right to send his children to school, girls are mentioned as well as boys,[4] but we do not know how far they profited by the permission. Women were included in the prohibition issued against the maintenance of schools by Lollards,[5] and Leach draws attention to an entry in the records of the Corpus Christi Gild, Boston,[6] for the year 1404, which speaks of 'Matilda Mareflete, schoolmistress in Boston, (magistra scolarum),'[7] and if women could be teachers they must themselves have had some education. This instance is, however, apparently the only case which has up to now been discovered of a woman teacher in an elementary school; Mr. Leach is of the opinion that it could not have been the Boston grammar school, because the Chancellor, in whose hands the

[1] *Liber Niger*, 45 [2] *Ibid.*, 51. [3] *Italian Relation*, 22. [4] *Rot. Parl.*, III, 602. [5] *Ibid.*, 584. [6] In the Gild Certificates in the Public Record Office. [7] *Victoria County Hist.*, *Lincolnshire*, II, 451.

appointment lay, would not have licensed a woman.[1] Nuns often taught the daughters of the gentry; the little nunnery of Swyn, in Yorkshire, Thorold Rogers tells us, received several girls as boarders.[2] Amongst the *Chancery Proceedings* is a petition which states that Laurens Knyght, gentleman, arranged that his two daughters, aged seven and ten respectively, should live with the Prioress of Cornworthy, Devon, and that she should teach them, and should receive weekly for their meat and drink twenty pence.[3] There were different standards of education for men and women. Women were not expected to understand Latin, but letters to nuns were written in French, and the nuns of Sempringham were forbidden to talk Latin, while it was enjoined upon boys at school and young men at Oxford and Cambridge.[4] The general education of women was not entirely neglected. Bryan Roucliffe, writing to Sir William Plumpton about his little granddaughter, says, 'Your daughter and myn . . . speaketh prattely and french and hath near hand learned her sawter.'[5] As she was only four years old she was certainly not backward for her age. But the wills of the period do not give the impression that parents thought it necessary to make special provision for the education of their daughters; probably knowledge of household management and of domestic work was considered more suited to them than any other kind of learning.

The development of higher education in the fifteenth century, as far as we can see, was not assisted by the economic changes of the period;

[1] *Victoria County Hist.*, *Lincolnshire*, II, 451.
[2] *Work and Wages*, 166. [3] *Early Chanc. Proceed.*, 44/227.
[4] Leach, *Victoria County Hist.*, *Lincolnshire*, II, 471n.
[5] *Plumpton Corr.*, 8.

on the contrary, it may even have suffered through them. There are numerous complaints of the decay of the Universities; Henry VI, in a letter to the Provincial Synod of Canterbury, laments 'siquidem in ipsis diminutus jam est studentium numerus; nemirum cum sit merces seu fructus studii nullus aut modicus'[1]; and the year this letter was written (1438) the number of students was a thousand.[2] The Universities continually bewailed their poverty, which may have been partly due to the depreciation in the value of their lands through the diminution of the profits of agriculture,[3] but which was certainly largely the result of the low estimation in which scholarship was held at this time. University education was not popular, and very few were ready to provide adequate means for it[4]; and those who did endow new colleges at Oxford and Cambridge were not merchants and traders, but members of the Royal Family and ecclesiastics.[5] Humphrey Duke of Gloucester, was one of Oxford's most generous patrons; his magnificent gift of books supplied one of the University's greatest needs,[6] and did much to restore it to its old position.[7] His interest in the New Learning was not, however, shared by his countrymen,[8] and England lagged behind other nations in its adoption of the new doctrines.[9] He did, however, inspire some of his immediate successors to carry on his work[10]; and a

Higher education.

[1] Bekynton, *Letters*, No. xxxix. [2] Wylie, *Henry IV*, Vol. III, 414; and *Humphrey Duke of Gloucester*, by K. H. Vickers, 402. [3] Traill, *Social England*, II, 235. [4] Vickers, *Humphrey Duke of Gloucester*, 402. [5] Henry VI; Margaret of Anjou; Margaret, the mother of Henry VII; R. Flemmyng, Bishop of Lincoln; Chichele, Archbishop of Canterbury; Waynflete, Bishop of Winchester; and Alcock, Bishop of Ely, were among the benefactors of Oxford and Cambridge (Willis, *Architectural Hist. of Cambridge*, Vol. I, Introd., Cronological Summary, lxxxiv, etc). [6] Vickers, 402. [7] *Ibid.*, 406 and seq. [8] *Ibid.*, 344. [9] *Ibid.*, 419. [10] *Ibid.*, 423 and 421.

few scholars devoted themselves to the study of Greek learning, in spite of the general apathy. Sellyng, a monk of Christ Church, Canterbury, visited Italy, and on his return to England established a school of Greek at Canterbury.[1] Grocyn, a fellow of New College, lectured publicly on the Greek language at Oxford, some time between 1496 and 1500.[2] His lectures 'mark the opening of a new period in our history,'[3] and bore splendid fruit in the sixteenth century; but it cannot be said that any general enthusiasm for higher education was manifested in England during the fifteenth century, or that much advantage was taken of the opportunities for studying classics provided by foreign Universities. We read in the *Chancery Proceedings* that Thomas, son of John Herford, was sent to school at Pisa[4]; but it seems to have been unusual to send children abroad for education.

Evidences of the spread of education.

But although the English were not at this time 'addicted to . . . the study of letters,'[5] they were, we believe, keenly alive to the advantages to be derived from the spread of elementary education, and we have in the records of the period evidence of the results of the growing desire for knowledge. The *Paston Letters* show that not only men and women of good position, but their dependents and servants also, persons like Richard Calle, who sold 'kandyll and mustard in Framlyngham,'[6] and Sir John Fastolf's servant Payne, were able to read and write. The Cely and Stonor Papers give a similar impression. The Celys and Sir William Stonor[7] were merchants of the Staple, and their business entailed a consider-

[1] Gasquet, *Old English Bible*, 309-10. [2] *Ibid.*, 310 and seq. [3] Green, *Short Hist. of the English People*, 298. [4] *Early Chanc. Proceed.*, 226/47, date 1493-1500. [5] *Italian Relation*, p. 22. [6] *Paston Letters*, V, 21. [7] *A.C.*, Vol. XLVI, No. 175.

able amount of correspondence, because much of it was carried on in Calais; so much indeed that, in the case of the Celys, the junior member of the firm lived there. Numerous communications passed between him and the other partners at home, and thus foreign trade was a direct incentive to the diffusion of education. The handwriting is sometimes bad and illegible,[1] and the spelling very variable; for example, a simple word may be spelt in three or four different ways in the same letter[2]; but none of the writers seem to have any difficulty in making their meaning clear, and they appear to express themselves easily. The *Household Book of Anne Duchess of Buckingham*[3] is written in a small, legible hand, and though a few pages are untidy, on the whole it is well kept. It is in Latin, but English words are used occasionally, and we have expressions such as 'pro haling & draghing iiij dol. vini'[4] and 'kynderkyn de bere duble & ale.'[5] There are also some very quaint examples of the mixture of languages in some of the churchwardens' accounts; for example, 'Item, pro le pascal tapyr' and 'Item, uno peynter pro peyntyng de la Rodelofte.'[6] The scribes' knowledge of Latin was probably rather superficial. The accounts of bailiffs afford proof, as Thorold Rogers has pointed out, that they were not wholly illiterate, and he also refers to the bills written by artisans for New College, Oxford. They were not, he says, the work of adept penmen, but show that artisans knew how to write out an account.[7] The Account Book of Robert Brigandyn, clerk of the King's ships (10–13

[1] For example, that of Richard Cely the Elder, Vol. LIII, No. 7, and No. 97 in Vol. XLVI. [2] Chandler said he noted seventeen modes of writing Waynflete's name (*Life of William Waynflete*, p. 13). [3] Add. MSS., 34, 213. [4] *Ibid.*, f. 21. [5] *Ibid.*, f. 22 d. [6] Hobhouse, *Tintinhull Accounts*, 188. [7] Thorold Rogers, *Work and Wages*, 165.

H. VII) is a beautiful specimen of penmanship.[1] Yet the *Churchwardens' Accounts* do not seem to have been written by themselves, but by professional scribes, as payment for making them up is often mentioned.[2]

Amongst the *Chancery Proceedings* there is a petition from the warden of Stansfeld Church against Richard Brasyer of Norwich, which states that Richard purposely omitted a clause in the indenture made between them, and that he being 'not lettered nor vnderstondyng,' was deceived, and thought it was there when it was missing.[3] Several other petitioners bring forward the same plea that they have been cheated because they were 'nothynge letteryd' . . . 'nor vnderstode not what was wretyn.' In some instances the occupations of the petitioners are stated, and they included a fuller and a weaver,[4] a dyer,[5] a glover,[6] a Dutch beer-brewer,[7] and a knight.[8] When inquiries were made touching Sir John Fastolf's will, in May and June, 1466, twenty witnesses were examined, and of these eleven were described as 'illiterate,' and they consisted of five husbandmen, one gentleman, one smith, one cook, one roper, one tailor, and one mariner. The term 'literatus' was applied to seven persons; that is to say, two husbandmen, two merchants, a tailor, a mariner, and one other whose occupation was not specified.[9] The two remaining witnesses were Stephen Scrope, who could write, as we know, and a man who had been a schoolmaster. It is obvious from these examples that a knowledge of reading

[1] *Aug. Office, Misc. Bks.*, 316. [2] *Medieval Records of a London City Church*, 168 and 204. Hobhouse, *Tintinhull Accounts*, 176 and 177, and 186. *Yatton Accounts*, 84. [3] *Early Chanc. Proceed.*, 24/138. [4] *Ibid.*, 31/146. [5] *Ibid.*, 44/265. [6] *Ibid.*, 50/413. [7] *Ibid.*, 59/44. [8] *Ibid.*, 15/143. Other cases in which the occupation is not given, 25/158, 59/50, 15/229, 16/277. [9] *Paston Letters*, IV, 237-44.

and writing was not universal, but that it was fairly widespread.

The economic changes of the period affected even the sports and amusements of the people. There are continual complaints that servants and labourers will not exercise themselves in the use of bows and arrows, as commanded by statute, but play 'coites, dices, gettre de peer, kayles & autres tielx jeues importunes.'[1] These games were stigmatized as unlawful, and, with the addition of a few others, were forbidden under pain of imprisonment.[2] As an excuse it was urged the high price of bows caused 'yomen to play unlawful games,'[3] and it was therefore enacted that aliens should bring four bowstaves into the country with every ton of merchandise they imported.[4] A few years later they were ordered to bring ten with every butt of wine[5]; but these measures were designed as much to injure the Venetians, England's most formidable trade rival, as to revive archery, and they did not succeed in the latter aim. Guns were beginning to take the place of bows and arrows as weapons, and archery was no longer the favourite national sport.

Amusements.

Great delight was still taken in hunting and hawking, and in some parts of the country considerable enclosures were made for the chase.[6] The right to take part in these sports had been made by Parliament dependent upon the possession of lands and tenements to the value of 40s. a year[7] in the case of a layman, and an income of £10 in the case of a priest. In the fifteenth century many merchants

[1] *Rot. Parl.*, III, 643, and 11 *H. IV*, c. 4. [2] 17 *Ed. IV*, c. 3, and *Rot. Parl.*, VI, 188. [3] *Ibid.*, VI, 156. [4] 12 *Ed. IV*, c. 2. [5] 1 *Ric. III*, c. 11. [6] I. S. Leadam, *Domesday of Inclosures*, II, 389. E. S. Gay, in *T. R. Hist. Soc.*, N.S., VII, 219. Campbell, *op. cit.*, II, 34 and 379. [7] 13 *Ric. II*, St. I, c. 13, and *Rot. Parl.*, II, 282.

and traders attained the requisite qualifications and took advantage of them. The Celys were especially fond of hawking, and there are many allusions to it in their letters[1]; and Richard the Younger on one occasion took his 'fawkener' with him when he went up to buy wool in the Cotswolds.[2] He and his father nearly involved themselves in serious trouble over the 'scleyng of an hartte,'[3] and old Richard decided to keep no more greyhounds in consequence.[4]

Card-playing became very popular about the middle of the fifteenth century, and in 1463 the importation of playing-cards was forbidden on the petition of the London card-makers.[5] The commercial spirit of the age entered even into games, and men of all classes played dice and cards for money, and this practice not unfrequently degenerated into gambling. A servant of the Earl of Warwick was playing cards, and 'a straunge man fill in to play' and lost 'a bowte the somme of xls.'[6] Robert Cely, the black sheep of the family, received thirty shillings 'to pay hys ostes' at Calais, but he 'playd hyt at dys every quartere.'[7] Women as well as men indulged in card-playing. Sir John Howard, we read, 'lent my lady Scalez to pley at cardez 8s. 4d.'[8] Even the pilgrims going to the Holy Land played cards and dice on board ship.[9] As a consequence of the evils which ensued from these games, it was ordered that 'noo Lorde, nor other person of lower estate, suffre any Dicyng or pleiyng at Cardes within his hous, . . . oute of the xii dayes of Christmasse.'[10] The Duke of Clarence

[1] *Cely Papers*, 79 and 81, and *A.C.*, Vol. LIII, No. 155.
[2] *Cely Papers*, 80. [3] *Ibid.*, 73 and 78. [4] *Ibid.*, 79.
[5] Strutt, *Sports and Pastimes*, p. 426. [6] *Early Chanc. Proceed.*, 31/507. [7] *Cely Papers*, p. 12. [8] *Howard Household Book*, I, 481.
[9] Wylie, *op. cit.*, III, 175.
[10] *Rot. Parl.*, V, 488, and 11 *H. VII*, St. II, c. 3.

threatened to dismiss any of his court who played 'any manner of game at the dice, cardes, or any other hassard for money '[1]; so it is clear that cards and dice were not the only gambling games. Mr. Martin has drawn attention to an instance of horse-racing in the *Chancery Proceedings*, upon the result of which a kind of wager was laid.[2] Bets were made on all kinds of matters, from the possible size of a hailstone[3] to the chances of succession to a bishopric.[4]

Mrs. Green thinks that the gaiety of the towns was sobered by the pressure of business and by the increase of the class of depressed workers, and that the old games and pageants lost their lustre and faded out of existence before the coming in of new forms of poverty and bondage, save where a mockery of life was given to them by the compulsion of the town authorities.[5] It is undoubtedly true that the Corpus Christi Play was in danger of disappearing in Canterbury at the end of the century; because the crafts which had maintained it were so reduced in number, and so poor. Consequently the Burgmote ordered that every craft which could not afford to do its part by itself should be incorporated with some other craft.[6] There was also a good deal of discord in Coventry concerning the performance of pageants. The Smiths asked to be relieved from the burden of contributing to the 'Cotelers pachand,'[7] and the 'cardemakers, sadelers, masons and peyntors,' which had been as 'oone fellauship in beryng Costys . . . to ther pagent,' wished 'to departe and to breke þer felauship.'[8] These troubles

[1] *Ordinances of the Royal Household*, p. 91. [2] *Early Chanc. Proceed.*, 67/49, quoted in *Archælogia*, Vol. IX, Second Series, p. 11. [3] *Early Chanc. Proceed.*, 66/282. [4] *Ibid.*, 202/13. [5] Mrs. Green, *op. cit.*, I, 152. [6] *Ibid.*, 151, and Accounts of St. Dunstan's, Canterbury, in *Archælogia Cantiana*, Vol. XVII, 147. [7] *Coventry Leet Book*, 115–16. [8] *Ibid.*, 205.

happened in the first half of the century, when the affairs of the city were in a flourishing condition and when it could afford to keep four minstrels of its own,[1] and to give the King's minstrels twenty shillings at the time; so it is obvious that poverty was not the cause of the evils, but that they were probably mainly due to bad feeling between the crafts. 'Throughout the fourteenth, fifteenth and sixteenth centuries, we have continuous evidence of the popularity and frequent production of Miracle Plays in nearly every part of England.'[2] The list of the performances of pageants given by Miss Toulmin Smith in her *Yorks Plays* also shows that they were very much appreciated.[3] Household Books mention payments to minstrels and players from different towns, as well as to those in the employment of great nobles; for example, Lord Howard gave 'to the Plaiers of Esterforde' 3s. 4d.[4]; and Metyngham College paid 12d. to three 'lusoribus & trepidatoribus de Becclys.'[5] Churchwardens' accounts allude to all kinds of amusements: Christmas plays,[6] the mock courts of the Play Kings[7] and King's revels,[8] hocking,[9] Robin Hood exhibitions[10] at the village butts, and Church-ales.[11] All these amusements were used as means of obtaining money to provide for the expenses of the parish church, but their frequency proves that the people still cared for games and pageants and that the spirit of gaiety had not died out in England.

[1] *Ibid.*, pp. 59 and 121. [2] A. W. Pollard, *Eng. Miracle Plays*, xxii–iii. [3] *York Plays*, edited by Miss L. T. Smith, pp. lxiv–vii, and xxxii–iii. [4] *Howard Household Book*, II, p. 148; other references to similar payments, 104, 146, 336, 519. [5] Add. MSS. 33, 987, f. 82 d. [6] Hobhouse, 184. [7] *Ibid.*, xiv, and 183. [8] *Ibid.*, 3, 5, 7. [9] *Ibid.*, xx. [10] *Ibid.*, contributions from this source, p. 4, 10, 11, 12, 14, etc. [11] *Ibid.*, 89, 177, 181, etc., and Accounts of Bishop Stortford, Herts, quoted by Toulmin Smith in *The Parish*, pp. 502–3, and Accounts of St. Mary's, Elham, in *Archælogia Cantiana*, Vol. X, p. 66.

CHAPTER VIII

THE EFFECTS PRODUCED BY THE ECONOMIC CHANGES OF THE FIFTEENTH CENTURY UPON THE DEVELOPMENT OF NATIONAL CHARACTER

ECONOMIC changes exercised a considerable influence upon the development of national character and intellectual life in England. As we have already seen, a greater value was set upon education and more opportunities were provided for it, than in earlier days, but the middle and lower classes profited by them rather than the upper. The intellectual development of the age was, therefore, to a great extent the intellectual development of these classes, and their characteristics are impressed upon it. They wished to be successful in commerce and to make money, and they did not care for books which would not help them to attain these objects. This is perhaps one reason why the literature of the period did not reach a high standard, and why the Revival of Learning aroused so little enthusiasm in England that only a few exceptional men took an interest in it.

Intellectual development.

The spread of education increased the number of those who could read, and thereby created a larger demand for books. The value set upon them was often very great.[1] Books were sometimes pledged as security for debts,[2] and were very often left as legacies by will.[3] The Bishops

[1] For examples see *Early Chanc. Proceed.*, 47/18, 48/511, 51/253, 111/84. [2] *Ibid.*, 217/11, and 231/63. [3] *Ibid.*, 55/127, and *Early Eng. Wills*, pp. 49–51.

of Lincoln and Salisbury prized some books, left to them by the late Abbot of Westminster, so highly that they laid petitions concerning them before the Privy Council.[1] A good deal of money was spent on the embellishment of books. Edward IV paid 'for bynding, gilding and dressing of a booke called Titus Livius 20s.'[2] For the 'coveryng & garnysshing of six books' the King bought six yards of 'cremysy figured velvet,' 'a corse of silk, a naille of blue silk weying' nearly two ounces, laces, tassels, 'botons of blue silk and gold,' 'claspes of coper and gilt,' and other articles.[3]

In early days the copying of manuscripts was mainly the work of the monks, but by the fifteenth century they had ceased to supply the market, and professional scribes were employed,[4] like William Ebesham, who transcribed various books for Sir John Paston. He was paid 'ijd a leaff'[5]; but sometimes writers charged by the letter, from a penny to fourpence a hundred, according to the quality of the work.[6] It is not surprising that books were scarce when every word had to be copied by hand, and we find that even colleges had so few that in the statutes of St. Mary's College, Oxford,[7] it was laid down as a rule that no scholar should occupy a book in the library above an hour, or two at the most, so that others should be hindered from the use of the same.[8] Henry V showed considerable interest in literature, but even he was forced sometimes to borrow books.[9] The number

[1] *Proceed of the Privy Council*, V, 140-1. [2] N. H. Nicolas, *Wardrobe Accounts of Edward IV*, p. 125.

[3] Nicolas, *op. cit.*, p. 152. [4 and 6] *Camb. Hist. of English Literature*, II, 307. [5] *Paston Letters*, V, 3. [7] St. Mary's College was founded as a seminary to Oseney Abbey in 1446 (Warton, *Hist. of Eng. Poetry*, edition of 1840, p. lxxxix). [8] *Ibid.* [9] Syllabus to Rymer's *Fœdera*, II, 640.

which could be produced by scribes was wholly inadequate when reading was no longer confined to scholars, but all sorts and conditions of men wished for books, and it was, Caxton tells us, on account of the labour of writing and the numbers of books wanted that printing was introduced into England.[1] Before the end of the century printing-presses were set up in London,[2] Westminster,[3] Oxford,[4] and St. Albans[5]; but they could not print enough books to satisfy the needs of the public, and, in an age of rigid protection, books were imported duty free.[6]

The special characteristic of the English press was that it produced books in the vernacular.[7] 'Caxton left the glory of restoring the classical writers of antiquity . . . to the learned printers of Italy,'[8] and gave the people the classics of their own land,[9] in their own tongue. It is worthy of note that Pecock, the most enlightened man of his age, wrote his greatest work, the *Repressor*, in English, and that he compiled a smaller and simpler edition of *The Donet*, called *The Poor Men's Mirror*, in the hope that even the poor would purchase so cheap a book.[10] Fortescue generally wrote in Latin, but his last treatise on his favourite subject, the *Monarchia*, or the Difference between an Absolute and a Limited Monarchy, was in English; and as he wrote this book to please Edward IV, it has been suggested that the use of the vulgar tongue was due to that King's perception of the importance of influencing the opinions of the common people.[11] Moreover, whereas most of the political songs of the

[1] Quoted in *William Caxton*, by Gordon Duff, p. 21. [2] *Ibid.*, 47. [3] G. Duff, *Printers, Stationers and Bookbinders of London and Westminster*, 45. [4] and [5] G. Duff, *Early Printed Books*, chap. ix. [6] 1 *Ric. III.*, c. 9. [7] G. Duff, *William Caxton*, 13, and *Camb. Hist. of Eng. Literature*, II, 311. [8] G. Duff, *William Caxton*, p. 14, quoting Disraeli. [9] *Ibid.* [10] *Camb. Hist. of Eng. Literature*, II, 294. [11] *Ibid.*, II, 297.

fourteenth century were in Latin, the majority were in English in the fifteenth.[1] By the end of the century, too, the Chroniclers had begun to write in English[2]; and this use of the national language was the result of the intellectual development of the nation. Reading was no longer confined to the learned, who understood Latin, and both authors and printers found it worth while to produce books for the people. The result of the spread of education may also be seen in the multiplication of school-books.[3]

The desire of the middle classes to fit themselves to occupy the position in society which their wealth had gained for them shows itself in the great demand for books on manners and etiquette. Caxton brought out a *Book of Good Manners* at the request of a mercer, who had been helped by reading it,[4] and it became so popular that it was reprinted four times before the close of the century.[5] Wynkyn de Worde, who studied public taste carefully, issued many books of this kind.[6] The *Boke of Curtasye*, published by the Early English Text Society in *Manners and Meals*, enables us to see the nature of the instruction that was required. We gather that the readers had very little idea of how they ought to behave, but that they were exceedingly anxious to learn, and that they felt that every one, 'gentylmon, ȝomon, or knaue,' needed 'nurture for to haue.'[7]

Legal works were produced in considerable numbers, especially by Lettou and Machlinia[8]; and

[1] This may be seen by comparing the two volumes of Wright's *Political Songs*, the first dealing with the fourteenth century and the second with the fifteenth. [2] For example, Capgrave and the author of the *English Chronicle*. [3] Especially by the St. Alban's Press (G. Duff, *Early Printed Books*, p. 158). [4] Morley, *Eng. Writers*, VI, p. 331. [5] *Camb. Hist. of Eng. Literature*, II, 315. [6] G. Duff, *Early Printed Books*, p. 142. [7] *Manners and Meals*, 299.

[8] G. Duff, *Printers, Stationers and Bookbinders of London and Westminster*, p. 36 (cf. T. Roger, *Agriculture and Prices*, IV, 20).

this is not surprising when we remember the extraordinary amount of litigation which went on, and how necessary it was for every man who possessed property to have some knowledge of law, if he wished to keep it safely. The discontent caused by the inequalities in wealth, which were beginning to be so marked, found vent in the Robin Hood ballads, a series of poems which cannot be accurately dated, but which certainly reflect the spirit of the fifteenth century in many ways, and which were very much appreciated at this time. Moralities and Miracle Plays were also very popular, and they performed the important function of helping to render the growth of the drama possible. The humour of the fifteenth century, though rough and coarse, was vigorous, and was therefore not without effect upon the comedy of the next generation. Thus it will be acknowledged that economic changes had some share in determining the lines upon which the intellectual development of the nation should progress, and in deciding what kind of literature should be produced. It was perhaps for this reason that the literature of the period was not of a very exalted type, but was homely and commonplace.

Artistic development.

The artistic development of the nation also owed some of its most characteristic features to the tendencies of the age. The attention devoted in this century and the latter part of the fourteenth to the building and rebuilding of churches,[1] market crosses,[2] and municipal buildings was the result of the growing wealth of the middle classes. In some cases churches, which had remained unfinished since the visitation of the

[1] E. S. Prior, *A Hist. of Gothic Art in England*, p. 427, and F. Bond, *Gothic Architecture in England*, 133.
[2] Turner and Parker, Part ii, Vol. III, 279, 327.

Black Death, were completed, and we see in them Decorated and Perpendicular architecture side by side,—a striking memorial in stone of the history of the period. Judging from the lists given by Rickman[1] and Mr. Francis Bond,[2] the counties of York, Norfolk, Suffolk, Gloucester, Somerset, and Kent were most active in building. Lincoln, Warwick, Dorset, Northampton, Nottingham, Cambridge, and Worcester rank next to them. Thus it will be seen that those districts which accomplished most in this respect were, for the most part, those connected in some way with the woollen industry, either producing wool like Gloucestershire, or making cloth like Norfolk and Suffolk and Yorkshire. One or two details of the architectural history of the counties are of interest. The largest amount of building took place in Yorkshire, but that, perhaps, may be accounted for by the largeness of its area. It went on all through the century and was of all kinds : additions to York[3] and Beverley[4] Minsters, to Bridlington Priory,[5] and the erection and enlargement of parish churches[6] and of a Guildhall[7] at York. In Suffolk attention was mainly devoted to building parish churches[8]; in Worcester to enlarging monasteries.[9] Amongst towns Bristol[10] deserves special commendation ; but Londoners were not behindhand, and their achievements included lengthening the nave of Westminster Abbey[11] and the rebuilding of the Guild-

[1] Rickman, *Styles of Architecture in England*, pp. 295–313.
[2] F. Bond, *Gothic Architecture in England*, pp. 638–56.
[3] Rickman, *op. cit.*, 308. [4] Bond, *op. cit.*, 638. [5] *Ibid.*, 639. [6] *Ibid.* Hedon and Howden churches, Rickman, 295. [7] Turner and Parker, *op. cit.*, III, 304 and 334. [8] Churches at Blythburgh, Long Melford, Southwold, Walberswick. Bond, 639, 648, 653–4. Ipswich and Bury St. Edmunds, Rickman, 297 and 299. [9] Malvern and Little Malvern Priories, Bond, 649 and 648, south aisle of Abbey Church at Pershore, Rickman, 301. [10] Bond, 639. [11] *Ibid.*, 655.

hall, which 'of an olde and lytell cotage' they made 'into a fayre and goodly house.'[1]

Occasionally these churches were built by rich individuals, as for example the nave of Northleach Church, in Gloucestershire, which was the work of John Fortey, a wool merchant[2]; but as a rule they owed their existence to the united efforts of all the parishioners. The 'Receipts and Expenses in the Building of Bodmin Church' illustrate the means taken to raise the money, and prove how willing every one was to do his part; the total amount collected was £268 17s. 9½d.,[3] no small sum for a little place like Bodmin, and there were also gifts of labour, windows, and trees. The gilds gave in money £86 11s. 5d., and £24 13s., and the latter sum was the outcome of a collection of pennies and half-pennies from the members, and they also gave wax worth £4 13s. 4d.[4]; £50 8s. were provided by voluntary gifts, in which four hundred and sixty persons joined, and amongst them were fourteen 'servi' and two 'famulæ.' Only eight people gave more than a pound; the largest contribution was £6 13s. 4d., and the smallest 1d.,[5] and so it is evident that even the very poor did something to help on the work. Churches built thus with the people's money and labour seem to reflect the spirit of their builders. The great substantial churches of Norfolk, with their solid square towers, are typical of the sturdy matter-of-fact craftsmen who gave them being, as well as of their former populous and wealthy parishes; and the grander examples of architecture—such as King's College, Cambridge, and St. George's Chapel,

[1] *Chronicles of Fabyan*, 576. [2] Rickman, *op. cit.*, 306. Cley Church, Norfolk, is one of a group of churches built by a wealthy wool-exporting community. [3] *Camden Miscellany*, Vol. VII, pp. iii–iv. [4] *Camden Misc.*, Vol. VII, p. vi. [5] *Ibid.*, 42–9.

Windsor—embody the love of magnificence and of elaborate decoration, which was characteristic of the age. They have a florid beauty of their own, but in their repetition of the same form of ornament and their continual use of straight lines, they betray the same lack of imagination and of artistic feeling which is noticeable in much of the literary work of this period.

Churchwardens' accounts and other documents show that a great deal of money was spent on accessories, especially rood-lofts, or painted screens, altars and vestments. At Yatton, £3 10s. 4d. was paid for 'ymages to the rodeloffte yn number lxix'[1]; and the cost of painting, carving, and setting up the rood-screen in St. Mary-at-Hill was £7 2s. 1d.[2] The monastery of 'Our Lady of Syon' engaged a carver to make an 'alter table' and said it was to be 'of ten Storys of our lady,' and to be 'right a grete and costely wark,' and he was to receive for it £60 and meat, drink, fuel, and other things necessary for all that worked with him.[3] One of the churchwardens of Yatton parish church records that he paid 'for a sewte of vestments and a cope £26.'[4] The crosses used in processions must have been rather a heavy item of expenditure. We read in the *Chancery Proceedings* that the late parson of Ashprington Church left £20 for one, and the parishioners added another £10.[5] It was the fashion to have elaborate tombs, and the Countess of Warwick left careful directions concerning her own: it was to be adorned with an image of herself, with Mary Magdalen at the head, and St. John the Evangelist and St. Anthony, one on each side of her.[6] People in those days seem to have been very

[1] Hobhouse, 98. [2] *Medieval Records of a London City Church*, 225, 228. [3] *Early Chanc Proceed.*, 189/5. [4] Hobhouse, 113. [5] *Early Chanc. Proceed.*, 233/16. [6] *Early Eng. Wills*, 117.

fond of painting and gilding, and there are many entries of payments for work of this kind.[1] It is possible that we should have thought their taste rather gaudy, but it is difficult to speak with any certainty upon this point because so much that they did has perished. There is an interesting example of mural painting in the church of St. Thomas, Salisbury: it is a fresco, attributed to the fifteenth century, and it represents the Last Judgment. The composition is crowded, and the drawing not very good, but the colours are pleasing; they may, however, have been a little crude before time had mellowed them. Windows were a great feature in fifteenth-century churches, and we know that many of them were very beautiful[2]; and some of the carving of screens and pews is also very fine.[3] Apart from these achievements there is not much evidence of the existence of artistic talent; the illustrations of books printed in England are not of great merit, and are quaint rather than beautiful. On the whole it cannot be said that the artistic development of the nation made much progress at this time.

Attitude towards religion.

The work done by the people in building and adorning their churches also possesses great interest from another point of view, because it reveals their attitude towards religion; and whatever verdict may be passed upon their æsthetic qualities, their zeal for maintaining their places of worship cannot be questioned. Churches were largely kept up by voluntary contributions, and the gifts and bequests made for this purpose were extraordinarily numerous. The

[1] 'Maistress Agnes Breten did do gilte and paynte the Tabernacle of our lady . . .which cost xxvij li.' *Medieval Records of a London City Church*, p. 142. [2] For example, the great east window in York Minster. [3] Especially in the churches of Norfolk.

wills of the period contain many legacies for making steeples,[1] repairing chapels,[2] and many similar objects. Those who had no money gave goods and chattels—gowns,[3] rings,[4] girdles,[5] cows,[6] lambs,[7] and all kinds of things—which were sold for the benefit of the church. Others gave their labour, like some washer-women of Tintinhull, who took nothing for washing the linen of the church.[8] It is pleasant to find that the keenness of the struggle for existence had not killed generosity, but it must be acknowledged that religious enthusiasm was not the only motive which inspired it. Combined with this feeling there was in most men a very strong desire to do honour to their native places, and to make their own church more magnificent than any other; a sentiment which is illustrated by the bequest of a man named Joy, who left money to provide a chrismatory in Southwold Church, wishing it to be so splendid 'that noon shuld be like unto yt in Suffolk.'[9] There was also another motive mingled with men's love for their churches, and that was anxiety to secure the welfare of their souls in the next world, and therefore most of them made bequests upon the condition that prayers should be offered for them after death,[10] and in many cases left money to pay for dirges,[11] or to found chantries in which priests should sing masses for their souls.[12] Consequently the number of obits and chantries increased greatly during this period, and there was a commercial tinge in the view that prayers could be bought for money; at least, the contract with the clergy was drawn up in a business-like way.

[1] *Early Eng. Wills*, 23, 58, 76. [2] *Ibid.*, 18, 69, 120. [3] Hobhouse, 5. [4] *Ibid.*, 8, 13. [5] *Ibid.*, 20. [6] *Ibid.*, 12. [7] *Ibid.*, 23. [8] *Ibid.*, 183. [9] *Early Chanc. Proceed.*, 98/17. [10] *Ibid.*, 24/147, 38/274, 22/147. [11] *Early Eng. Wills*, 16–17. [12] *Ibid.*, 25.

Another result of the mercenary spirit of the age and its lowered ideals may be seen in the lengths to which the sale of indulgences was carried. The practice was common in the days of Chaucer, but in the fifteenth century it reached unprecedented dimensions, and one of the earliest uses of printing was devoted to this purpose. A poem called 'The Stacyons of Rome,'[1] written about the year 1440, enumerates the different places in that city at which indulgences might be obtained, and the quantities were in some cases enormous; fourteen thousand years of pardons and Lents could be procured at the High Altar at St. Peter's, on St. Peter and St. Paul's day. The writer of the poem was very eager to draw attention to the superiority of the shrines of Rome, so that his readers might go there, rather than to St. James of Galicia or elsewhere. The visits of pilgrims must have been quite a source of revenue to towns which possessed popular shrines. Indulgences were granted, not by the Pope alone, but also by others to whom the necessary authority was delegated, such as the papal collector-general in 1439,[2] the Hospital of the Holy Trinity and of St. Thomas the Martyr, Rome,[3] and the prior of the Charterhouse.[4] They were granted, as a rule, on condition that the recipient expressed penitence for the sins remitted, and gave a contribution to the funds of the charity, for the benefit of which they were issued[5]; but the monetary side of the transaction seems to have been more prominent than the religious. It must not be thought, however, that all power of appreciating the beauty of Christianity had died out; some of the poems published by Dr. Furnivall in his valuable

[1] *Political, Religious and Love Poems*, ed. by Furnivall, 145.
[2] *Chanc. Misc.*, Bundle 15, File 6, No. 6. [3] *Ibid.*, No. 7.
[4] *Ibid.*, No 10. [5] *Excheq. Q.R. Eccles.*, 6/51.

collection of *Political, Religious and Love Poems*,[1] show that this was not the case. One or two of them, and in particular 'Quia Amore Langueo,' are absolutely pure in sentiment, and appeal only to exalted motives.

Nevertheless, it is to be feared that the lower type of religious thought was the more general, and this, combined with the deterioration of the clergy, tended to make the Church unpopular, and was perhaps one of the causes of the vigour of Lollardy during the first twenty years of the century. This movement, which had been started by scholars and theologians,[2] was carried on mainly by poor and unlearned men, especially after the death of Lord Cobham. As we have seen, their doctrines spread in the fifteenth century to Lincoln, Norfolk, Suffolk, Essex, Buckingham, Middlesex, and Somerset.[3] Most of these counties were, as we know, centres of industrial life, and amongst those who had the courage to die for their faith were several tradesmen and artisans—like Badby, the tailor, of Evesham,[4] and Richard Hounden, a wool-packer.[5] Unfortunately for themselves the Lollards tried to uphold their doctrines by appealing to force, in 1414[6] and 1431[7]; and they were consequently treated with great severity by the Government as enemies of order as well as heretics, with the result that, although they were not crushed out of existence, they became unobtrusive.[8] The underground character of Lollardy from this time makes it difficult to estimate the effects of its influence upon the nation, but from the continuance of the practices against which Wycliffe had preached we must

[1] *Early Eng. Text. Soc.*, O.S., 15, re-edited 1903. [2] Trevelyan, *op. cit.*, 339. [3] *Ibid.*, map. [4] *Ibid.*, 335. [5] Gairdner, *Lollardy and the Reformation in England*, I, 159. [6] Ramsay, *Lancs. and York*, I, 179. [7] *Ibid.*, I, 436–7. [8] Gairdner, *op. cit.*, I, 162.

conclude that the bulk of the people were not affected by his teaching. Pilgrimages were more popular than ever, as the number of licences issued for conveying pilgrims proves[1]; and if men could not go themselves, they often left money to pay others to go for them after their death.[2] Chantries and chantry priests were also multiplied. The large numbers of books of devotion and of religious works issued by Caxton and other printers show the interest taken in these subjects. The author of the *Italian Relation* noticed how frequently English people went to church. 'They all attend Mass every day,' he writes, 'and say many Paternosters in public.'[3] The Duke of Clarence ordered that every holyday, matins, mass, and evensong should be celebrated for his household, 'and that every gentylman, yeoman and groome, not having resonable impediment, be at the seid dyvine service.'[4] The care taken by the coroner's jury to state in cases of sudden death, whether the deceased had received the rites of the Church or not indicates the value that was set upon them.[5] Taking all these facts into consideration, it seems clear that there was no general revolt of the laity against the doctrines or authority of the Church.

Moral character. The economic changes of the period produced more striking effects upon the moral development of the nation than upon any other side of its character, and some of these effects have already been suggested[6]; but the special illustrations given in the following pages are devoted to the moral rather than to the material aspect of

[1] *Cal. French Rolls*, 1422–4, ms. 15 and 14; 1433–4, ms. 14, 13, 11, 10, 9; 1444–5, ms. 10, 9, 8, 7, 5, 4; and many others. [2] *Early Eng. Wills*, 53, 65. [3] *Italian Relation*, 23. [4] *Ordinances of the Royal Household*, 89. [5] *Coroners' Rolls*, 63, m. 3; 61, ms 1, 4, 7.
[6] For example, evasions of the Usury laws and fraud by customers.

the question. There cannot be any doubt that the standard of commercial morality was very low, or that eagerness for monetary gain blunted men's sense of honesty and fair play. Accusations of cheating and deception were brought against artisans of all kinds—'fesours de Draps de layn,'[1] worsted weavers,[2] fishmongers,[3] tanners,[4] and many others. Merchants, both English and alien, frequently smuggled,[5] and even respectable merchants of the Staple, like the Celys, were occasionally guilty of discreditable tricks. The Lieutenant of the Staple had ordered that the quality of the wool to be sold should be tested by certain selected sarplers; but William Cely, after his sarpler had been cast out, secretly substituted another better sarpler for it, and so obtained a more satisfactory award.[6] In the course of the negotiations concerning commercial intercourse carried on between England and Flanders, in 1478, the Flemings declared that the English were in the habit of buying by a big pound and selling by a small one; and that they mixed their washed and unwashed wool.[7] The dealings of lawyers would not always bear the light of day: Godfrey Grene, who was acting on behalf of Sir William Plumpton, wrote to his patron describing the trouble he had taken to obtain sureties for him—'I fand one,' he says, 'that hath bene of old a supersedias mounger, & was agreed with him that he shold gett me a man to aske it, and he and the man shold have had vs for their labour.' The man played him false, but he adds, 'I may nott arreast him nor strive with him for the mony, nor

[1] *Rot. Parl.*, III, 541, and *Early Chanc. Proceed.*, 30/33. [2] *Rot. Parl.*, V, 619. [3] 22 *Ed. IV*, c. 2. [4] 2 *H. VI*, c. 7, and *Little Red Book of Bristol*, II, 111–12. [5] *Rot. Parl.*, III, 510; IV, 454; V, 55. [6] *Cely Papers*, 160 and 162. [7] Rymer's *Fœdera*, XII, p. 66, quoted in *Cely Papers*, xxiii, xxiv.

for the decept, because the matter is not worshipfull.'[1] In the *Chancery Proceedings* we have an action, on behalf of the King, brought against persons for obtaining a writ of supersedias and a writ of exigent by 'vntrewe, sotell and disseyuable meens.'[2] Charges of forgery were very common, and were made against all kinds of persons,[3] but this was a sin which apparently had never weighed very heavily on the medieval conscience.

One of the great causes of dishonest practices was the use that was made of bribery. No one, not even the King himself, was above taking a bribe. Sir William Plumpton was anxious that his son's claims to the family estates should not be questioned, so it was arranged that William Gascoigne should name to the escheator the men whom he wished to be empanelled, and that he should pay him four pounds for his office and twenty shillings for his reward.[4] 'Entreat the sheriff as well as ye can by reasonable rewards, rather than fail,' wrote Sir John Fastolf to Howys.[5] The city of Exeter kept the Chancellor in fish while its lawsuit was going on,[6] and the wardens of the parish of St. Mary-at-Hill gave a dinner to the chief judge when they were at law with the prioress of St. Helen's, and sent gifts of food and money to persons likely to be of service to them in the matter.[7] The Venetians systematically bribed the English collectors of customs, and the Senate issued injunctions as to the amount they should spend on it.[8] The corruption of juries seems to have been a matter of frequent occurrence; the Justices in

[1] *Plumpton Corr.*, p. 31. [2] *Early Chanc. Proceed.*, 25/218. [3] *Ibid.*, 9/357–61, 14/23, 14/24, 15/18, 32/47, 19/212. [4] *Plumpton Corr.*, lxxxvii. [5] *Paston Letters*, II, 235. [6] Freeman, *Exeter*, 159. [7] *Medieval Records of a London City Church*, 179, 190–1, 203. [8] Atton and Holland, *op. cit.*, 40–1.

the Star Chamber were asked whether a certain offender should be fined, or whether the matter should be referred to a jury, and they all said that he should be fined, because it was likely that the jurors would be corrupted by him.[1] An Act passed in the reign of Henry VI speaks of 'the great Damage and Disherison that cometh by the usual Perjury of Jurors impanelled upon Inquests, . . . which Perjury doth abound and increase daily more than it was wont, for the great Gifts that such Jurors take of the Parties in Pleas sued in the said Courts,' and it ordered that in such cases the plaintiffs should recover damages and costs.[2] The penalty was not, however, sufficiently heavy, and a more severe Act was passed against perjury in the time of Henry VII, which dealt especially with London.[3]

In these respects the commercial expansion of England had a bad effect upon the development of national character, but in other ways it was beneficial. Trade gave Englishmen training in practical affairs, and taught them to manage for themselves much business which had hitherto been done for them, and so it taught them to be capable and self-reliant. Foreign commerce brought them into contact with other nations, which suggested new ideas to them and widened their mental horizon; and this was an experience which they greatly needed, for they were naturally very intolerant of aliens. Moreover, trade was in those days carried on in the face of many difficulties, and the travelling it involved was attended with many hardships and not a little danger. The roads were full of pitfalls, and not by any means always free from robbers; the sea was even more perilous, for it was swarming

[1] *Proceed. of the Privy Council*, III, 313. [2] 11 *H. VI*, c. 4.
[3] 11 *H. VII*, c. 21.

with pirates. Merchants could not follow their calling unless they had a great deal of courage and perseverance, and unless they were willing to run risks; and thus their daily occupations engendered in them a spirit of enterprise and a love of adventure. The greed for gain, which was the ruling passion of the age, gave direction to their energies, and therefore, during the last quarter of the century the English began to copy the Portuguese, and to send out exploring expeditions to distant lands beyond the sea, and it is significant that they started from Bristol, the city which played so large a part in the commercial life of the time. The first expedition apparently sailed in 1480, to seek for the fabulous islands of Brazil, and the Seven Cities; but it was unsuccessful, and some other attempts were also failures.[1] In 1497 a party of explorers started under the leadership of John Cabot, crossed the Atlantic, and discovered land, which was possibly Cape Race, but the exact spot is not known[2]; and in 1498 another expedition also reached land on the other side of the ocean.[3] The disappointment felt in England when Cabot returned without any gold or gems, silks or spices,[4] proves effectually that desire for wealth was the chief motive which inspired the English adventurers, and when they found that none was to be had, their interest died down. These expeditions therefore had little immediate result, but they were full of promise for the future, and they are memorable as the first efforts of England to obtain a knowledge of the world outside Europe, and as the first signs of the spirit which enabled her in after years to build up an empire beyond the seas.

The development of their faculties and the spread

[1] Raymond Beazley, *John and Sebastian Cabot*, 41-2. [2] *Ibid.*, 73. [3] *Ibid.*, 109. [4] *Ibid.*, 110.

of education ought to have fitted the middle and lower classes to take an active part in political life, yet they seem to have cared little for the affairs of the nation. The towns, as we have already noticed, only joined in the Wars of the Roses when they were obliged, and did not care in the least which of the rival Houses won; their chief aim was to curry favour with the victor. In the poem 'How the Wise Man tauȝht His Son,' the father warns his son to 'desire noon office for to beere,' for fear that he should displease his neighbours and bring trouble upon himself.[1] A curious complaint was made in 1416 'that many citizens of the City of London . . . blessed with affluence and sufficiency of property and means,' induced a crowd of people to come to the Guildhall to shout and make an uproar to the effect that such a one must be mayor or sheriff, in order that they themselves might escape office; and in consequence, it was ordered that a fine of £100 should be imposed upon any person who formed a party or held meetings for the purpose of avoiding office.[2] The year before the ordinance was passed a man had been imprisoned for refusing to be an alderman, but afterwards he had consented to undertake the duty.[3] Occurrences of this kind were, however, very unusual; men were as a rule quite willing to take public posts in their own towns, partly, perhaps, because it gave them an advantage over trade rivals. It was unquestionably because they were so wrapped up in town politics that they cared so little for the good of the nation; yet an even stronger reason for their negligence may be seen in their selfish absorption in their own private business.

Political development.

[1] *Manners and Meals*, p. 49. [2] Riley, *Memorials of London*, 637. [3] *Ibid.*, 601–2.

There are, nevertheless, undoubted signs that the power of the middle class was growing steadily. The House of Commons gained some valuable privileges from the Lancastrian kings, including the right to initiate money bills,[1] and freedom of debate.[2] When Warwick and Clarence rebelled against Edward IV, in 1470, they considered the opinion of the people of so much importance that they addressed manifestoes to them, before they landed in England.[3] Philip de Commines says that Edward IV owed his restoration to the aid of the rich burgesses of London,[4] and however this may be, it is certain that he depended largely upon the support of the traders and merchants, and favoured them greatly, and that Richard III and Henry VII did the same. Thus the fifteenth century witnessed the beginning of the rise of the middle class, which was one of the most momentous events in the political history of the country.

Conclusion.

The effects produced by economic changes upon the development of national character were of a mixed nature, partly good and partly bad. For a time they caused moral confusion, but ultimately, by arousing new ambitions and opening out larger possibilities, they rendered the growth of the nation inevitable. Some very unpleasant traits of character were prominent—lawlessness, selfishness, and greed of gain—but they must not be wholly attributed to the inherent depravity of the people, but must be considered mainly as the outcome of the phase through which they were passing. Old institutions were crumbling away, and new ones were not firmly established; they were subjected to the influence of new ideas,

[1] Ramsay, *Lancs. and York*, I, 110. [2] *Ibid.*, I, 29.
[3] *Ibid.*, II, 356. [4] *Cronique and Hystoire . . . par . . . Phelippe de Commines*, xliv. d.

and assailed by new temptations. It is hardly surprising that for the moment they were overwhelmed, and lost their mental balance, and that they misused or left unused powers, which they had not hitherto possessed. Their worst feature was their inability to see that there was anything higher than material aims, or anything more to be desired than their own personal advantage, and it was owing to this state of mind that they so seldom rose above the level of commonplace achievements. Their sins were not those of a dying nation, but rather those of one emerging from immaturity, and in spite of their failures, there were signs of latent strength and abundant evidence of forces at work, which were making for the progress of the race.

APPENDIX

A. Petition of Artificers for the Prohibition of the importation of Wrought Goods (1463–4) [*abbreviated*].

Pyteuously shewen and compleynen Artificers, Handcrafty men and women . . . howe they all . . . been gretely empoverysshed . . . by the grete multitude of dyvers chaffares and wares, . . . beyng full wrought and redy made to the sale, . . . brought into this reame of Englond and Lordship of Wales, from beyonde the see, aswell by Merchauntez Straungers as Deynsyns and other persones, wherof the moost part in substaunce is disceyvable, and nought worth in regarde to eny mannes occupation or profite; and also by the meanes of the grete nombre and multitude of Aliens and Straungers of dyvers nations, beyng Artificers, housholders and dwellers in dyvers citees, tounes, boroughs and villages, within the seid reame & lordship usyng such handcraftes, and havying & settyng a werke grete nombre of people in their houses of their owne nations, & noon other, dailly occupiyng the seid handcraftes, by the which the seid Artificers straungers be contynuelly occupied and gretely enriched, and all the other artificers beyng the kynges lieges, gretely empoverysshed, and not a werke. And over that, grete part of the tresour & richesse of the seid Reame and Lordship . . . is daily conveyed & caried oute of the seid Reame & Lordship to the grete hurt of the Kyng and the empoverysshing of his seid Reame and Lordship, by cause wherof his liege subgettez beyng Artificers, may not lyve by their Craftes and occupations, as they might doo in dayes passed, but many of theym aswell housholders as journey men servauntes and apprenticez in grete nombre, at this day be unoccupied, and lyve in grete ydelnes, poverte & ruyne, which often tymes causeth hem to fall to riotte, vyces & mysgovernauncez. . . . Wherfore please youre wise discretions . . . to pray the Kyng to ordeyn that noo marchaunt, the Kynges born subget, deynsyn or straunger bryng, sende nor conveye . . . into this reame of Englond & Lordship of Wales, eny of theese wares or thinges underwriten . . . wollen bonettes, eny wollen cloth, laces, corses, ribans, frenges of silke and of threde, threden laces, throwen silke, silke in eny wise enbrauded, golden laces, tyres of silke or of gold, sadles, styropes, or eny harneys longyng to sadelers, spores, moleyns for bridels, aundyrnes, gredyrnes, eny manere lokkes, hamers, pynsons, fyretonges, drepyngpannes, dyses, tenys balles, poyntes, laces, purces, gloves, gurdels, harneys for gurdles of iron, of laton, of stele, of tyn or of alkamyn, eny thyng wrought of eny taued lether, eny manere peltry ware, tawed botes, shoen, galoches or corkes, knyves, daggers, wodeknyves, boytkyns, sheres for taillours, cisours, rasours, shethes, cardes for pleiyng, pynnes, patyns, paknedles, eny manere peynted ware, forcers, caskettes, rynges of coper gilt or of Laton, or chauffyngdisshes, candelstickes hangyng or stondyng, hangyng lavours, chauffyng - balles, sakeryngbelles, rynges for curtyns, ladles scomours, counterfett basons, ewers, hattes, brusshes, cardes for wolle or white wyre . . . uppon peyne to forfeit theym . . . unto the ende of the terme of x yeres.—*Rot. Parl.*, Vol. v., p. 506.

B. Extracts from the 'Early Chancery Proceedings.'

1. A money-lending transaction, to illustrate later Medieval opinion regarding Usury. (Date of Bundle, 1475–1480 and 1483–1485.)

To the right reuerend ffader in God, the Bisshop of Lincoln and Chaunceler of Englond.

Right humble besechith vn to your lordshyp your Oratour William Elryngton of Durham, mercer, that where as he nowe iiij yeres past and more had for a stoke of on Richard Elryngton the som of xxx li., wherefore your said Oratour was by hys obligacion bondyn vnto the said Richard in xl li. and odde syluer; which som of xxx li. your said Oratour shuld haue to be imployd in marchaundise, duryng the space of vij yeres, yeldyng yerely vnto the said Richard, for the lone thereof iiij li. of lawfull money of Englond, and at the vij yeres yend to yeld hole vnto the said Richard the said som of xxx li.; wherevppon your said Suppliant occupyed the said som by the space of ij yere, and payd yerely vnto the sayd Richard iiij li.; and after that your said Oratour rememberyng in his conscience that that bargayn was not godly nor profytable, intended and profred the said Richard hys said som of xxx li. a gayn, which to do he refused, but wold that your said Oratour shuld performe his bargayn. Neuerthelese, the said Richard was afterward caused, and in maner compelled, by spyrituall men to take agayn the said xxx li., whervppon (to) fore sufficient record the said Richard ffaithfully promised that the said obligacion of xl li. and couenauntz shuld be canceld and deliuered vnto your said Oratour, as reson is. Nowe hit ys so that the said Richard owith and ys indetted by his obligacion in a gret som of money to one John Saumpill, which ys nowe maire of Newe Castell, where fore nowe late the said Richard, by the meane of the said mayer, caused an accion of dett apon the said obligacion of xl li. to be affermed, (to) fore the maire and Shyreff of the said Towne of Newe Castell, and there by the space almost of xij moneth hath sued your said Oratour, to hys gret cost and this aynst all trowgith and conscience, by the mighty favour of the said maire, by cause he wold the rather attayne vnto hys dwete, purposith nowe by sotill meanis, to cast and condempe wrongfully your said Oratour, in the said som of xl li. to his gret hurt and vndoyng, withowte your speciall lordship be vnto him shewid in this be halfe, wherefore please hit your said lordship to considre the premise, therevppon to graunt a certiorari, direct vn to the maire and Shireff of the said Toune, to bryngvpp (to) fore yow the cause, that hit may be there examined and rewled as conscience requirith for the loue of God and in way of charyte.—(Bundle 64, No. 291.)

2. An example of the use and abuse of trusts. (Date of Bundle, 1467–1472 ; and perhaps also 1433–1443.)

To the right reuerent fader in God the
Bisshop of Bathe & Welles, Chaunceller of Englond.

Mekely bisechith your gracious lordship your pour Oratour Raaf Weld that where, as he late beyng seased of a mees and lxxx acres of land with th' appertenauncez in Pluckle, in the Counte of Kent, in his demesne, as of fee, and so seased, therof infeffid John Bocher to haue to hym and his heirz, in fee, to thuse and behof of the said Raaf and his heirz, and to th' entent to refeffe the said Raaf and his heirz, whenne he were by theme therto requyred. By force of the whiche the said John was seased of the said mees and lande, in his demesne, as of fee, to th' entent abouesaid. And howe be it that your said bisecher oft tymes sithen the delyuere of þe said astate, in maner and forme afforerehersed made, hath requyred the said John to make astate to hym of þe said mees and lande with þ'appertenauncez, the which to do the said John at all tymes hath refused, and yet doth, agayn all right and conscience. Please it your gracious lordship to considère the premysses, and to graunt a writte sub pena to be direct to the said John Bocher to appere affore your lordship, in the Chauncerye of our souerain lord þe Kyng, there to answere to the premysses, and to be examyned and ruled vppon and in the premysses, as right and conscience shall requyre, for the loue of God and in wey of charite.

Plegii de pro (sequendo)
Johannes Butte de London, Gurdeler.
Willelmus Salter de eadem, Pynner.

Early Chancery Proceedings, Bundle 38, No. 4.

3. Capture of a Pinnace by English pirates. (Date of Bundle, 21–28 Henry VI; and perhaps also 33–35 Henry VI.)

To the most Wurshipfull & reuerend
ffadyr in God, the Archebisshop of Cauntirbery,
Chaunceler of Inglond.

Mekely besecheth your pour bedeman John Warburton that where as he late in a Spynas, that he bought in Britayn, chargid with Wyne, oyle and oþer goodis and merchandisez, sailed toward Inglond, come vpon the see certain Rouers of Inglond and toke the same Spynas & merchandises, and brought hem to Portesmouth & hem ther sold & dispoyled as them list, yn vndoyng of your said besecher, with owte your gracious remedie; and aftyrward gracious lord it lyked to your goode grace to make your lettres to be wrete to the lord Lisle, for parcell of the same merchandisez, be request of whiche your lettres, the said lord Lisle deluiered a none all that come to his handez þerof, that is to say, the same Spynas & j ton of Gastard. Please it to your good & gracious lordship to considere this matier, and to ordeyne so aftyr your high discrecon that your said besecher may haue the remenaunt of the said marchaundisez, for the loue of God & in werk of Charite.

Early Chancery Proceedings, Bundle 15, No. 139.

4. An attempt to claim a free man as a 'neif.' (Date of Bundle, 10 Richard II to 14 Henry IV.)

A tresreuerent piere en Dieu & son treshonoure & tresgracious Sieur, leuesque Dexcestre, Chaunceller Dengleterre. Supplie vn poure home William fitz John Culne, que come il soit de frank estate & condicion, & il & toutz ses auncestres de toute temps dount memoire ne court sount & ount estes de mesme la condicion, saunz ceo que ascun cleyme ou chalange ad este fait de dit William ou de ascun de ses ditz auncestres; vient ore vn John Shortgroue, ffermer, de certeins terres & tenements dun Georgĕ Belamy, & cleyme le dit William come neif appertenaunt as terres & tenements, & ad pris & areste le dit William a Vpton, en le Countee de Hereford, & luy ad amesne de dit countee tantque en Gales, & luy illeoqes detient en forte & dure prison, en perpetuel destrucion de dit William sil neit votre tres-gracious aide. . . .

Early Chancery Proceedings, Bundle 3, No. 110.

5. References to cases of lawlessness in different parts of the country, to show the prevalence of the evil.

Cases in	Cornwall........	6/260, 27/138, 27/415, 43/49.
,,	Devonshire	6/164, 12/251, 27/168, 28/289.
,,	Somerset	6/265.
,,	Warwick	29/343.
,,	Worcester	3/72.
,,	Norfolk.........	6/55, 31/322.
,,	Suffolk	5/165.
,,	Kent	6/159, 6/267.
,,	Surrey	4/5.
,,	Cambridge	4/135, 6/146.
,,	Nottingham	3/138.
,,	Northampton ...	3/126*a*.
,,	Yorkshire	3/141, 6/188, 13/85, 45/219.
,,	Bedford	32/270.
,,	Essex	4/172.
,,	Hertford	20/157, 25/82.
,,	Buckingham	27/267, 31/474.
,,	Leicester	27/429.
,,	Dorset	6/268, 31/475.
,,	Derby	39/62.
,,	Hereford	11/171.
,,	Berkshire	6/220, 6/224.
,,	Westmoreland ..	6/196
,,	Sussex	45/378.

The above are a few out of many cases of breaches of the peace recorded in the *Early Chancery Proceedings*.

6. Some items from an inventory of the goods of William Ferre, mercer, to show the quantity of plate possessed by men of the middle class. (Date of Bundle, 1480–1483.)

In primis, a Gobelet couerd, of siluer and gilt with iij ssawcours, weying xxi vncez iij quarters.

Item, ij salt-sellers gilt, couered, weying xvij vncez.

Item, a maser, gilt, weying ix vncez.

Item, dozen spones knoppes gilt, weying xij vncez.

Item, ij peces of siluer, couered, chaced, parcels gilt, weying xxxvj uncez.

Item, a standing nott gilt, with a coueryng, weying xxij vncez.

Item, iij gilt girdellis, weying xvij vncez and iij quarters.

Item, harneys for a girdell parcell gilt, weying iij vncez and iij quarters.

Item, ij standing Goblettis, couered, and a fork of siluer parcell gilt, weying xv vncez iij quarters.

Item, a maser couered gilt, weying xxxviij vncez and iij quarters.

Item, ij peces of siluer, weying x vncez.

Item, xij spones, weying xiv vncez.

Item, a maser, the bonde gilt, weying v vncez.

Item, ij saltsellers, chaced, parcell gilt, weying xiv vncez.

Item, a Cradell of siluer and gilt, with a Childe theryn, massee.

Item, ij tokkyng girdillis, the bocles and pendauntis of siluer and gilt.

Item, a Agnes Dei with a vernacle of siluer & gilt with moder of perle.

Item, A knopp of siluer & gilt with a blew stone for a maser.

Early Chancery Proceedings, Bundle 61, No. 500.

C. Information from various sources, placed together for purposes of comparison.

1. A few specimens of prices, to show the value of money and the cost of living.

(a) *Cost of transit and travelling*—

Hire of a horse for 15 days	6s. 8d.[1]
Carriage of a cart-load of hay from Stafford to Writell	6d.[2]
Carriage of fish (value 3s. 8d.) from Winchelsea to Writell	14d.[3]
Carts laden with provisions going from Maxstock to Kymbolton, a day	2s.[4]
Cart carrying fuel, by the day	8d.[5]
Carriage of a butt of wine from London to Kymbolton	8s.[6]
Paid to four bargemen from 'Queynhith' to Westminster	16d.[7]
Carriage of 1 quarter, 3 bushells of salt, from 'Quenhith' to 'Bredstrete' (London)	1½d.[8]
Carriage of a wey of salt from Lowestoft to Metyngham College	12d.[9]
Carriage of 6 packs of cloth from Stoke to Ipswich	3s.[10]
Carriage of 2 loads of timber from Dorking to Kingston	18d.[11]
Boat-hire from Harwich to 'Mantyre'	6d.[12]

[1] *Early Chanc. Proceed.*, 12/128. [2] Add. MSS., 34, 213, f. 6. [3] *Ibid.*, f. 13. [4] *Ibid.*, f. 31 d. [5] *Ibid.*, f. 33. [6] *Ibid.*, f. 44. [7] *Ibid.*, f. 74 d. [8] *Ibid.*, f. 109 d. [9] Add. MSS., 33, 986, f. 69. [10] *Howard Household Book*, I, 340. [11] *Ibid.*, 525. [12] *Howard Household Book*, II, 201.

(b) *Prices of wool and fells—*

' 15 lbs lanae '	2s. 6d.[1]
' pro 2 duodecim pellibus & dimidia de Sherlynggis	3s. 9d.
pro 2 duodecim pellibus & 9 cum lana	6s. 10d.[2]
' una petra lanae '	3s.[3]
20 wull felles	13s. 4d.[4]
Sherlenges . . . a dozen	2s.[5]
Wool, per stone (in 1465)...........	40d.[6]

(c) *Prices of clothing and jewellery—*

' A kertell of Reede '	10s.[7]
' A ffurre of Coony regge '	6s. 8d.[8]
' 30 dosein hattes prys '	£32 10s.[9]
' 7 pakkys of Irish yarn '	£38.[10]
' Shoes for the ' henxmen and fotemen of Henry VII, per pair	6d.[11]

Clothes for the Queen, Sir John Howard, &c.—

Scarlet, per yard	8s.
Satin, per yard	12s.
Crimson Velvet, per yard..........	35s.
Damask russet, per yard	9s.
Cloth of gold, per yard	£8 6s. 8d.[12]
Kendal cloth, per yard	4½d.[13]
' fyne crymysyne engreyned,' per yard	15s.[14]
Holland cloth, per ell	8½d.[15]
Green sarcenet, per yard	5s.[16]
' For makyng a gowne of tauny saten '	4s.[17]

[1] Add. MSS., 33, 985, f. 133. [2] Add. MSS., 33, 987, f. 57 d. [3] *Ibid.*, 33, 988, f. 25. [4] *Howard Household Book*, II, 237. [5] *Ibid.* [6] *Paston Letters*, IV, 172. [7] *Early Chanc. Proceed.*, 16/599 (date, 23 *H. VI*). [8] *Ibid.* [9] *Ibid.*, 30/55. [10] *Ibid.*, 10/44. [11] [9] Campbell, *op. cit.*, II, 18. [12] *Ibid.*, I, 237 (date, 1 *H. VII*). [13] *Howard Household Book*, II, 219. [14] *Ibid.*, I, 162 (date, 1465). [15] *Paston Letters*, IV, 289 (1467). [16] *A.C.*, Vol. XLVI Letter 239 (1479). [17] *Early Chanc. Proceed.*, 88/42.

'2 plyte of fyne lawne'............	21s. 5d.[1]
Ermines . . . the 'timber'..........	18s.[2]
'4 boge skynnys'	8s.[3]
'53 White lambe skynnes'.........	13s. 4d.[4]
2 'girdeles of corses harnessed with Siluer'	£2 13s. 4d.[5]
Marten's fur for a gown............	£17.[6]
'a floure of golde with a lyon . . . dyamondes and 2 rubies	£6 13s. 4d.[7]
'a tablet of golde . . . with baleyce and peirlis,' weighing 8½ ounces	£16.[8]
A chain of Gold, weighing 19½ ozs...	£32 11s. 8d.[9]

(d) *Prices of wheat, and other kinds of food*—

Wheat, at Yatton, in 1445, the bushell	7d. or 8d.[10]
,, in Norfolk, in 1474, a comb..	2s. 4d.[11]
36 quarters of wheat (17 *H. VI*).....	£20.[12]
10 combs of wheat (4 *H. VII*)......	£1 6s. 8d.[13]
Sheep, each	1s. 10d.[14]
5 Oxen, each	13s. 4d.[15]
3 little pigs......................	15d.[16]
1 capon........................	8d.[17]
2 lambs........................	2s. 2d.[18]
40 sheep	£4.[19]
A shoulder and brest of mutton	5d.[20]
6 geese	1s.[21]
3 barrels of herrings..............	£1 6s. 8d.[22]
2 'coddis'	1s.
20 'plais'......................	8d.
2 soles.........................	5d.
2 haddocks.....................	4d.[23]

[1] *Howard Household Book*, I, p. 384 (1466–7). [2] Campbell *op. cit.*, I, 228 (1 *H. VII*). [3] *Early Chanc. Proceed.*, 105/40. [4] *Ibid.* [5] *Early Chanc. Proceed.*, 16/599. [6] *Ibid.*, 97/44. [7] Campbell, *op. cit.*, II, p. 321. [8] *Ibid.* [9] *Howard Household Book*, I, 154–5. [10] Hobhouse, p. 81. [11] *Paston Letters*, I, 283. [12] *Early Chanc. Proceed.*, 12/205. [13] *Ibid.*, 86/10. [14] *A.C.*, Vol. XLVI, No. 60. [15] Add. MSS., 34, 213 (date, 5 *Ed. IV*), f. 77 d. [16] *Ibid.*, f. 47. [17] *Ibid.* [18] *Ibid.*, f. 9. [19] *Ibid.*, f. 59. [20] *Howard Household Book*, I, p. 435. [21] *Ibid.*, II, p. 75. [22] *Early Chanc. Proceed.*, 17/161. [23] Add. MSS., 34, 213, f. 11.

3 dols of Red wine	£15.[1]
a hogshead of White wine	£1 4s.[2]
3 butts of malmesey	£14.[3]
Ale, the barrel	3s. 4d.[4]
1½ barrel of Beer	3s.[5]
12 lbs. of Jordan almonds	3s.
12 ,, Dates	6s.
6 ,, 'reysouns of Corauns'	1s. 3d.
1 ,, Pouder of gynger	1s. 4d.[6]
30 ,, Pepper at 12d.	30s.
30 ,, Cinnamon at 20d.	50s.
4 ,, Cloves at 2s. 6d.	10s.
4 ,, Mace at 2s. 8d.	10s. 8d.[7]
'Suger' per lb.	10d.[8]

(e) *Payments for the board of various persons*—

Board of prisoners:

7 Frenchmen	3s. 4d. a week each.
Sir Th. Dalalaund, kt.	10s. ,,
2 Scotch gentilmen	6s. 8d. ,, ,,
a preest	6s. 8d. ,,
The erle of Surrey	40s. ,, [9]
3 men of the erle for 4 weeks	30s.(2s. 6d. a week)."

Thomas Welleys, husbandman, agreed to pay 6d. a week for the board of his kinswoman, Margaret Kyvet.[10]

2. List of occupations, to illustrate the division of labour in the fifteenth century.

Baxter	*Early Chanc. Proceed.*, 28/223.
Bed-maker	,, ,, ,, 64/284.
Blexster	,, ,, ,, 15/47

[1] *Ibid.*, f. 21. [2] *Ibid.*, f. 22 d. [3] *Early Chanc. Proceed.*, 64/281. [4] *Ibid.*, 20/155. [5] Add. MSS., 33, 986, f. 69 d. [6] *Howard Household Book*, I, 328. [7] Add. MSS., 34, 213, f. 86. [8] *Ordinances of the Royal Household*, p. 103. [9] Campbell, *op. cit.*, I, 208. [10] *Early Chanc. Proceed.*, 67/38.

Brasier .... *Early Chanc. Proceed.*, 66/232.
Brigandine-maker ,, ,, ,, 32/279.
Broiderer .... ,, ,, ,, 60/209.
Brown-baker ..... ,, ,, ,, 45/300.
Bucklemaker ..... ,, ,, ,, 38/63.

Capper .... ,, ,, ,, 109/35.
Chandler .... ,, ,, ,, 61/374.
 'talughchaundeller' Sharpe, *Wills*, II, p. 576.
 'wexchaundeler' ,, ,, ,, 353.
'Chapemaker .... *Early Chanc. Proceed.*, 66/441.
'Chauntour' ..... ,, ,, ,, 101/16.
Clothpakker ..... Sharpe, *Wills*, II, p. 414.
Cofferer .... *Early Chanc. Proceed.*, 32/348.
'Cordener' ...... ,, ,, ,, 80/15.
Coverlet-weaver... ,, ,, ,, 48/50.
Currier .... ,, ,, ,, 109/57.

Fellmonger ..... ,, ,, ,, 67/194.
Filacer of the Common Pleas ,, ,, 61/431.

Galleyman ...... ,, ,, ,, 29/358.
Girdler .... ,, ,, ,, 11/194
Goldbeater .... ,, ,, ,, 48/476.
Goldfiner .... ,, ,, ,, 211/23.
Gold-wire-drawer ,, ,, ,, 47/100.

Hattermerchant .. ,, ,, ,, 97/16.
Honeyman .... ,, ,, ,, 64/1055.

Latoner .... ,, ,, ,, 64/286.
Lister .... ,, ,, ,, 215/30.
Lorimer .... ,, ,, ,, 11/366.

'Milpekker' ..... ,, ,, ,, 31/480.

Netmaker .... ,, ,, ,, 64/200.

Pasteler .... ,, ,, ,, 67/352.
Pewterer .... ,, ,, ,, 67/146.
Pouchmaker ..... ,, ,, ,, 82/67.
Pulter .... ,, ,, ,, 33/327.
Purser .... ,, ,, ,, 55/244.

Sherman .... ,, ,, ,, 11/231.
Spectacle-maker .. ,, ,, ,, 78/70.
Spurrier .... ,, ,, ,, 32/303.
Stockfishmonger .. *Sharpe*, *Wills*, II, 366.

Stoneslipper	*Early Chanc. Proceed.*			66/27.
Sugarfiner	,,	,,	,,	64/82.
Tapiser	,,	,,	,,	76/125.
Tonker	,,	,,	,,	61/261.
Vestment Maker ..	,,	,,	,,	63/178.
Waker	,,	,,	,,	64/552.
Waterbearer	,,	,,	,,	213/79.
Wheeler	,,	,,	,,	64/1006.
Wiremonger	,,	,,	,,	82/87.
Woadmonger	,,	,,	,,	64/9.
Woolman	,,	,,	,,	59/147.
Woolpacker	,,	,,	,,	51/106.
'Wyndrawer'	,,	,,	,,	32/441.

D. Privy Seal Letter (*'Benevolence'*) *referring to the King's necessities, to be further explained by the Commissioners appointed for this purpose, and requesting the loan of a considerable sum* (20 *July,* 4 *Henry VI*).

De par le Roy,

Chers et bienamez. Come pour la defense de nostre Royaume encountre noz rebeaux et ennemys et la brief expedition de nos guerres, nous conviendra necessairement avoir chevance et provision d'une grande somme de deniers, sicome plus au plain de par nous et nostre Conseil vous exposeront [names of Commissioners follow] lesqueux nous avons assignez, de l'avis de nostre dit Conseil, par noz lettres de Commission desouz nostre Grand Seal, pour communiquer et tanter ovec vous de et sur la chevance d'aucune somme notable par vous a apprester a nous en ceste nostre grande necessitee, et pour vous permettre pour et en nostre noun sufficeante seuretee de repaiement de tielle somme come vous nous vuillez en ce cas apprester. Si vous prions, tres cherement, q'en avancement de ceste besoigne, quel a l'aide de nostre Createur tournera au bien et transquilitee de nous, de vous, et de toute Christianitee, prendre vous vuillez le plus pres que vous pouvez en nous aidant a ceste foix par voie d'apprest d'une notable somme, tielle come par les sousditz commissioners de vous sera desiree, adjoustant nientmains a eux ferme foy et creance en leur relation a vous affaire de par nous et nostre dit conseil en celle partie. Donne sous nostre Prive Seal, a Westm[ester] le xx^{e} jour de Juylli.

Original letter in Exchequer, Treasury of Receipt, Privy Seals and Letters Patent for Loans, Bundle 1; cf. *Patent Roll*, 4 Henry VI, part ii, m. 9; *Cal.*, p. 355. Published in *A Formula Book of English Official Historical Documents*, edited by Hubert Hall, p. 98.

E. Extract from an Indenture of War made between Edward IV and Robert Donne (14 *Edward IV*).

Robert 'is reteigned and behest towardis the same our souueraigne lord to do hym seruice of werre . . . for an hool yere . . . with x Archers . . . takyng wagis for hymself of xijd by the day, and vjd by the daye by moyen of Reward, and for eueriche of the saide Archers vjd by the day' . . . .

. . . .

'Also our saide Souueraigne lord the Kyng shall haue the third parte of wynnyngis of werre, aswele of the saide Robert, as the thirdde of thirddes whereof eche of his Retenue shalbe answeryng vnto him of their wynnygis of werre duryng the tyme abouesaide, be it prisoners, prayes or other goodes or catallis whatsoeuer it be; of which thirddis and thirddis of thirddis the said Robert shall answere vnto our saide souueraigne lord in his Eschequier in England, by his othe, or by the othe of his deputie or deputies accompting for hym in this partie, and as touching the prisoners and prayes that duryng the said terme shalbe taken by the said Robert or any of his saide Retenue, the said Robert, or he or they that so shall take such prisoners or prayes, shall within viij dayes after the takyng therof, or assone as resonably, shall mowe certifie vnto the Constable & Marchall or oon of theym, aswele the names of the saide prisoners as their estate, degre & condicion and also the nature, quantite and value of their saide getingis, by estimacion, vpon peyne of forfeiture of the prisoners & wynnyngis abouesaid. Also the saide Robert shall haue alle maner prisoners that shall happe to be take by him, or any of his saide Retinue, duryng the tyme abouesaide, Except the Kyng his aduersarie, and alle Kyngis & Kingis sonnes his aduersaries of Ffraunce, and also alle lieutenauntis & Chiueteins havyng the saide aduersaries power, which shalbe & abide prisoners vnto the Kyng, our saide soueraigne lord, for the which he shall make resonable aggrement with the takers of theym.'—*Accounts Exchequer Q. R. Army*, 72/1 (last case in file).

F. Petition from the Prior of the Cathedral Church of St. Mary's, Coventry, that a vagabond monk might be attached by the secular arm (*November 6th*, 1455).

'Excellentissimo principi ac domino Henrico Dei gratia Regi Anglie et Francie & domino Hibernie, vester humilis Capellanus Johannes Shoteswell, prior ecclesie Cathedralis beate Marie de Couentre, salutem in eo per quem Reges regnant & regna cuncta persistunt. Celcitudini vestre regie notum facio, per presentes, quod quidam frater Johannes Lynby, monachus ecclesie predicte, sub ordine Sancti Benedicti ibidem professus, salutis sue immemor, spreta obediencia ordinis illius ac in mei predicti prioris capellani vestri predicti eius prioris ac superioris, & libertatis ecclesie preiudicium, ac se, de patria in patriam vagatur ac discurrit, in anime sue periculum ac ordinis predicti scandalum manefestum. Quapropter excellencie vestre supplico quatinus brachium regalis potencie solita gratia apponatis, vt per vestrum subsidium libertas ecclesiastica sub vestre defensionis clipeo tuta maneat & illesa, & vos exinde a Deo retribucionem condignam consequi valeatis, Qui vos ecclesie sue & populo per tempora conseruet diuturna. Data apud Couentre sexto mensis Novembris, anno Domini millesimo quadringentesimo quinquagesimo quinto.'—*Chancery Warrants for Issue*, Ser. 1, File 1759, No. 12.

BIBLIOGRAPHY

I. ORIGINAL AUTHORITIES (*a*) *Unpublished*—

Ancient Correspondence, Vol. 46 (*Stonor Papers*): Letters, 17, 47, 60, 62, 74, 100, 105, 115, 116, 119, 120, 160, 169, 196, 213, 233, 239, 240, 241, 263. Vol. 51: Letter, 100. Vol. 53 (*Cely Papers*, not included in the collection published by the Camden Soc.): Letters, 6, 58, 99, 125, 133, 146, 155.

Ancient Indictments, K.B. 8, No. 1 (*Baga de Secretis*): 17 *Ed. IV*.

Ancient Petitions, 299/14910, 306/15259.

Assize Roll, No. 862.

Augmentation Office, Miscellaneous Books, Vol. 316.

Chancery Miscellanea, 4/8 (*Household Book of the Lady Alicia de Brienne*), 15/6.

Chancery Warrants for Issue, Series I, Files 1759–69.

Coroners' Rolls, Nos. 60, 61, 63, 145, 147–50, 158, 168–70.

Domestic State Papers (*Charter to the Merchant Adventurers*), Charles II, Vol. XXVII, pp. 1–5.

Early Chancery Proceedings, e.g. Bundles 3–19, 20–2, 24–42, 44–7, 50–6, 58–62, 64–7, 76, 78, 80, 82, 88–9, 90–1, 94, 95, 97, 100, 101, 105–11, 183, 185–9, 190, 192–7, 200–2, 210, 211, 213, 216, 217, 219, 223, 226, 230, 231, 233, 234.

Exchequer Accounts, Q.R. Army, 42/32, 42/36, 44/24, 48/2, 48/3, 68/1, 72/1.

— *Q.R. Ecclesiastical*, 8/24, 6/51, 1/17.

— *Q.R. Miscellaneous*, 516/13.

— *Q.R. Wardrobe*, 406/22.

Lay Subsidies, $\frac{237}{27}$.[1]

[1] All the above documents are in the Public Record Office.

Additional MSS., 33, 985–33, 988 (*Accounts of Metyngham College*).[1]

— *MSS.*, 34, 213 (*Household Book of Anne Duchess of Buckingham*).[2]

ORIGINAL AUTHORITIES (*b*) PUBLISHED—

Ancient Songs and Ballads, collected by Joseph RITSON, 3rd edition, revised by W. Carew HAZLITT (1877).

BEKYNGTON, T., *Letters* (Rolls Series, No. 56).

Borough Customs, edited by Miss Mary BATESON (Selden Soc., Nos. 18 and 21).

CAMPBELL, Rev. W., *Materials for a History of the Reign of Henry VII* (Rolls Series, 1873).

Cely Papers, edited by H. E. MALDEN (Camden Soc., 3rd Ser., 1900).

Churchwardens' Accounts of Croscombe, Pilton, Yatton, Tintinhull, Morebath, and St. Michael's, Bath, edited by Bp. HOBHOUSE (Somerset Record Soc., 1890).

— *of St. Dunstan's, Canterbury*, edited by J. M. COWPER, in *Archælogia Cantiana*, Vols. XVI and XVII.

— *of St. Mary's, Elham*, edited by Scott ROBERTSON (*Archælogia Cantiana*, Vol. X, 1876).

— *of Hythe Church*, edited by Scott ROBERTSON and MACKESON (in *Archælogia Cantiana*, Vol. X).

— *of St. Mary-at-Hill, London. The Medieval Records of a London City Church*, edited by H. LITTLEHALES (Early English Text Soc., 1905).

— *of Receipts and Expenses in the Building of Bodmin Church*, edited by Rev. J. J. WILKINSON (*Camden Miscellany*, 1875).

Collectanea Anglo-Premonstratensia, edited by Francis A. GASQUET (Camden Soc., 3rd Ser., 1904), Vol. I.

COMMINES, Philippe de, *Cronique et Hystoire* (1523).

Coventry Leet Book, edited by M. Dormer HARRIS (Early English Text Soc., 1907), Part i.

[1] In the British Museum. [2] *Ibid.*

Débat des Hérauts, edited by M. P. MEYER (Société des Anciens Textes Français, 1877).

English Chronicle (1377–1461), edited by Rev. J. Sylvester DAVIES (Camden Soc., O.S. No. 64, 1856).

Early English Miscellanies in Prose and Verse, edited by J. O. HALLIWELL (*Warton Club Miscellany*).

ELLIS, Sir Henry, *Original Letters Illustrative of English History* (Three Series, 1825–46).

English and Scottish Popular Ballads, from the collection of F. J. CHILD (1905).

FABYAN, R., *The New Chronicle of England*, edited by H. ELLIS (1811).

Fifty Earliest English Wills, edited by F. J. FURNIVALL (Early English Text Soc., No. 67).

FORTESCUE, Sir J., *Works* (1869).

GAIRDNER, J., *Letters and Papers illustrative of the reigns of Richard III and Henry VII* (Rolls Series, 24).

Historical MSS. Commission, *9th Report*.

HOWARD, *Household Books* (Roxburghe Club, 1841 and 1844).

LEADAM, I. S., *The Domesday of Inclosures* (1897).

LEADAM, I. S., *The Inquisition of* 1517, in *Trans. of the Roy. Hist. Soc.*, VI–VIII (1892–4).

Liber Albus, in *Munimenta Gildhallæ* (Rolls Series).

Little Red Book of Bristol, edited by Francis Bridges BICKLEY (1900).

LYDGATE, *Minor Poems*, edited by O. J. HALLIWELL (Percy Soc., No. 2).

Naval Songs and Ballads, edited by C. H. FIRTH (Navy Record Soc., 1908).

Manners and Meals in the Olden Times, edited by F. J. FURNIVALL (Early English Text Soc., O.S. 32).

Ordinances and Regulations for the Government of the Royal Household (Soc. of Antiquaries, 1790).

Paston Letters, edited by J. GAIRDNER, 6 vols. (1904).

PECOCK, R., *Repressor of Over-much Blaming of the clergy* (Rolls Series, 1860).

PERCY, Bp., *Folio Manuscript Ballads and Romances*, edited by J. W. HALES and F. J. FURNIVALL (1867).

Plumpton Correspondence, edited by T. STAPLETON (Camden Soc., No. 4, 1839).

Political, Religious and Love Poems, edited by F. J. FURNIVALL (Early English Text Soc., No. 15).

Political Songs, edited by T. WRIGHT (Rolls Series, No. 14).

Proceedings and Ordinances of the Privy Council, edited by Sir N. H. NICOLAS (Record Commission).

Relation of the Island of England, edited by C. A. SNEYD (Camden Soc., O.S. No. 37).

RICART, *The Maire of Bristowe is Kalendar*, edited by L. T. SMITH (Camden Soc., 1872).

RILEY, H. T., *Memorials of London* (1868).

Rotuli Parliamentorum (Record Commission).

RYMER, T., *Fœdera* (London, 1711).

SMITH (J. T. and L. T.), *English Gilds* (Early English Text Soc., 1870).

Songs and Carols of the Fifteenth Century, edited by T. WRIGHT (*Warton Club Miscellany*, 1856).

Stafford Household Book, abstract, by Lord BAGOT, in *Archælogia*, Vol. XXV.

Statutes of the Realm, Vol. II (1817).

The Law Merchant, edited by C. GROSS (Selden Soc., 1908).

Wardrobe Accounts of Edward IV, edited by Sir N. H. NICOLAS.

Calendars—

EWALD, A. C., *Calendar of the French Rolls*, in *Reports of the Deputy Keeper of the Public Records*, Vols. XLIV and XLVIII.

Calendar of the Patent Rolls—

HARDY, T. Duffus, *Syllabus of Rymer's 'Fœdera,'* Vol. II (1873).

SHARPE, R. R., *Calendar of Wills proved and enrolled in the Court of Hustings*, London (1890).

II. LATER WORKS—

ADDY, S. O., *Evolution of the English House* (1898).

ASHLEY, W. J., *Early History of the Woollen Industry* (1886).

ASHLEY, W. J., *Introduction to English Economic History*, part ii (1888).

ASTLEY, H. J. D., *Memorials of Old Norfolk* (1908).

ATTON, H., and HOLLAND, H. H., *The King's Customs* (1908).

BEAZLEY, C. R., *J. and S. Cabot* (1898).

BEAZLEY, C. R., *Prince Henry the Navigator* (Hero of the Nations), 1895.

BELLOT, H. H. L., *The Inner and Middle Temple* (1902).

BOND, F., *Gothic Architecture in England* (1905).

BOURNE, H. R. FOX, *English Merchants* (1866).

Cambridge History of English Literature, edited by A. W. WARD and A. R. WALLER, Vols. I and II.

CAPES, W. W., *The English Church in the Fourteenth and Fifteenth Centuries* (Vol. III of *History of the English Church*, edited by Rev. W. R. W. STEPHENS and Rev. W. HUNT).

CARLISLE, Nicholas, *Endowed Grammar Schools in England and Wales* (1818).

CHANDLER, R., *Life of William Waynflete* (1811).

CHEYNEY, E. P., *Disappearance of English Serfdom*, in *English Historical Review* (1900).

CLOWES, Sir W. L., *History of the Navy*, Vol. I (1897).

CREIGHTON, Dr. C., *History of Epidemics in Britain*, Vol. I (1891).

CUNNINGHAM, W., *Alien Immigrants to England* (1897).

CUNNINGHAM, W., *Christian Opinion on Usury* (1884).

CUNNINGHAM, W., *Growth of English Industry and Commerce* (1905).

CUNNINGHAM, W., *Economic Changes* in *Cambridge Modern History*, Vol. I (1902).

DAVENPORT, Frances G., *Decay of Villeinage in East Anglia*, in *Transactions of the Royal Historical Society*, N.S., XIV (1900).

DAVENPORT, Frances G., *The Economic Development of a Norfolk Manor* (1906).

DENTON, W., *England in the Fifteenth Century* (1888).

DIXON, E., *Craftswomen in the Livres des Métiers*, in *Economic Journal*, Vol. V (1895).

DIXON, E., *Florentine Wool Trades in the Middle Ages*, in *Trans. of Roy. Hist. Soc.*, N.S., XII (1898).

DOUTHWAITE, W. R., *Gray's Inn* (1886).

DOWELL, Stephen, *History of Taxation and Taxes* (1888).

DUFF, E. Gordon, *William Caxton* (1905).

DUFF, E. Gordon, *The Printers, Stationers and Bookbinders of London and Westminster in the Fifteenth Century* (1899).

DUFF, E. Gordon, *Early Printed Books* (1893).

EDEN, Sir F. M., *The State of the Poor* (1797).

FABER, Richard, *Die Entstehung des Agrarschutzes in England* (1886).

FOX, F. F., *Some Account of the Ancient Fraternity of Merchant Taylors of Bristol* (1880).

FREEMAN, E. A., *Exeter* (Historic Towns Series, 1895).

FULLER, Th., *Church-History of Britain*, edited by J. S. BREWER (1845).

GAIRDNER, J., *Lollardy and the Reformation in England* (1908).

GASQUET, F. A., *The Old English Bible* (1897).

GASQUET, F. A., *Parish Life in Mediæval England.*

GAY, E. F., *The Inquisitions of Depopulation and the Domesday of Enclosures*, in *Trans. of the Roy. Hist. Soc.*, Vol. XIV (1900).

GIUSEPPI, M. S., *Alien Merchants in England in the Fifteenth Century*, in *Trans. of the Roy. Hist. Soc.*, N.S., IX (1895).

GREEN, A. S., *Town Life in the Fifteenth Century* (1894).

GROSS, C., *The Gild Merchant* (Clarendon Press, 1890).

HALL, Hubert, *History of the Custom Revenue in England* (1885).

HALL, Hubert, *A Formula Book of English Official Historical Documents* (1908).

HARRIS, D. M., *Life in an Old English Town* (1898).

HASBACH, Dr. W., *History of the English Agricultural Labourer*, translated by Ruth KENYON (1908).

HAZLITT, W. Carew, *The Livery Companies of the City of London* (1892).

HUDSON, W., *The Assessment of* 1334, in *Norfolk Archæology*, Vol. XII (1895).

HUNT, W., *Bristol* (Historic Towns Series, 1887).

HYNDMAN, H. M., *Historical Basis of Socialism* (1881).

JAMES, J., *History of the Worsted Manufacture in England* (1857).

JENSEN, O., *The Denarius Sancti Petri*, in *Trans. of the Roy. Hist. Soc.*, N.S., XIX.

JESSOPP, A., *Parish Life in England before the Great Pillage* (1901).

JUSSERAND, J. J., *English Wayfaring Life in the Middle Ages*, translated by L. T. SMITH (1889).

KITCHEN, G. W., *A Charter of Edward III confirming the Privileges of St. Giles' Fair, Winchester* (1886).

LAPSLEY, G. T., *Account Roll of a Fifteenth Century Iron Master*, in *Engl. Hist. Review*, Vol. XIV (1899).

LAMBERT, J. M., *Two Thousand Years of Gild Life* (1891).

LAW, A., *English Nouveaux-Riches in the Fourteenth Century*, in the *Trans. of the Roy. Hist. Soc.*, N.S., IX (1895).

LEACH, A. F., *Early Yorkshire Schools* (*Yorks. Archæol. Assoc.*, Record Series, Vols. XXVII and XXXII).

LEACH, A. F., *History of Warwick School* (1906).

LEACH, A. F., *Schools in Lincolnshire*, in *Victoria County History, Lincolnshire*, Vol. II.

LEACH, A. F., *A History of Winchester College*.

LEADAM, I. S., *Polydore Vergil in the English Law Courts*, in *Trans. of the Roy. Hist. Soc.*, N.S., XIX.

LEONARD, E. M., *Early History of English Poor Relief* (1900).

LEWIS, G. R., *The Stannaries : a study of the English Tin Mines* (Harvard Economic Studies, III).

LEWIS, J., *Life of R. Pecock* (1820).

LINGELBACH, W. E., *Organisation of the Merchant Adventurers*, in *Trans. of the Roy. Hist. Soc.*, N.S., XVI.

MACPHERSON, D., *Annals of Commerce*, Vol. I (1805).

MARTIN, T. C., *Some Chancery Proceedings of the Fifteenth Century*, in *Archælogia*, 2nd Series, Vol. IX (1904).

MICHEL, F., *Histoire du Commerce et de la Navigation à Bordeaux* (1867–70).

MORLEY, H., *English Writers*, Vol. VI (1896).

NICHOLLS, Sir G., *History of the English Poor Law* (1898).

NICOLAS, Sir N. H., *History of the Royal Navy* (1847).

OCHENKOWSKI, W., *England's Wirthschaftliche Entwickelung* (1879).

OMAN, C., *Political History of England*, Vol. IV.

OPPENHEIM, M., *The History of the Administration of the Royal Navy*, Vol. I (1896).

POLLARD, A. W., *English Miracle Plays*, 4th edition (1904).

POLLARD, A. F., *Factors in Modern History* (1907).

PRIOR, S., *History of Gothic Art in England* (1900).

PRYCE, G., *Memorials of the Canynges' Family* (1883).

RAMSAY, Sir J., *Lancaster and York* (1892).

RAMSAY, Sir J., *Expenditure of Edward III*, in *The Antiquary*, Vol. I (1880).

REDSTONE, V. B., *Social Condition of England during the Wars of the Roses*, in *Trans. of the Roy. Hist. Soc.*, N.S., Vol. XVI.

ROGERS, J. E. T., *History of Agriculture and Prices*, Vol. IV (1866).

ROGERS, J. E. T., *Six Centuries of Work and Wages* (1884).

RICKMAN, T., *Gothic Architecture* (1881).

RUDING, R., *Annals of the Coinage of Great Britain*, 3rd edition.

SAVINE, A., *Bondmen in England under the Tudors*, in *Trans. of the Roy. Hist. Soc.*, N.S., XVII (1903).

SAVINE, A., *Copyhold Cases in the Early Chancery Proceedings*, in *Eng. Hist. Review*, Vol. XVII (1902).

SCHANZ, G., *Englische Handelspolitik gegen Ende des Mittelalters* (1881).

SHILLINGTON, V. M., and CHAPMAN, A. B. W., *Commercial Relations of England and Portugal* (1907).

SMITH, J. T., *The Parish* (1857).

SMITH, L. T., *York Plays* (1885).

STOW, J., *Survey of London*, edited by J. STRYPE (1754).

STRUTT, J., *Sports and Pastimes of the People of England*, edited by W. HONE (1898).

STUBBS, W., *Constitutional History of England*, 4th edition, Vol. II (1896).

TRAILL, H. D., and MANN, J. S., *Social England*, Vol. II.

TREVELYAN, G. M., *England in the Age of Wycliffe* (1899).

TURNER, T. H., and PARKER, J. H., *Domestic Architecture of England* (1859–77).

VARENBERGH, E., *Histoire des Relations Diplomatiques entre Flandre et l'Angleterre* (1874).

Victoria County History, edited by W. PAGE: *Dorset*, Vol. II; *Lincolnshire*, Vol. II; *Gloucestershire*, Vol. II.

VICKERS, K. H., *Humphrey, Duke of Gloucester* (1907).

WALFORD, C., *Fairs, Past and Present* (1883).

WARTON, T., *History of English Poetry*, editions of 1840 and 1871.

WILLIAMS, E., *The Staple Inn* (1906).

WILLIS, Robert, *Architectural History of the University of Cambridge* (1886).

WORSFOLD, T. C., *Staple Inn and its Story* (1903).

WRIGHT, T., *History of Domestic Manners* (1862).

WYLIE, J. H., *History of England under Henry IV* (1896).

Books of reference—

Dictionary of National Biography ; *Draper's Dictionary*, by W. BECK.

Complete Peerage of England, Scotland, Ireland, &c., edited by G. E. C. (1887).

INDEX